BITTER RECKONING

BITTER RECKONING

Israel Tries Holocaust Survivors
as Nazi Collaborators

DAN PORAT

The Belknap Press of Harvard University Press
CAMBRIDGE, MASSACHUSETTS · LONDON, ENGLAND
2019

First printing

Library of Congress Cataloging-in-Publication Data
Names: Porat, Dan, 1964– author.
Title: Bitter reckoning : Israel tries Holocaust survivors
as Nazi collaborators / Dan Porat.
Description: Cambridge, Massachusetts : The Belknap Press of Harvard
University Press, 2019. | Includes bibliographical references and index.
Identifiers: LCCN 2019011292 | ISBN 9780674988149 (alk. paper)
Subjects: LCSH: World War, 1939–1945—Collaborationists. | World War,
1939–1945—Collaborationists—Public opinion. | War crime
trials—Israel—20th century. | Kapos—Europe—History. |
Israelis—Attitudes. | Concentration camp inmates as guards—Europe—
History—20th century. | Holocaust, Jewish (1939–1945) | World War,
1939–1945—Concentration camps.
Classification: LCC D810.C696 P67 2019 | DDC 940.53/18—dc23
LC record available at https://lccn.loc.gov/2019011292

In memory of my father, Shlomo Porat

CONTENTS

BITTER RECKONING

INTRODUCTION

IN JANUARY 1952, after a three-and-a-half-month trial, the Tel Aviv District Court issued its verdict in a case brought by the State of Israel against Yehezkel Jungster. Jungster was a Holocaust survivor whose wife and children had been murdered by the Germans. The lead judge, Pinchas Avishar, declared that Jungster "had made himself a tool in the hands of the barbaric Nazi regime in its plan to annihilate the Jewish people." Jungster, the court determined, had been a Jewish collaborator with the Nazis.[1]

Those present, who could see the defendant seated in the dock, must have had some trouble believing that the sickly man before them was as barbaric as claimed. Jungster, forty-one, suffered from a disease of the circulatory system; he had already lost his left leg and was losing his right leg to necrosis, had had one of his kidneys removed, and suffered from high blood pressure. The panel of three judges, however, explained that in 1943–1944, when Jungster was an inmate in the Grodziszcze and Faulbrück camps in western Poland, he had been a "heavily built man . . . , dressed in a leather jacket, shod in boots, who walked about with a rubber-coated metal-wire rod in his hand, beating at a whim anyone who crossed his path." Jungster had served as a kapo—a concentration camp prisoner who was assigned by the SS to a position supervising other prisoners within the camp. Witnesses testified that Jungster beat his victims, often aiming for their genitals, even when no Nazi was in sight.[2]

The case of Jungster was just one of about forty so-called kapo trials that took place in Israel between 1950 and 1972. The story of these trials is as yet little known, because only in recent years has the Israel State Archives made the transcripts of some of these trials publicly available. During these trials, Jewish functionaries, such as camp supervisors and ghetto policemen, faced indictments for their behavior during the Holocaust. Israeli prosecutors brought charges against them for having collaborated with the Nazis in assaulting Jews and inflicting grievous injuries. They were accused of blackmail and of surrendering victims to the Nazis, of membership in enemy organizations, of the murder of prisoners, and even of war crimes and crimes against humanity.[3] In two-thirds of these cases the courts sided with the prosecution, and all but one of those convicted were sentenced to prison, for an average of twenty-six months behind bars.

This book asks a number of interconnected questions about these trials of Jews accused of collaboration. What motivated the trials in the first place? How did the judicial and social treatment of collaborators change over time? What was the relationship between the kapo trials and the two high-profile Holocaust trials that took place in Israel during this period—those that centered on the Nazi Adolf Eichmann and the Hungarian Jew Rudolf Kastner? Were Jewish and non-Jewish collaborators viewed as equally culpable? How did the meaning of collaboration change between the immediate aftermath of World War II and the 1970s? And finally, what implications has the suppression of these stories had on our memory of the Holocaust?

The obliteration of these functionaries from Jewish collective memory, I believe, has allowed for the rise of an overly simplistic view that conceives of all victims as heroes. In a contemporary culture that tends to venerate Holocaust survivors, the idea that a victim might have behaved in a questionable manner seems inconceivable. The prevalent view today, however, was not the dominant one for the first twenty years after World War II, when many believed that the victims as a group, and especially those who had served in leadership positions in ghettos and camps, shared responsibility with the Germans for the catastrophe that had befallen them. By focusing on the kapo trials and their development, this book traces the changing attitudes toward those accused of collaboration.

* * *

When Allied forces broke open the gates of concentration camps in 1945, they discovered not only piles of corpses and dozens of gravely ill inmates but also survivors who were seeking revenge. Many of those who were liberated sought retribution not just against the Germans but against former Jewish functionaries in the camps and ghettos as well. Freed inmates lynched and beat Jews who, as ghetto policemen, had surrendered them and their family members to the Nazis or who, as kapos in concentration camps, had harassed or abused them.

This violence continued outside the liberated camps. To quell the brutality, leaders in the reemerging Jewish communities in European towns and displaced persons (DP) camps channeled these disputes into honor courts, which were established to resolve ordinary disagreements among members of the community. These courts, presided over by prominent individuals, also examined the moral behavior of functionaries and issued social punishments such as public denunciations and excommunication from the community. In most instances, these judgments succeeded in curbing the violence within the community; they also helped it rebuild its self-identity as a wholesome society, free of impure elements that had contaminated it.

When survivors immigrated to Mandatory Palestine, the same kinds of intra-Jewish clashes that had been seen in Europe erupted in public spaces there. Two institutions in pre-state Israel operated similarly to the honor courts in Europe: *Landsmanschaften* (communal organizations of expatriates from a specific city or country) and the World Zionist Congress honor court weighed in on accusations against functionaries. But these institutions were inadequate for addressing the dozens of disputes that flared among the survivors. Media commentators and public figures called upon the heads of the Yishuv, the Jewish community in Mandatory Palestine, to alleviate tension by establishing a public committee of socially prominent figures to deliberate these cases and issue social punishments. The leadership chose, however, not to establish such a committee, deeming social penalties insufficiently severe for those accused of cooperating with the Nazi mission to annihilate the Jewish people.

It was only after the establishment of the State of Israel and after a repeated demand from a high-ranking police officer that the Ministry of Justice drafted a bill setting up a system for trying functionaries in criminal court, where they would face their accusers. The Nazis and Nazi Collaborators Punishment Law, passed by the Knesset in 1950, inaugurated what became known as the kapo trials, which would go on for the next twenty-two years. Over those two decades, the kapo trials went through four main phases, moving from an initial perception of Jewish ghetto and camp functionaries as perpetrators equivalent to the Nazis to a final perception of them as victims.

During the first phase (August 1950–January 1952), alleged collaborators were subjected to uncompromising treatment. Israeli legislators and prosecutors zealously sought retribution against these Jews, whom they viewed as partners with the Nazis in their crimes against European Jewry. Legislators formulated the law so as to put Nazis and their Jewish collaborators on equal footing, a perspective that failed to take into account the antithetical worlds in which they lived. Only in the sentencing phase did the law make provision for the functionaries' position as victims themselves, allowing in very limited cases some measure of leniency.

Like the legislators, prosecutors viewed anyone who had filled a position under the Nazis as guilty until proven innocent. Prosecutors charged almost every defendant, even those who had allegedly beaten only a single camp inmate, with "crimes against humanity," the same charge leveled against members of the Nazi leadership in the Nuremberg trials. When judges noted that the charge of crimes against humanity was suitable only for actions committed against a mass of people, prosecutors would replace the charge with "war crimes," an offense also punishable by death. In the first year and a half of the kapo trials, district courts sentenced six former kapos to an average of almost five years of imprisonment and issued one death sentence, in the case of Yehezkel Jungster.

In the second phase (February 1952–1957), functionaries were cast not as Nazis but as Jewish collaborators of the Nazis. This phase began after the court sentenced Jungster to death; to prevent any further such rulings, the prosecutors, who seem to have never anticipated that the court would issue a death sentence, rushed to change all indictments that included charges that could potentially carry the death penalty, and they almost never again brought charges of war crimes or crimes against humanity against Jewish functionaries. Shortly thereafter, the Supreme Court, to which the Jungster case had been automatically appealed, overturned Jungster's death sentence. In doing so, the Supreme Court adopted the new line drawn by prosecutors between Nazis and their Jewish collaborators: the former could face charges of crimes against humanity and war crimes, but the latter could not. In all other respects, the justice system continued to view the functionaries as equal to the Nazis, and the trials continued.

Outside the courtrooms, however, doubts began to emerge as to whether functionaries should be prosecuted at all. In theater and the media, artists and journalists asked if it was possible to judge "those who were there." The defamation trial of Rudolf Kastner, head of the Budapest Rescue Committee, although not one of the kapo trials, exacerbated such doubts. This case began when Israel's attorney general, Haim Cohn, brought charges against a journalist for defaming Kastner. Survivors had accused Kastner of collaborating with Adolf Eichmann; in exchange for Kastner's collaboration in the extermination of half a million Hungarian Jews, they claimed, the Nazis helped him save more than a thousand of his own family members and cronies. The district court ultimately ruled against Kastner, who had become the de facto defendant, concluding that he had "sold his soul to the devil" by collaborating with the Nazis. In defense of Kastner, Cohn voiced skepticism about the court's ability to judge those who had acted in the Holocaust, stating that "this is a matter between them and Heaven."[4] Cohn, however, did not extend this sense of doubt from the Kastner defamation case to the kapo trials. He still believed in the court's ability to weigh the motivations and actions of functionaries.

In the third stage (1958–1962), the legal system viewed most functionaries as men and women who had committed wrongs but had done so with good intentions. In 1958 the Supreme Court reversed the district court decision in the Kastner trial, effectively clearing him of collaboration, on the grounds that a person could have legitimately done something wrong, including cooperating with the Nazis, because he believed that sustaining a good relationship with the Nazis would enable him to save Jews in the future. Even if he had made a mistake, the court determined, one could not judge him for that. As a result of this ruling, Cohn reformulated the policy of the attorney general's office, in one case even ordering prosecutors to withdraw an indictment. From this point forward, prosecutors filed charges only against functionaries they believed had aligned themselves with the Nazis' aims. During this period some survivors had also come to believe that it was time to put aside past controversies and move on. Others, however, still called for putting alleged collaborators on trial.

The Eichmann trial in 1961, and the trial of Hirsch Barenblat two years later, marked the shift to the fourth and final stage of the kapo trials (1963–1972). In this phase the legal system viewed functionaries as ordinary victims, a change that signaled a full reversal from the initial view of functionaries as guilty until proven innocent. One of the goals of Eichmann's prosecutor, Gideon Hausner, was to remove the charge of collaboration from kapos and policemen. In his selection of witnesses for the Eichmann trial, he portrayed functionaries as harmless and in some instances even heroic. The prosecution drew a stark distinction between innocent Jews, including functionaries, and evil Nazis. The negative image of those who were victims but at times acted in ways that benefited the perpetrator vanished.

Shortly after the conclusion of the Eichmann trial, a young and ambitious Israeli prosecutor, David Libai, temporarily challenged the new perception of functionaries as innocent. After Hausner retired, Libai filed an indictment against the former head of the Jewish police in the Polish town of Bedzin, Hirsch Barenblat. The indictment included one count, hardly ever deliberated in an Israeli court, that charged Barenblat with membership in a hostile organization, "one of whose aims was to assist in carrying out actions of an enemy administration against persecuted people."[5] If Barenblat was convicted on this count, it would mean viewing anyone who had joined a Jewish Council or police unit as guilty of aiming to assist the Nazis, regardless of intent or actions. Libai hoped that just as Hausner had utilized the Eichmann trial to prosecute the entire Nazi regime, so he could use the trial of Barenblat to attain a conviction of the entire Jewish leadership in the councils and the police.

Halfway through the trial, however, Libai's superiors in the Ministry of Justice ordered him to remove this count from the indictment. After the Tel Aviv District Court issued a guilty verdict against Barenblat on other counts, the case was appealed to the Supreme Court. The justices ruled that the prosecution had been wrong to indict Barenblat for membership in a hostile organization. Justice Moshe Landau, who had headed the panel that tried Eichmann, declared that it was hypocritical to judge the functionaries, ordinary men and women who had lived in a morally upside-down world, by the standard of those living safely in Israel. The functionaries had taken up their positions not with the aim of promoting the goals of their persecutors but in the hope of saving themselves and their families. The court cleared Barenblat of all charges.[6]

Yet the Supreme Court continued to hold that in cases in which functionaries had acted in "sadistic" or "monstrous" fashion, they should face trial.[7] In the court's view, in extreme cases victims' actions could be subjected to legal scrutiny, as indeed occurred in a 1972 case against a woman accused of cruelly treating camp inmates.[8] With that legal procedure, the kapo trials came to an end, following the implicit directive of the Supreme Court in the Barenblat verdict to try only the most severe cases of cruel behavior.

* * *

This book focuses on those in Israel's judicial system who investigated, prosecuted, and judged Jewish functionaries. I document the shift in how Israel's legal authorities conceived of these men and women: from seeing them as equal to Nazis to viewing them as completely free from blame for any questionable actions. At the same time, I portray the drama within the confines of the courtrooms, where survivors' accounts were pitted against each other. In a few cases, I oppose a court's ruling. Courts have a duty to carefully follow the letter of the law and weigh each piece of evidence brought before them. However, I, as a historian, can evaluate the actions of protagonists in a more circumstantial and contextual manner and can avail myself of evidence unavailable to the court.

While the book traces the entire course of these trials, it focuses more attention on eight of them. I have chosen these eight cases for two reasons. First, some of them mark important milestones in the development of the kapo trials. Thus the several legal procedures of Julius Siegel (1946, 1949, 1952–1953) help highlight the form of justice deployed against functionaries both in Jewish honor courts in Europe and in Israeli courts. The case against Andrej Banik (1951), the only non-Jew tried in the kapo trials, was the first of these trials to take place in Israel. The case of Yehezkel Jungster (1951–1952) resulted in distinguishing collaborators from Nazis and exempting the former from the death penalty. The Barenblat trial (1963) represents the judiciary's adoption of the view that it was impossible and inappropriate to judge ordinary men and women who chose to take on leadership positions to save themselves.

A second consideration in selecting these cases has to do with the moral issues they posed to judges. Four of the cases resulted in a clear guilty verdict: those of Elsa Trenk (1951), Siegel, Jungster, and Jacob Honigman (1951–1952). Four other cases resulted in acquittal: those of Banik, Barenblat, Raya Hanes, and Pinchas Pashititzky. Yet the acquittals were very different from each other. The Hanes case (1951–1952) highlights the complexity of serving as a kapo in a death camp, of someone who sought to do the right thing but at the same time was forced to act in ways that seemed harsh. Hanes is an example of a person who managed to deftly maneuver between the Nazis' malicious intent and the goal of saving people, a position that was not understood by many of the inmates she oversaw. In the acquittal of Pashititzky (1951–1952), by contrast, the court cleared the defendant but at the same time severely censured him for his choices and actions in a labor camp. Taken together, these eight cases present the complexity of assessing the moral behavior of these men and women.

* * *

Initially, when I began poring over the thousands of pages of transcripts of these trials, I had a hard time taking a position about the appropriateness of prosecuting these alleged collaborators. At first I asked myself how one could judge those who had gone through hell on earth, men and women who had lost entire families, experienced unimaginable hunger, and lived under conditions of brutal oppression, striving only to survive. Why had Israeli prosecutors indicted these survivors? Was this part of the dominant trend in Israeli culture in the 1950s, when it was common to accuse diaspora Jews of "going like sheep to the slaughter" and taking part in their own annihilation? In bringing these indictments, I believed, the State of Israel had failed miserably to understand the victims' plight, and it should not have placed them on trial. In its search for scapegoats, it had done a disservice to innocent survivors.

Then I began reading the harsh stories recounted by survivors in the courtrooms, and my view swung to the opposite side. One witness described how, in 1942, the commander of the Jewish police entered the town orphanage, climbed to the attic, found dozens of pale children, dragged them down the stairs, and handed them over to the Nazis to be transported to Auschwitz.[9] Was this not an act that deserved punishment? Another witness, a former camp prisoner, had seen her cousin collapse in the barracks and rushed out to get her water, only to be blocked upon her return by a Jewish kapo who cursed her, grabbed the bowl of water, poured it out, picked up a stick, and beat the prisoner.[10] Yes, I thought, it was the Nazis who had subjected these women to the inhumane conditions of the camp, but did the status of victim permit the kapo to beat this inmate and many others so viciously, even when no German was in sight? How could one justify such gratuitous violence by one human toward another?

In considering these cases, I oscillated from viewing these inmates as innocent scapegoats to seeing them as criminals. It was an essay by Primo Levi on what he called the "gray zone" that first laid out for me the irresolvable tension between the perceived guilt of such victims and our inability to judge them. Levi, an Italian-born Holocaust survivor, writes, "The condition of the offended does not exclude culpability, which is often objectively serious, but I know of no human tribunal to which one could delegate the judgment." Oppression, he holds, does not sanctify victims. Functionaries—not minor ones such as lice checkers or messengers but rather kapos, who frequently used violence—served, in Levi's words, as "collaborators" and so are "rightful owners of a quota of guilt." Yet he goes on, "I believe that no one is authorized to judge them, not those who lived through the experience of the Lager [camp] and even less those who did not."[11]

Levi believes that we must suspend our judgment of these functionaries. Those who did not experience the exhaustion, the hunger, the fatigue, and the humiliation that resulted in "the death of the soul" cannot judge those who assumed positions as functionaries; even those who shared those experiences cannot judge. Yet, argues the scholar Adam Brown, Levi's suspension of judgment does not mean that, for Levi, it is not important to attempt to evaluate their actions, even if no conclusion can be reached.[12] Levi notes that the gray zone between perpetrator and oppressed is filled "with obscene or pathetic figures (sometimes they possess both qualities simultaneously) whom it is indispensable to know if we want to know the human species." We must study these functionaries, those men and women whom Levi—despite contending that judgment is impossible—labels as "sadists," individuals "fatally intoxicated by the power," who "collaborated" and "committed atrocities."[13] However, as I assess their behavior, I believe one must always remember that the kapos were indeed victims of the Nazi perpetrators, who placed them in a morally bankrupt world, a world we will never fully understand.

Years earlier, before the publication of his essay on the gray zone, Levi expressed a very different view that "it is very hard indeed to judge. . . . But they should be judged."[14] So too thought the Israeli Knesset when in the summer of 1950 it passed the Nazis and Nazi Collaborators Punishment Law.[15] The primary intention in establishing this law was to judge "the Nazis' assistants," those survivors who had allegedly collaborated with their oppressors. In the view of some Israeli legislators, the Jewish men and women who would face trial had served as "murderers and betrayers," "collaborators," and "war criminals."[16] In this Knesset legislation and in the kapo trials that ensued, there was no place for a gray zone, only for verdicts of guilty or innocent.

* * *

While my aim in this book is to unpack the historical development of the kapo trials, I believe it is important that I spell out my own view about the appropriateness of placing these individuals in front of a court to evaluate their past behavior. I recognize that the social unrest within the community of Holocaust survivors required Israeli authorities to channel accusations into a system that would help resolve disputes and minimize violence. And indeed, the process of judging suspects did successfully curtail the violence between survivors.

Although Israel's criminal courts system was successful, overall, in channeling social unrest, I believe that the establishment of social courts instead of, or in addition to, criminal courts would have allowed for a greater public reckoning with the questionable actions of individual Jews during the Holocaust. The suggestion of establishing social courts had been floated in the pre-state period but was rejected by the heads of the Jewish community in Mandatory Palestine. Such courts could have addressed crimes that a state prosecutor could not include in a legal indictment. In addition, judges would not have been limited in their rulings by a specific choice of words in the law. Instead, the committees could have weighed the actions against a broader moral code established by its members, who would be survivors as well. Such committees could have issued social judgments ranging from verbal condemnation to social excommunication. They would have achieved social order in Israel, as they had in the DP camps, and generated a deeper public discussion about the role of victims in the Holocaust.[17]

The trials that took place through the mid-1950s did help calm the tensions among survivors. Although those trials were socially justified, however, no social good came from the trials conducted following the Kastner trial that ended in 1958. That trial created a heated public discussion that underscored the complexities of victims' actions during the depths of the Holocaust. After that, the office of the attorney general should have ceased to file indictments. From that point on it was clear to all that no social good would come from trying alleged collaborators.

In addition to examining the trials and their legitimacy, this book traces changing views among Israelis about how to treat alleged collaborators. In the 1950s, Israelis had taken a negative view of survivors in general and an especially vindictive approach toward the leaders of the Jewish communities and those who had assumed positions of responsibility in the ghettos and camps. Israelis commonly viewed the leaders of the Jewish communities, Jewish police, and kapos as a group that had relentlessly collaborated with the Nazis in their persecution of the Jewish people. This view then shifted radically to one that acknowledged the victimization of those who just a few years earlier had been viewed as traitors to the nation—sometimes even characterizing them as heroes. It became impossible to imagine a scenario in which a Jew could beat, let alone murder, one of his brethren.

Israeli society has moved from one extreme to another, from charges of complete guilt to sweeping vindication, a shift that I believe indicates a lack of acknowledgment of the spectrum of possible types of victims in the Holocaust. By focusing on the extremes, observers have eliminated the possibility of a person behaving in a harmful and merciless manner as a functionary while at the same time being a victim, or of a functionary serving the Nazis at the same time that she acts to assist prisoners. Having been a victim does not place a person in a morally superior position, and having been a kapo does not define a person as cruel. The human stories revealed in the kapo trials demonstrate the complexity of the position of victims, a complexity that we must comprehend if we wish to truly try to understand—and to the degree possible—overcome the Holocaust.

CHAPTER ONE

FROM REVENGE TO RETRIBUTION IN POST-NAZI EUROPE

In 1945, American forces liberated the sick and starving inmates of Bad Tölz, a subcamp of the Dachau concentration camp. A week later, in early May, a Jewish American officer arranged for a memorial ceremony. It was held nearby in the movie theater of what had been the SS officer school. Former inmates gathered in the theater, some leaning on walking sticks and others supporting ailing friends.

At the head table sat an American officer. Beside him sat those who as kapos had until recently overseen the inmates in the camp. The audience of liberated Jewish inmates listened quietly as the chair of the gathering delivered his opening remarks. Next to speak was one of the former kapos seated at the head table. During his speech, some in the audience began to squirm with discomfort. Another former kapo seated at the head table rose to speak. A buzz went through the crowd. Then, from the front of the theater, a former inmate sprang to his feet. With all eyes focused upon him, the man raised his fists and faced his fellow inmates, saying angrily, "We are speaking here about the German SS men, but before we judge them, let us take revenge on the Jewish SS men among us!"

Members of the audience leapt upon the former kapos. For a few moments the Americans in the room were stunned. Lube Meskup, the girlfriend of one of the former kapos, Itzik Gritzmacher, and herself a former kapo, blocked the hall doors in an attempt to save her boyfriend, who had sprung out the window. The crowd proceeded to beat her. The mob then caught up with Gritzmacher and beat him, crying "Murderer!" and "Nazi!" They also latched on to the other kapos and beat them. Moments later, the American soldiers pushed the crowd back and prevented the killing of the former kapos.[1]

Survivors attack a former kapo at Bergen-Belsen concentration camp.

Similar scenes were repeated in liberated camps and towns across Poland, France, Greece, Holland, and elsewhere in Europe. For some survivors, liberation was not a time to celebrate freedom or mourn the loss of loved ones but a time to take revenge and settle accounts.

Following the liberation of Auschwitz in late January 1945, survivor Nathan Urbach heard someone crying, "Save me! They're killing me!" He then saw two young men viciously beating a former kapo, Eliezer Gruenbaum. Urbach ran to a nearby block of French prisoners and urged them to come to Gruenbaum's aid. The Frenchmen, who had known Gruenbaum before liberation, rushed out and saved their friend.[2] But that was not the fate of many others. There was a rumor that shortly after liberation, Jews in Munich murdered hundreds of other Jews who had been accused of collaboration.[3] While this rumor was undoubtedly exaggerated, the lynching of functionaries did indeed occur. In January 1945 in the Buchenwald concentration camp, freed inmates identified five former kapos and killed them.[4]

As these events show, blame for the atrocities of the Holocaust was not restricted to Germans alone. At this time, many believed that the Germans could not have created such horror without the collaboration of some within the leadership of the Jewish community. In the eyes of the liberated, it was not only members of the Jewish leadership who were responsible but also many of the Jewish functionaries in ghettos and camps. The Jewish policemen who had personally handed them or their relatives over to the Nazis and the kapos who had controlled their lives in the camps were responsible for their suffering. In 1945, many directed their vengeance at those who had overseen or harmed them directly. Only later would a broad vision of Nazi crimes emerge, recognizing the sophistication of the Nazi machine in utilizing victims to serve as their own destroyers.[5]

In a few outstanding cases, kapos and policemen condemned themselves. In May 1945, a group of thirty men liberated from the Grodziszcze labor camp gathered to deliberate on the fate of their former supervisors. Some, they decided, would be spared; others would be beaten severely; yet others deserved death. They resolved to kill the former head kapo, Jacob Rosenzweig. Equipped with a pistol, they entered the area that had housed the German camp commanders. But when they entered one of the apartments, they found that Rosenzweig had hanged himself from the ceiling with a belt.[6]

A former Jewish policeman from the Otwock ghetto, Calel Perechodnik, felt a deep sense of guilt for having taken part in the deportation of his wife and daughter to the Treblinka extermination camp. Imagining himself speaking to his wife, as she sits on the floor of a train car, he wrote, "You are sitting, and there is one thing that you do not understand. How is it possible? Your Calinka, who loved you for ten years, was loyal to you, guessed at and fulfilled all your thoughts and wishes so willingly, has now betrayed you, has allowed you to enter the cattle car and has himself remained behind." He could hear his deceased wife accuse him: "You are guilty. You caused our destruction! You are guilty." And he could never forgive himself for the death of his wife and daughter.[7]

Stanislav Adler, a policeman from the Warsaw ghetto, committed suicide in 1946. In the memoir he left behind, Adler wrote, "The moral dissolution caused in the Order Service [the Jewish police] by the roundups for the labor camps did not manifest itself in any deeds. It stopped at moaning and swearing at the fate that brought one to such detestable service. Evidently, it was preferable to catch than to be caught. I can't recollect an instance of anyone leaving the Order Service in that period [of 1941]. . . . Like the others, I did not take immediate measures to quit at once." But, unwilling to take part in the roundups of Jews, Adler did in the end arrange to be reassigned from the Jewish police to a different position.[8]

Violence erupted not only in the liberated camps but also in the towns to which survivors returned in search of siblings, parents, and acquaintances. Sometimes, instead of finding family members, survivors met those whom they regarded as their tormentors. In those instances, survivors either acted independently to avenge themselves on perceived collaborators or handed them over to the local police, charged with purging those who had associated themselves with the Nazi regime. In the Praga neighborhood of Warsaw, Antek Zuckerman, the head of the Jewish underground, encountered a mob beating a Jewish policeman. He broke through the crowd and handed the man over to the Polish police.[9]

* * *

In early 1946, David Ben-Gurion, head of the Jewish Agency, visited displaced-persons (DP) camps in Germany. In Munich, where many gathered to greet him, a representative of the survivors took the podium to deliver a welcome speech. At the sight of this survivor, three members of the audience leapt up and cried, "Scoundrel! Kapo! You were with the Nazis!"

"Their eyes were on fire; they wanted to murder someone," Ben-Gurion reported to the board of directors at the Jewish Agency in Jerusalem. "After five years of observing the daily murder of their fellow Jews, they have lost every remnant of humanity."[10]

Three years earlier, in a speech commemorating the death of Joseph Trumpeldor, who was killed while valiantly defending a Jewish outpost in the northern part of pre-state Israel, Ben-Gurion had told listeners of a similarly heroic uprising in the Warsaw ghetto. He saw that event as highlighting the very different deaths of most European Jews, who, he said, had lived and died in submission, "dying in solitary confinement, with their hands and legs bound." Zionism, he proclaimed, introduced a "new kind of death," the heroic death.[11]

In the years that followed, a number of Jews who had been raised on Zionism in pre-state Israel joined the British Army's Jewish Brigade to battle the Axis and "lend a hand to the remnants of [the] Jews." In the summer of 1945, units of the Jewish Brigade were stationed in the town of Tarvisio in northern Italy. From there, a select group of Jewish Brigade soldiers conducted revenge operations, by one estimate executing a hundred Nazis, including Gestapo and SS men.[12]

But these soldiers' acts of revenge were not limited to Germans. In at least two cases, members of the Jewish Brigade were implicated in the killing of Jewish former kapos. While the unit was stationed in Milan, soldiers learned that survivors at a Jewish refugee house at 5 Via dell'Unione had identified a kapo in their midst. Four Jewish Brigade soldiers raced from their base to the house, where they found an agitated crowd encircling a tall, athletic, and healthy-looking individual.

The soldiers took the alleged collaborator to their camp and established a kangaroo court, with two sergeant-majors and a sergeant serving as judges. Witnesses accused the man of having beaten and killed inmates in a concentration camp. One survivor, who had been summoned from another refugee center in Magenta Villa to give testimony, started shrieking at the sight of the defendant. The defendant turned pale. "He killed my brother," the witness screamed. Others recounted how the man had murdered children with a cudgel.

The defendant did not deny the accusations. When asked why he had beaten children to death on the eve of Yom Kippur, he simply responded, "Because the Germans told me to do it."[13] He also said in his testimony: "Do you know what a Jew is? When you leave him alone he falls upon food like an animal. That is why I beat them, so they would not stampede all at once."[14]

No witness spoke in defense of the accused. For the self-appointed judges, who had grown up in Mandatory Palestine under a Zionist ideology that taught them to be independent, courageous, and powerful modern Jews, the collaborator was the embodiment of the worst type of diaspora Jew: submissive, frightened, selfish, and corrupt. Unlike survivors, whose acts of vengeance emanated from the personal expe-

Jewish police detain a former kapo who was recognized in the street at the Zeilsheim displaced persons camp, near Frankfurt, Germany.

rience of suffering, these soldiers acted in retaliation against those who, according to their ideology, had wounded the honor of the Jewish people. It is possible, too, that their encounters with the rage of survivors shaped their own anger toward such functionaries.

The "court" issued a death sentence, which was carried out immediately. One of the judges, Yisrael Libratovsky, took the first shot, followed shortly afterward by a second bullet from another Jewish Brigade soldier, Abu (Avinoam) Horwitz. When the unit commander, Yehudah Surkis, learned of the "trial" and "sentence," he summoned the soldiers who had been involved and told them they would be courtmartialed. But this never happened. The lives of former camp functionaries were cheap.[15]

In another instance, a Jewish Brigade medic stationed at the Jewish refugee house at 5 Via dell'Unione reported that refugees had just identified another kapo. Minutes later, Sgt. Meir Davidson, along with a unit corporal who had been summoned by the medic, entered the refugee house to find an enraged and agitated crowd demanding revenge.

Davidson called for any person who knew the alleged collaborator to come forward. At first no one did. It was enough for a man to be dressed in a leather jacket, boots, and breeches and to have a full head of hair and gold teeth for survivors to infer that he had served the Germans and benefited from it. Then one refugee from the Mauthausen concentration camp identified the man. The survivor had lived in Block 3, and this kapo had been in Block 11. He had never seen the kapo beat anyone, the survivor said, "but a kapo must be bad; he must be a killer, a murderer." Many survivors believed that anyone who held a position for the Germans was culpable. Viewing all functionaries as guilty of collaboration allowed survivors to overlook their own lack of resistance. The Jews' submission to the Nazis, the reasoning went, resulted from their leadership's deception and their repression by the Jewish policemen and kapos.

For days, Davidson interrogated the accused in the unit's guardroom, but the questioning yielded no results. "Can silence and a person's clothing be indicative of their guilt? Could he be suppressing an agonizing past?" Davidson asked himself. Unable to resolve the dilemma, he decided to release the man and arranged for him to stay at the Magenta Villa refugee center. There, though, several refugees ended up identifying him. One night, five of them pulled the suspect out of the storage room where he was resting and dragged him down to a nearby creek. They tied him up and sat him by the water's edge. Then the survivors woke two soldiers from the Jewish Brigade and told them to go down to the creek, where the soldiers were informed that they were to serve as observers to a trial. Witnesses gave testimony, and the kangaroo court issued a death verdict. The five survivors pulled the prisoner into the river, where they repeatedly dunked his head under water until he eventually died.[16] After sunrise, a group of women from the villa went down to the creek to wash laundry. There they found the suspect's body, his face disfigured and his gold teeth missing.

Years later Davidson still felt the burden of guilt for not ensuring the man's safety. He asked, "What have I done? Do I have blood on my hands?"[17]

Justice in Communal and State Courts

Violence against functionaries also raged in DP camps in Austria, Italy, and Germany, which were home to hundreds of thousands of former inmates, mostly from Eastern Europe. The heads of the DP camps established honor courts to deal with disputes and misdemeanors of all kinds. These courts also examined accusations of collaboration during the war. Cases came before the honor courts either as the result of a complaint filed by survivors against their supposed tormentors or as the result of individuals' requests to clear their names.[18]

In early 1946, as an American major named Abraham Hyman stood in the public square of the Landsberg DP camp in the American Zone near Munich, a cry of "Kapo!" pierced the air. Within seconds he saw people rush out, surround the accused, and start beating him. The camp police broke up the mob, taking the accused with them and placing him in detention. A few months after witnessing the incident, Hyman returned to the camp's honor court to observe the trial of the former kapo, whom the witnesses accused of having beaten prisoners attempting to retrieve potato peelings from the garbage in a concentration camp. Three survivors sat as judges: the head of the DP camp, a community leader, and a former Lithuanian judge. Usually such panels included at least one person with a legal background, while the others were people who had standing within the community. All, including the prosecutor and the defense lawyer, were survivors. Those who just weeks earlier had fiercely attacked the accused now served as an audience and "filled the 'court-room' as calm observers and watched the proceedings with amazing detachment," Hyman wrote.[19]

The court convicted the defendant but, apparently accepting his argument that he had beaten inmates to deter them from eating from the garbage and so contracting dysentery, gave him a light sentence. Had survivors taken their own revenge on this alleged collaborator, the chances are that the punishment would have been disproportionate to the crime, as frequently happened in cases of vigilante justice. But honor courts calibrated retribution to the nature of the crime and other circumstances. While the public viewed all functionaries as traitors, the courts had a nuanced view of them. Punishment ranged from a reprimand to a

Sitting in judgment at a court in a displaced persons camp, Hofgeismar, Germany.

cut in social benefits, a ban on holding any public position, or even banishment and excommunication from the community.[20]

Weeks later, Hyman saw the former kapo walking safely around the Landsberg camp. Hyman wrote that "the trial was, in my opinion, conducted in harmony with the highest standards of the common law tradition" and that the court's ruling "showed the finest example of judicial temperament."[21] Only in exceptional cases did the court order the camp police to detain suspects, and very few of the convicted were ever imprisoned.

The defendants tried by these courts were accused of a range of behaviors. The least serious involved verbal abuse; more serious infractions included disloyalty to the community and betrayal of Jews; the gravest involved physical abuse. In each of these cases the defendants had by their behavior placed themselves outside the Jewish community to varying degrees, and the punishment distanced the guilty in varying degrees from the community to which they now wanted to belong.

Usually the courts had no law or statute to rely on, and mostly focused on what the panels' members considered to be moral or immoral behavior within the context of Nazi rule. In Munich one panel wrote, "In the absence of definite regulations . . . that would define the mere belonging to the ghetto police or similar body as a criminal act, the rehabilitation commission sat in judgment over this case in the same way as over all other cases: namely, in agreement with general principles of jurisprudence, basing judgment on concrete evidence of guilt or innocence."[22] The panelists had no written law to follow except their own "general principles of jurisprudence." Judges mostly did not consider mere membership in the Jewish Council or police, or serving as a kapo, to be a criminal act. Instead they examined the behavior and intentions of the defendant while he or she acted in such a role.[23]

The courts and their different punishments were a means of dissipating, in an orderly and civilized manner, the tensions and violence surrounding alleged collaborators in the survivor community. Violence was channeled through acceptable social institutions. These courts were instrumental in calming social tensions among survivors and also served a retributive function, punishing those who had contributed to the disruption of social order during the war. Furthermore, the courts helped to rebuild the community of survivors in the DP camps into a healthy society, cleansed of members who had acted immorally. The trials and punishments constructed a society that viewed itself as having dealt with its turncoats. In examining its members for disloyalty, the community of survivors followed a path similar to that taken by European states, where the postwar authorities established courts to cleanse their societies of traitors.[24]

Officials of the United Nations Relief and Rehabilitation Administration (UNRRA) in the DP camps in Germany viewed these courts as effective, but when the American army and the military government learned about the honor courts, they initially forbade them as extrajudicial. In early 1947, the army ordered an honor court at the Reinhardt-Kaserne DP camp, located in the German town of Neu-Ulm, to close. The director of the UNRRA area team reported, "The Court was abolished, as already stated, immediately on receipt of the administrative order, stating they were illegal." But she went on to write that "the usefulness of the Court in Camp Administration was very great; its proceedings were conducted with great dignity and impartiality and it enjoyed the full confidence of the Camp Director and of the displaced persons."[25]

A UNRRA district director in Stuttgart, A. T. Berney-Ficklin, accepted that the existence of honor courts was formally prohibited, but he found a way to preserve them. In a letter to his subordinates he wrote in reference to the army directive that "in effect, this means that Courts as such cannot be permitted, but that the Camp Director may use Committees of responsible Displaced Persons to assist him in maintaining discipline by administrative action as indicated." Except for murder cases, where the US military government required that the defendant be brought before its own courts, the "committees" continued to issue judgments on various issues, including the behavior of alleged collaborators during the war.[26]

In 1947, local honor courts in DP camps in the American Zone of Occupation, in southwestern Germany, ceased dealing with cases involving collaboration. Instead, a "rehabilitation committee" established by the Central Committee of Liberated Jews in Munich became the main forum for cases of collaboration. In the Soviet-occupied zone in Berlin, an honor court likewise heard cases of alleged collaboration. These two courts alone heard a total of a few hundred cases. For the most part, the hearing of cases ended in 1949, when the DP camps were largely emptied out.[27]

* * *

Even before the end of World War II, the Polish Republic established state courts to try functionaries who had served under Nazi rule. Between 1944 and 1950 the Polish state courts tried 1,375 cases of Germans and *Volksdeutsche* (Polish citizens of German ethnic origin) for their actions in the camps and ghettos, and 370 cases that included Poles as well as Ukrainians and members of other groups. These courts also heard the cases of 44 Jews accused of collaboration, focusing on the intention of the accused to act against the Polish nation or against individuals within it.[28]

The physician Leon Gross stood trial for allegedly selecting Jews for death and giving lethal injections to inmates in the Plaszow camp. Testimony in his favor by the notorious camp commander Amon Goeth did not help him, and the Polish state court sentenced Gross to death. He was executed in December 1946. Another Jew, Mendel Grünszpan, was tried for having beaten fellow inmates at the Rzeszow camp. The state court sentenced him to one year's imprisonment. Chana Lender was accused of mistreating inmates when she was head of the Jews at the Parschnitz camp. The court sentenced her to five years in prison.[29]

In the most prominent case against a Jew in postwar Poland, on January 7, 1946, the Polish state court issued a verdict regarding Michal Weichert. During the war, Weichert had served as the head of the Krakow-based Jewish Aid Office, an organization that dispensed medicine and other aid from abroad to Jews across Poland. The prosecution argued that Weichert had helped the German cause through his activity in the Aid Office, because the organization presented the Nazi regime to the international community as supporting Jews rather than exterminating them. The court accepted the prosecution's argument that Weichert's activities had harmed the unity and standing of the Polish state. The judges stated, however, that a conviction required proof of intent to act against the Polish state, and because the prosecution had not established Weichert's intent, he could not be convicted.[30]

The clearing of Weichert's name took the Jewish community by surprise. The heads of the community, especially those who had served in the underground and who during the war had killed collaborators as a means of deterrence, viewed Weichert as a traitor. Already during the war, in 1944, the Jewish Fighting Organization issued in absentia a death sentence against him. His acquittal in January of 1946 by the Polish state court led to the rapid establishment of the Jewish communal court in Poland. In the newspaper of the Central Committee of Polish Jews (CCPJ), *Dos naje lebn,* an article appeared under the pen name Cincinnatus calling on Jews to examine their own community:

> We will be committing a sin towards future Jewish generations if we falsify the historical truth by covering it up. Of all the people in Europe, we have undoubtedly the greatest account to settle with German Hitlerism. . . . But we must have the courage to state that our people do not consist entirely of innocent martyrs. Our standing will be no less in the eyes of the world if we brand and try our own turncoats and traitors.[31]

The writer of this article believed that the Jews, who were more severely affected than other groups under the Nazis, should not shrink from judging their own "turncoats and traitors." The impossible position of functionaries in camps and ghettos, who strove in many cases to preserve their families' lives as well as their own, was not yet considered an acceptable reason for their actions.

With the approval of the Polish authorities, the board of the Jewish community decided to establish a communal court to try Jewish functionaries accused of collaboration and betrayal. The goal of such a tribunal, as stated in its charter, was to cleanse "Jewish society of people who, for one reason or another, collaborated with the Nazi authorities during the occupation" and to unmask "traitors of the Jewish nation, who have tens and hundreds of victims on their consciences and still pass, or seek to pass, for respectable people."[32]

To bring these men and women to justice, the CCPJ delegated the investigations to the Central Jewish Historical Commission, a group established at the end of the war to collect evidence about the events that took place during the Holocaust. In the four years of its operation, from 1946 to 1950, the Historical Commission collected the names of 2,000 suspects. Prosecutors from the legal office of the CCPJ conducted approximately 150 investigations and submitted 28 indictments to the communal court. Those courts convicted eighteen of the accused, and five of them were also tried by a Polish state court.[33]

Three years after its establishment, the communal court heard the case against Weichert and pronounced him guilty of misleading Jews in Poland and abroad regarding the fate that awaited them. The court barred Weichert from serving in any leadership position in the Jewish community. The conviction also forced Weichert to leave his positions in research and cultural institutions associated with the Polish Jewish community. Theaters, both Jewish and Polish, would not support his projects. To make a living he sold his library and found work as a cashier. Social ostracism by both the Jewish community and the Polish cultural establishment inflicted a powerful social punishment.[34]

In the eyes of the Polish court that had acquitted Weichert, he was not a collaborator because he did not share the goals and aims of the Nazi regime. But the Jewish communal court convicted him as a collaborator because, in its view, anyone who could have resisted but did not do so failed "to behave as befits a Jewish citizen." For the Jewish court, like the larger Jewish community, no viable option existed between resistance and collaboration. The postwar Polish Jewish community pursued those few who had acted as Weichert had done, and once it had rid itself of them it could portray itself as a community constituted entirely of resisters.[35]

A Jewish Police Commander in a State Court

In late January 1948, Judge Walewski, of the District Court of Sosnowiec, traveled to nearby Bedzin to hear case 304/47, *The Republic of Poland v. Henryk (Hirsch) Barenblat*. Hirsch Barenblat, a resident of the town of Bedzin, Poland, escaped during the war to Slovakia to save his life and was extradited to Poland in 1947. He had been behind bars for seven months awaiting trial.[36] His indictment included accusations that "as a policeman, then as deputy commander, and, from November 1942, as commander of the Jewish militia [in Bedzin], he acted to cause harm to Polish citizens of Jewish nationality through house searches, arrests and deportations to the death camp of Auschwitz, where most of the deportees were murdered."[37]

Barenblat denied the allegations. In the summer of 1941, Barenblat, a skilled musician, was offered and accepted a job with the Jewish Council (Judenrat) of Bedzin as the coordinator of its cultural activities. This position, he claimed, obliged him to wear a police uniform, though he was not a policeman; rather, he conducted an orchestra of forty musicians who performed concerts for the entertainment of the Jews of Bedzin. Months later, the Germans ordered that all cultural activities in Bedzin be shut down, and Barenblat's job as a cultural coordinator and conductor ended abruptly.

It was then, Barenblat told the court, that he "was asked to join the Jewish police" for a second time. He consented. He testified that as a policeman he performed only administrative tasks. In March or April 1942, Barenblat stated, an unspecified person informed him that he had been "nominated to be the chief of the Jewish police." Thus, he claimed, he unintentionally ended up in a position he had never sought.

In his account, Barenblat always spoke in passive language, never stating that he had joined the Jewish police out of his own volition. According to Barenblat, positions had always been offered to him. This scenario seems very unlikely, as many Jews strove to join the police to

Hirsch Barenblat, head of
the Jewish police in Bedzin,
Poland.

better their own position. Serving in the Jewish police offered better
living conditions and for a time protected one's family from deportation.
Of the many who sought these positions, only a few were able to join
the police.

In addition to claiming that he had not wanted to join the Jewish
police, Barenblat also presented a second line of defense. As commander, Barenblat argued, he held no responsibility for police conduct. To distance himself from his subordinates' actions, he portrayed
himself as a police officer not directly involved with acts perpetrated
against Jews. All he did was relay to the policemen lists of names that
he received from the Jewish Council. When the policemen paraded men
and women to the station, Barenblat added, "I did not know what was

happening with them." Under oath he continued to assert that "there were no instances of me mistreating anyone whatsoever. . . . It just was not done. . . . I neither hurt, beat up, nor abused anyone." In fact, he maintained, the opposite was true: the Jewish policemen suffered at the hands of the Jewish populace, he asserted without elaboration.

He claimed to bear no responsibility for what occurred at the bottom of the chain of command. Like many Nazis after the war, he shifted responsibility up the chain. He argued that his superiors on the Bedzin Jewish Council and those who oversaw them at the Sosnowiec Central Office of the Jewish Communities in Eastern Upper Silesia were responsible for the roundups, abductions, and imprisonments that the Jewish police carried out. As police commander, "I received orders from the Jewish community authorities, but I myself did not give orders to anyone else."

He also pointed to the reputation of the heads of the Jewish community to explain his actions. In the Jewish Council as well as in the Jewish police, there were reputable people who had contributed to the community for many years, and he had no reason to doubt their orders. Throughout his testimony, Barenblat emphasized that the Jewish police was an organization established and commanded by the leaders of the Jewish community, not by the Germans. Thus, his argument went, he was acting under Jewish orders and not under the orders of the German enemy.[38]

Twenty-three witnesses testified. In the years 1942–1943, prosecution witnesses stated, the Jewish police in Bedzin, headed by Barenblat, faithfully served the Nazis. In the view of these witnesses, and contrary to the defendant's own argument, Barenblat did bear responsibility for the actions his subordinates conducted under his command. Fearing abduction by the Jewish police, Jewish residents had to peek out of their windows to ensure that no policeman was in the vicinity before going out into the street. Simcha Zlotowski, a merchant, testified that one day he was walking through the town's old market when he came across Barenblat standing with a few of his subordinates. Suddenly one of the policemen seized Zlotowski, who was subsequently deported to a labor camp in Sosnowiec. In Zlotowski's opinion, it seemed that the policeman had acted under Barenblat's supervising eye, though he admitted, "I am not able to say if it was Barenblat who

ordered the other policeman to arrest me." Like Zlotowski, other prosecution witnesses did not have direct knowledge of the defendant's
commands or actions. "I heard that the defendant used to mistreat
people; however, I never witnessed it myself," declared Nathan
Piorun.[39]

Unlike the testimony of these witnesses, Isaac Wacksman's touched
directly on Barenblat's actions. Wacksman was working in a tailor shop
in Bedzin when news came that the Jewish police had arrested his
cousin Ester Fylenda and her daughter. Wacksman bribed Barenblat,
who promised that he would release Wacksman's relatives shortly. The
night passed, but Wacksman's cousins remained locked in the police
building. In the morning, a train loaded with Jews stood in the station
ready to depart for Auschwitz. Wacksman ran to the station and reminded Barenblat of his promise to free his relatives. Barenblat refused to honor his promise. "Instead, he hit me in the face and kicked
me. . . . They were all very bad and indecent people," Wacksman said
of the police and the Jewish Council, an overarching statement that
reflected the prevailing view among many survivors.[40]

Unlike prosecution witnesses, defense witnesses tended to look at
Barenblat's behavior in relative terms. "Many people in the ghetto believed that if someone else had been in Barenblat's shoes, the situation
would have been much worse," asserted factory owner David Kleinman.
Conditions at the Kamionka labor camp were "much changed for the
better" when Barenblat arrived in August 1943, testified a housewife
named Rozka Felczer. Given the circumstances, the twenty-four-
year-old Felczer said, "nothing bad can be said about the defendant.
Surely anyone would have acted as he did or maybe even worse given
the context of the [Nazi] occupation." In both cases the defense witnesses emphasized the context of Barenblat's actions.[41]

Then a former member of the Jewish underground, Maria "Kasia"
Szancer, took the witness stand. Kasia had smuggled people and documents in and out of the Bedzin ghetto. Both Polish and Jewish society
held members of the resistance movement in high esteem, and it seems
that in this case her account carried greater weight than those of "ordinary" survivors. Kasia encountered Barenblat shortly after the Nazis
shipped his wife off to Auschwitz. Barenblat smuggled Kasia out of
German custody in a bread cart. She fell in love with her rescuer and

Kasia Barenblat, second wife of Hirsch Barenblat, who testified in his defense.

they married, a relationship the Polish court seems to have ignored when examining her testimony.

Kasia told the court that Barenblat had not wanted to take the position of police commander but was ordered to do so by the Jewish underground in town. "The leaders of the underground thought Barenblat was a good match for the position since he could help people, and through him the organization could have access to the ghetto," she told the court, an account that other underground activists refuted.[42]

In early March 1948, the state court pronounced its verdict:

> It is well known that despite the fact that they acted under the command of the German authorities, the Jewish police or *Ordnungsdienst* took part in a set of actions of oppression against the Jewish population. Nevertheless, it is not possible to treat it as a criminal organization, and also it is not possible to treat membership in the police as a crime. Therefore, in order to convict any policeman and even the police commander of crimes against the Jewish people, one

must point to harmful acts that the defendant committed against the Jewish public in Bedzin and at the same time [show] that these actions benefited the German occupation authorities.[43]

The Polish state court held that mere membership in the Jewish police or the Jewish Council did not suffice to convict someone of membership in a criminal organization. The concept of a "criminal organization" had been developed three years earlier at the London Conference on Military Trials and pursued in the Nuremberg trials. The Nuremberg tribunal determined that organizations such as the SS and the Gestapo were criminal in nature and that anyone with knowledge of their criminality could be found guilty of membership in a hostile organization. The Polish court, however, would not recognize the Jewish organizations as criminal organizations. These institutions served the Germans in their actions against the Jews, but to convict an individual for membership in these institutions, the prosecution had to prove that the defendant intended to serve and in fact benefited the German authorities. The question of whether the Jewish Council and Jewish police should be considered criminal organizations would re-emerge in Barenblat's 1963 trial in Israel.[44]

The court rejected most of the prosecution testimony as hearsay. Even the actions of Barenblat's subordinates did not implicate him. Only evidence of a direct command or action by Barenblat would be considered incriminating. Just two witnesses, Wacksman and Sela Dykman, had given accounts pertaining to events that they personally had experienced and that related directly to Barenblat. But the court found that both testimonies were inconclusive and riddled with contradictions. In contrast, "a series of serious and objective witnesses presented the defendant in the most positive light as a man who frequently helped the Jewish people and on multiple occasions, at the risk of his own life, saved [his brethren] without hesitation." In the view of the court it was improbable that a person would both risk his life to save others and also send individuals to their deaths. The Polish state court concluded that "it has been decided to acquit Henryk Barenblat."[45]

Barenblat was freed after eight months behind bars, but his legal ordeal was not yet over. In mid-1948, the Jewish communal court requested Barenblat's file. The prosecutors of the CCPJ read the Polish state court transcripts and then collected a few more testimonies. Some of these testimonies, according to the prosecutors, justified the filing of a complaint against Barenblat to a Jewish communal court. In May 1949, CCPJ lawyers submitted an indictment against Barenblat, an indictment that would never come to trial.

For the CCPJ lawyers assigned to the honor court, the fact that Barenblat had served as a policeman, deputy commander, and commander of the Jewish police indicated that "the defendant facilitated the implementation of the plans of the Nazi occupier." Unlike the judges in the state court, the lawyers of the CCPJ deemed that Barenblat had "taken an active part in the deportations," indicating that they regarded serving the occupation forces in a diligent manner as a criterion of guilt, even without intent being proven. The indictment stated that the history of the Jews of Bedzin and the area "on the one hand testifies to the bravery of those who joined the resistance movement and fought against the Nazis." On the other hand, there were those who, "in exchange for a little power and influence from the Central Office [of the Jewish Communities of Eastern Upper Silesia] headed by Moniek Merin, and for the promise that their own lives would be saved, gave up defenseless fellow Jews to the hands of the Nazis." No middle ground existed between the resistance movement and the Jewish Council. The only legitimate choice was the underground.[46]

The indictment against Barenblat dedicated considerable attention to his part in the deportation of August 12, 1942, which came to be known as the Great Punkt. A few days before that, the Jewish Council in Bedzin and Sosnowiec had posted notices calling on all Jews of the two neighboring towns to assemble at the local sports field for the Germans to verify their documents. To assuage anxiety, the Jewish authorities urged residents to appear in their best clothing. Despite skepticism among Jews, on the day of assembly a witness wrote, "At 5:00 A.M. Jews began streaming [onto the sports fields], so as not to be late, God forbid. . . . Mothers pushed their young ones in strollers, the old and sick were brought in carts and carriages, all dressed in their finest clothing, as if they were going to a celebration."[47]

At 11:00 A.M. the Germans surrounded the field. They divided the thousands of assembled Jews into three groups: one destined for release, one to be shipped to a labor camp, and one to be reexamined. Families were separated. Fathers attempted to switch groups to reunite with their children, as did wives who wanted to stand by their husbands. People pushed and shoved, cried and howled. On that day and the following ones, the Germans deported thousands of Jews from Bedzin and Sosnowiec to Auschwitz for systematic murder.[48]

Based on the witness Zlotowski's account to the Polish state court (testimony that was dismissed by that court as hearsay), and on the basis of new testimony by a handful of others, the legal office of the CCPJ concluded that in the Great Punkt, Barenblat ordered the Jewish policemen to prevent Jews from crossing from one group to the other. He supervised the aggressive actions of the police, who kicked and beat anyone who attempted to move between the groups. From this point onward, the prosecution argued, in contrast to the view of the Polish state court, it became clear based on their actions that the Sosnowiec Central Office of the Jewish Communities in Eastern Upper Silesia and the institutions of the Jewish Council and the Jewish police served as "loyal tools in the hands of Nazis." Witnesses refuted Barenblat's argument that "when people tried to leave the groups, 'police made sure to protect the Jewish population.'"[49]

Barenblat was "deeply loyal to the evil institutions of the Jewish police and the Jewish Council," the prosecutors argued in their indictment, indicating that—unlike the Polish state court—they viewed these Jewish institutions as criminal organizations based on their actions and not on their intentions. But had this case come to trial, it is not at all clear that the Jewish honor court would have seen the Jewish organizations in that way. In fact, honor courts in DP camps in Germany also refused to recognize them as criminal organizations. While behavior within these organizations could face scrutiny, membership in them could not be considered voluntary.[50]

Careful not to impugn the Polish court, the prosecutors implied that the testimony of Kasia Szancer, the heroic underground fighter and Barenblat's wife, had misled the state court judges. Kasia had corroborated her husband's statement that the underground had urged him to take the position of police commander. This was highly unlikely, argued the CCPJ prosecutors, who saw the resistance and the Judenrat as diametrically opposed, because "the resistance movement believed that taking on any official function in the Jewish police force was reprehensible behavior harmful to the interests of the Jewish people."[51] Indeed, this negative view of the Judenrat and the Jewish police dominated the underground movement. One member of the Bedzin resistance movement, Hayka Klinger, wrote in her diary about the August 1942 deportation that "today, after the shameful acts of deportations, we have nothing whatsoever to do with them."[52]

The CCPJ prosecutors heard testimony about both the deportations in August 1942 and those that had taken place a few months earlier, in May, from resistance movement member Henryk Diament, who now resided in Vienna. In his account, Diament testified that in August 1942 he saw Barenblat ordering his men to prevent the escape of a group destined for deportation that had been transferred from the sports field to the Judenrat orphanage. Diament stated that Barenblat was responsible for the "diligence" with which the Jewish policemen guarded those destined for deportation. "If he had not ensured such diligence in following orders, they would surely have 'looked the other' way when people tried to escape." This behavior was no coincidence, argued the witness. Barenblat was dedicated to fulfilling German commands despite his knowledge that the deportees were destined to die. He had not simply acted on behalf of the Germans; rather, he had acted diligently on their behalf.[53]

For unknown reasons—possibly Barenblat's refusal to participate in the voluntary proceedings of the communal court—the prosecutors never presented the testimonies and materials they had collected to the communal court. The Polish state court and the prosecutors in the Jewish communal court held diametrically opposed positions regarding Barenblat, a disagreement that stemmed from the different nature of the legal procedure each of them utilized. On the one hand, the Polish court acted on the basis of a set of laws that determined what behavior was acceptable, and it applied a narrow legal approach to the examination of evidence. On the other hand, the prosecutors of the Jewish communal court interpreted the case on the basis of their personal understanding of the events, following neither law nor precedent, and the only question they considered was what behavior was morally befitting a Jewish citizen. The Polish court determined that Barenblat's actions lacked intent to serve the perpetrators, and that only proving such intent could allow conviction. The prosecutors

of the Jewish court viewed Barenblat as someone whose actions had
served the Germans and who thus had betrayed the Jewish nation.[54]

In 1963, fifteen years after the legal office of the CCPJ prepared its
indictment, an Israeli prosecutor presented allegations against Barenblat in Tel Aviv District Court. There, some of the same witnesses
would once again confront one another regarding Barenblat's actions
during the Holocaust. And the prosecutor would ask the court to address the question of the legal and moral responsibility of the Judenrat
and the Jewish police, asking whether they should be viewed as criminal organizations.

Moral Judgment in a Communal Court

One of the approximately 150 investigations undertaken by prosecutors of the legal office of the CCPJ in Warsaw was the case of Julius
Siegel. According to witnesses, Siegel harassed and beat inmates in a
workshop in Bedzin and "took an active part in deportations to Auschwitz and to the gas chambers." As in the case of Barenblat, the prosecutors stated that Siegel "took an active role," indicating that he had
acted diligently in the service of the Germans. He was not simply a desk
clerk at the Judenrat, the prosecutors held, but rather helped to facilitate
the deportation and persecution of Jews. However, after collecting a few
witness accounts, the commission dropped the case when it learned
that the accused had moved abroad.[55]

A textile engineer by training and a former Austrian officer in World
War I, Siegel headed a DP camp in Padua, Italy. It was not uncommon
for those who had served as heads of the community during the war to
continue to take responsibility after liberation, as happened in the case
of Itzik Gritzmacher, the former kapo at Bad Tölz who later assumed
a position of leadership. Besides having an inclination to take such
positions, frequently those who had served as functionaries during the
war were in better health and so were more able to serve as heads of
survivor communities. But in Padua, former residents of Bedzin identified Siegel and filed a complaint. The camp police arrested him and
placed him in detention.

Over the years, in Europe and in Israel, Siegel would face a total of
five court proceedings, which resulted in two verdicts, each of which

portrayed his conduct during World War II in a different light. The first opened in June 1946 in the DP camp of Cremona, in one of the communal courts that refugees established throughout Italy and elsewhere in Europe. To grant the court social legitimacy, the camp leaders held an election to select the judges. The residents chose eight men and one woman to serve on the panel.

The prosecutor, Zeshuta Itzhak, leveled grave accusations against the fifty-one-year-old defendant, whom he defined as an active facilitator of Nazi operations. The indictment made a general statement that "in the time of the German occupation Siegel was an active assistant to the occupiers, and many Jews died because of his actions, while others were sent to the camps because of his assistance, and still others were beaten by him." The indictment, however, did not include any specific charges or events, only promising to bring testimonies "from many witnesses, who know him personally and who can confirm the accusation."

The absence of specific charges in the indictment, which would be unthinkable in a criminal court, relates to the nature of the panel. As a communal tribunal, the court centered its deliberation on the ethics of Siegel's behavior and was open to hearing any testimony about his conduct and to deliberating on any of his actions and choices without specific accusations being leveled against him. In one such communal DP court in Rivoli, Italy, it was stated that the court "does not function according to laws and clauses formulated according to legal principles, but rather according to a social rationale and principles of national ethics."[56] The fact that the court did not restrict itself to any specific legal code could have made it difficult to mount a defense for the accused party. Still, the one key point for the court was the defendant's loyalty or disloyalty to the Jewish nation.[57]

First on the stand was the defendant, who turned down the court's offer to hire an attorney and chose to represent himself. In his account he sought to portray himself as a Jewish leader who had preserved his nation's honor in the face of German oppression. This strategy did not work in his favor; on the contrary, Siegel's own testimony, which preceded that of the prosecution witnesses, conveyed his close association with the Nazis. In what sounded like the boastful account of a person completely enamored of himself and out of touch with the views and feelings of the survivors in the DP camp, he proudly listed for the court all the positions he had held under the Germans, whom he had served throughout the war. When the Germans occupied the town of Bedzin, they appointed him as head of the Jewish workforce. They later appointed him *Judenältester* (Jewish elder) in the Brande labor camp and *Lagerältester* (camp elder) in the Sakrau camp. Very satisfied with his work, the Germans then made Siegel the *Judenältester* of the Gross-Masselwitz camp, and shortly thereafter in the Rossner workshop in Bedzin. When he arrived in Auschwitz, Siegel proclaimed, the Germans were waiting for him and immediately placed him in "a high-ranking position." Siegel declared to the court that "he found favor with the Germans," who admired his ability to administer and organize "his" Jews.

The Nazis liked his work so much, Siegel continued, that they arranged for the Nazi German press to interview him. He claimed to be the only Jew during the war whom the Nazi German press interviewed. "Siegel the Jew was famous throughout Europe," he boasted. He had never taken his hat off in reverence to a German "and he always saluted as an equal." He would not allow them to address him with informal second-person pronouns, demanding that they use only formal pronouns. By portraying himself as a leader on equal footing with the Germans, he believed, he could show the court that he had preserved the honor of the Jewish nation.

Even when he seemed to admit wrongdoing, it served his goal of self-promotion. Speaking at times in the third person about himself—as is customary in speaking German in official settings—and at times in first person, he testified, "It would not be honest if he said that he had never beaten a Jew. I beat [Jews] sometimes, but only out of pure fatherly love," implying that he held the same legitimate right to strike Jews that a father was then considered to have in relation to his children. Siegel claimed parental authority over "his Jews." Asked by one of the judges if he had also beaten Jews when no Germans were present, he acknowledged that he had. Not surprisingly, in future proceedings in Italy as well as Israel, as he came to comprehend the hostile feelings toward functionaries, Siegel would significantly alter his story.[58]

Prosecution witnesses described Siegel as greatly devoted to the German occupiers. "All his concern was to serve the interests of the

Germans, and never was he concerned with the interests of the Jews," Barish Wacksberg testified.[59] This was a theme that would recur in most of the other trials as well, in which defendants were often described as equivalent to, or worse than, the Germans. After all, in the eyes of former inmates it was these supervisors who had overseen them and directly executed the actions that harmed them. They frequently did not know the Germans who handed down the order to the functionaries, whom they knew by name.

A former inmate from the Sakrau camp described how, like a typical German, Siegel had demanded order and discipline. He beat and harassed laboring Jews. He would boast about his close relations with Heinrich Lindner, the German in charge of the local Schmelt industrial organization (and who was said to have treated Jews horribly and deported them), and said he had frequent discussions with him. Morris Herschteil, a prisoner in one of the labor camps in which the defendant served as supervisor, asserted, "In our camp, Siegel was seen as someone who had sold his soul to Lindner."[60]

Like the Germans, witnesses suggested, Siegel held anti-Semitic views. Once he ordered fifty bearded Jews to stand to one side at work. The Nazis rushed them to a local market, where a crew filmed the Jews "chasing" the Nazi soldiers for a propaganda movie. They also staged a scene of one Jew choking a German. "Siegel was present and laughing cynically," the witness related. In portraying Siegel as a Jewish anti-Semite, the witnesses presented him as one who not only acted in the service of the Germans but identified with their views of Jews as well. Describing Jewish functionaries as Nazis was also a tactical move that presented the functionaries to the court as the true culprits, devoted to the task of annihilating the Jews. Victims viewed functionaries like Siegel as equivalent to Nazis.

In November 1941, on the first anniversary of the establishment of the Sakrau labor camp, Siegel—who frequently dressed in a green outfit, breeches, and shiny riding boots, wielding a whip and wearing a monocle—gave a celebratory speech, even suggesting that the Germans would win the war.[61] The witness Moritz Herschteil reported to the court that he heard Siegel proclaim that the Jews should do "diligent work to serve the Germans. If the Germans win the war, they will surely designate for us, the Jews, a place where we will be able to work."

With these words uttered in the courtroom in Cremona, the witness placed Siegel in association with people such as Chaim Rumkowski, the head of the Lodz ghetto, and Moniek Merin from Sosnowitz, men who believed that the more productive the Jews proved for the Germans, the greater the chance that the Germans would save them from deportation—a view already strongly opposed by the Jewish rebel movement during the war. The "work and be saved" approach promoted by these leaders required residents to work to exhaustion and legitimized the German deportation of the weak and unproductive Jews from the ghettos to the camps.[62]

In June 1946, Siegel's trial was halted. The central Jewish communal court in Rome, which was established by the Refugee Center (the organization of Jewish refugees in Italy), proclaimed that the DP camp courts, including the one in Cremona, had no jurisdiction over the matter.[63] But mere weeks later, the dispute over the authority of the courts was resolved and Siegel's trial reopened in the Jewish Center for the Diaspora in Milan. The new prosecutor, Isador Tshorny, replaced the earlier charge against Siegel of "taking an active role" in the deportation and death of Jews with the explicit accusation of "betrayal of the Jewish nation." The earlier implicit accusation of treachery now appeared explicitly in the indictment.

Having heard the prosecution witnesses in the previous proceeding, Siegel had had time to reconsider his position and his account. Previously, probably because of his lack of acquaintance with the court, as well as being overly confident in his own abilities, Siegel had declined to retain counsel or to call witnesses. But for the court in Milan he submitted a list of eighteen witnesses, thirteen of whom lived in Munich and one of whom lived in Palestine. The court rejected his motion to await the arrival of the witnesses, apparently seeing it as a delaying tactic. It permitted Siegel to summon only two defense witnesses located in Italy, but even those two, for reasons unknown to both the prosecutor and the defendant, would not appear. The court gave the defendant twenty-four hours to hire a defense attorney, but on the following day Siegel arrived in court alone and announced he was unable to locate one. He would again represent himself.[64]

Unlike his account in the first trial, Siegel's testimony in the second trial no longer presented him as a close associate of the Germans. He made no reference to the Germans' appreciation of his work, to his close relations with Nazi officials, or to his earlier claim that "Siegel the Jew was famous throughout Europe." Now he presented himself as a victim: the Germans had controlled him, and he had had no choice but to act as he had done. His job was to recruit workers, "which was demanded by the Germans." But his earlier testimony in front of the court in Cremona partially trapped him. Responding to the Milan court's questions, he again admitted that he had beaten Jews, but this time he did not portray it as an action of "fatherly love." Instead, he expressed remorse, saying that he now understood that it was a crime. Siegel explained, "I was very nervous, and after each instance I always regretted it." He also justified his misconduct by pointing to the misbehavior of the Jews he had overseen, arguing that "among Jews there were bodily filth, a lack of willingness to work, and a habit of stealing bread; and I had no other way to respond."[65]

On July 19, 1946, Siegel made his closing statement, in which he admitted wrongdoing, speaking about himself in the third person: "He beat Jews, and not only when the Germans were watching. He honestly regrets this." He asked the court for mercy, as "he is over 50 years old and wishes to end his life in a way that will benefit his nation and country." Siegel also found a way to cast his role in the deportations in a less negative light. When the Germans demanded one thousand people for deportation, the Judenrat rounded up two thousand and released those who paid bribes. Unlike other corrupt members of the Jewish Council, "I did not accept bribes," Siegel proclaimed.[66]

On the same day, the court announced its verdict. It denounced the self-loving Siegel for "daring" to serve as the head of the DP camp in Padua. Based on his first account to the Cremona court, the Milan court detailed Siegel's many positions as an indication of his dedication to the Germans. Siegel, the court determined, acted out of "free will" to assume positions of power "to advance his personal prestige." The court found that his motivation was self-promotion, but indicated that it found no evidence he had gained personal financial benefit. The judges found no mitigating circumstances, and saw Siegel's behavior as a symptom of his warped personality and as an attempt to bolster his own position and power. Furthermore, the court concluded, the defendant had acted out of "loyalty to the Germans."

The judges framed their verdict in moral terms. "In the darkest time of the history of the People of Israel, in the sad days of the annihilation of European Jewry, the defendant Siegel did not attain the required standard." The court's view of the required standard, like that of the communal courts in Poland and elsewhere, was resistance. Siegel did "not assist his brethren in opposing the perpetrator by all means and in every way possible—but on the contrary, he sometimes did more than he was ordered [by the Germans], and on his own initiative beat his fellow Jews." The court concluded that Siegel acted in a "criminal manner that was harmful to the Jewish public." It decreed that Siegel could never again hold any public position in the Jewish community and ordered that the verdict be publicized in Jewish newspapers.[67]

But the self-centered Siegel remained determined to clear his name. Although he had already obtained a visa for the United States, in the summer of 1948, a year after the verdict was issued, he visited the Israeli consulate in Rome. He sought permission to immigrate to the newly established Jewish state, where he hoped to clear his name. Israel, however, would not permit Jews suspected of collaboration to immigrate. "For a long time," wrote Israel's consul in Rome, Aryeh Stern, to the Foreign Ministry in Tel Aviv,

> this person [Siegel] has turned up at our offices with a request to allow him to immigrate to Israel. . . . He claims that the accusations against him were exaggerated and distorted and he does not see the verdict as just. He has only one ambition, and it is to immigrate [to Israel], have his trial reviewed by an Israeli court, and accept any punishment, even the harshest, that may be inflicted upon him. His deep desire [is] to serve in the Israel Defense Forces, in any position, and in doing so to prove his faithfulness to his nation.[68]

After consulting with the Jewish communal court of Rome, the consul made an exception to the practice of not issuing immigration papers to those accused of collaboration. On October 1, 1948, immigration papers in hand, Siegel boarded the ship *Kadimah* in Genoa and traveled to Israel, where he would face three additional court appearances.[69]

CHAPTER TWO

TENSIONS AMONG SURVIVORS
IN MANDATORY PALESTINE

IN EARLY DECEMBER 1945, bus number 6 traveled down King George Street in Tel Aviv, picking up early evening commuters. At one stop a man and a woman in their thirties boarded and took their seats. As the bus drove off, the eyes of one of the passengers locked onto the new male commuter. The passenger became more and more upset as he continued to stare at the man who had just gotten on. Jumping to his feet, the passenger approached the new commuter.

"Are you Haim Molchadsky from Bedzin?" the agitated man asked in a quavering voice. No response. He asked the question again: "Are you Haim Molchadsky from Bedzin?" Silence. The questioner turned pale and started screaming in Yiddish, "You killed my family! You are responsible for the death of thousands of Jews!"

Other passengers crowded around. One slapped the new commuter's face; another hit him on the head. Others called for the driver to stop the bus. At the junction of Dizengoff Street and King George Street, the driver pulled the bus over. The man and woman leapt off. Passengers jumped off after them, and the scuffle spilled out into the street. Passersby also joined in. The pack of attackers surrounded the pair and blocked their escape. A policeman approached the scene. Together with passersby he broke through the crowd and pulled the couple away.

In the police station's interrogation room, the accused man admitted that he was indeed Molchadsky, the former head of the Bedzin Jewish Council and the person to whom police commander Henryk Barenblat had answered. The thirty-five-year-old Molchadsky, who before the war had headed the Bedzin branch of the Jewish National Fund (Keren Kayemet LeYisrael), had arrived in Mandatory Palestine a few

weeks earlier. He described to the police how when the Nazis had occupied Bedzin they appointed him head of the Jewish Council's social
department. This position, which required him to select those who
would go to work camps, made him many enemies, he stated. Then
the Germans promoted him, making him head of the Jewish Council
(Judenrat). But in the end he, too, was deported and suffered in Auschwitz, he told his police interrogators.[1]

This episode is just one of dozens of similar encounters in which
acts undertaken in the camps in Europe reverberated on the streets of
Tel Aviv. Retribution was carried out not only by survivors directly affected by alleged collaborators but also by people who had arrived in
Mandatory Palestine before the war and had not suffered in Europe.
Many residents of Tel Aviv and the rest of Mandatory Palestine had
family members who had perished in Europe, and they sought to avenge
the dead. Some also assaulted the suspected traitors to uphold the honor
of the Jewish nation, which they believed had been disgraced by people
such as Molchadsky and the members of the Judenrat.

A few weeks after Molchadsky's encounter on the bus, on the afternoon of Saturday, January 5, 1946, two brothers, Nechemia and Benjamin Friedrich from the Polish town of Ostrowiec, encountered their
townsman Shmuel Vishlitzky in the center of Tel Aviv. They suspected
that he had revealed the hiding place of their thirty-one-year-old aunt
Leah and her ten-year-old daughter. A scuffle ensued, but the bloodied
Vishlitzky broke away from the mob and ran for his life. Some of his
assailants pursued him, but he disappeared from sight. They combed
the bustling junction of Allenby Street and Ben-Yehudah Street for
hours, searching behind garbage cans and in stairwells for the alleged
collaborator, but to no avail.[2]

Those accused of assisting the Nazis frequently did not stay
silent. Two days after disappearing in the center of Tel Aviv,
Vishlitzky reemerged in the editorial room of *Ha-Mashkif*. Far worse
than the physical pain, he told the editors, were "the mental humiliation and torments." He denied any association with the Nazis. He
said that when he had arrived in Palestine three months earlier, he
had heard rumors accusing him of handing over a family to the Gestapo. He had then contacted the Tel Aviv offices of the *Landsmanschaft* of Ostrowiec and demanded a public inquiry. The subsequent

investigation had cleared his name, and the accusers had asked his forgiveness. Nevertheless, Vishlitzky appealed to the public in Tel Aviv "to help me prove my innocence. After all, will our town not turn into Sodom when each person chooses to take justice into his own hands?"[3]

In their quest to absolve themselves of accusations of collaboration, some survivors, like Vishlitzky, turned to their *Landsmanschaften* with requests that those organizations intervene in their cases. In July 1946, a survivor wrote to the *Landsmanschaft* of the Polish town Dabrowa Gornicza, accusing another survivor of serving as a *Judenältester*. While the writer was not seeking revenge, she did demand that the supervisor be tried and "completely removed from society."[4] Plaintiffs in Israel turned to the social institutions of the *Landsmanschaft* just as in Europe they would have turned to a communal court or to an honor court. But in the Yishuv, where many hoped to remove any remnant of exile tradition from the public sphere, such organizations did not hold the same sway that they did abroad. Vishlitzky's clearing by the *Landsmanschaft* had no effect and he, like others accused of collaboration, remained vulnerable to attacks.

Three weeks after being spotted on the Tel Aviv bus, Molchadsky, a self-proclaimed "miserable and unfortunate man," sent a letter to the daily newspaper *Haaretz* denying the calumny of collaboration. In his letter, Molchadsky asked that instead of the *Landsmanschaften* a different institution evaluate the cases of those accused of collaboration. He wrote, "I have turned to the responsible Zionist institutions with a request to investigate my case or put me on trial," adding that even in "the harshest of days I prayed for the day when I would have the opportunity to submit an account of my actions to the Zionist institutions in charge . . . I therefore repeat my request that I be granted an opportunity to present my case to the responsible authorities in whatever form or fashion [they] find fit." Unlike the *Landsmanschaften*, Zionist institutions, representing a movement that advocated Jewish independence, did hold sway among members of the Yishuv and were accepted as a fair arbiter. But the heads of these Zionist institutions showed reluctance to take upon themselves the judgment of Jewish collaborators with the Nazis.[5]

* * *

Newspapers in the Jewish community in Mandatory Palestine called on the Yishuv leadership to establish a committee to investigate accusations against alleged collaborators. In March 1945, one newspaper estimated that 250 alleged betrayers had entered Mandatory Palestine.[6] According to a writer in one of the socialist newspapers, it would have been possible to save many more Jews "if we had not been betrayed from within." The writer continued, "Isn't it essential to appoint a public *investigative committee* to assess concrete accusations? Isn't there, perhaps, a need for us to establish a court to try our own war criminals?" If Jews did not take Jewish criminals to task for their actions, the speaker feared, the Soviets would one day expose the Jewish traitors from within and form a "blot on the Zionist movement" by pointing to "those who amassed a fortune in the business of annihilating the Jews." A committee established by the Zionist authorities would save face for the Jewish nation.[7]

The writer dismissed an argument that would be frequently expressed in later years: "Do not judge your fellow man until you have stood in his place" (*Pirkei Avot*, 2:4). He believed that such reluctance to judge was dangerous in Mandatory Palestine. The absence of a court would result in anarchy, he thought. The public demanded judgment and it was essential to deal with the Jewish nation's "war criminals," he stated, referring to the accused with a term that the Allies used in reference to the Nazis and their accomplices.[8]

In addition to the black mark on the Zionist movement, another reason to establish a court was the anarchy and violence that reigned in public places in Mandatory Palestine. Many newspapers of divergent stances called for an institutional response. The liberal *Haaretz* turned to the heads of the Jewish community in the Land of Israel, demanding that "the organizations in charge express their view on this sad issue that is troubling the Jewish public."[9] A Revisionist party newspaper concurred and stated that "an investigation is required against people who have been accused of such serious charges!" The editors added that "in light of the recurring incidents of this kind, which are becoming more common, it is essential that a public institution investigate and deal with those among us upon whom such heavy allegations weigh."[10] Following the attempted lynching of a vendor at a shoe shop on Allenby

Street in Tel Aviv, *Yediot Aharonot* wrote that there was an urgent need for a people's court to judge such cases.[11]

In the absence of authorized social institutions, such as a court or a special committee, to deliberate on the various cases, violence continued to spread unabated. While the violence mostly concerned the community of survivors, at times it also touched on those who were not part of that community, as in the case of a man who had immigrated to Mandatory Palestine before the war. In April 1946, a scar-faced man entered the editorial room of the tabloid *Iton Meyuhad*. The man, forty-one-year-old Asher Berlin, who worked selling tickets in a movie theater, told a reporter that a few months earlier, in a dark alley not far from the intersection of Allenby and Ben-Yehudah, a group of men had surrounded him. Within seconds he felt knife blades penetrate his belly and slash his face. Passersby ran to his aid, but one of the attackers warned them, "Don't interfere. Two years ago he informed on Jews to the Gestapo." A few minutes later, after the attack was over, passersby rushed Berlin to a nearby hospital, where emergency surgery saved his life.

"Mr. Berlin wept bitterly in our editorial office, and with tears nearly choking him, cried bitterly about the false accusations that had literally been laid on him with knives," wrote the newspaper. Berlin went on to tell the editors, "If there was even a shred of truth in the accusations against me, I would cut my throat with my own hands." The truth was that Berlin had arrived in Tel Aviv twenty-two years earlier, in 1924, and had never since set foot in Europe. Even after the attempt to assassinate him, rumors continued to circulate in Tel Aviv that this ticket seller had collaborated with the Nazis. "Someone might fall victim to an error on the part of these unknown upholders of Israel's honor, thanks to an uninvestigated rumor or to similarity in face or name," concluded the editors of *Iton Meyuhad*. "The anarchy that is raging in our public places has gone beyond all bounds and must be controlled."[12]

As this last account makes clear, it was not only the preservation of the image of the Jewish nation and the street violence that motivated those who called for the establishment of a communal court, but also the quest for national retribution. In a national-religious newspaper, a columnist demanded trials of the "withered Jews who served as heads of Jewish Councils, officers in the Jewish Police or other jobs, who assisted the Germans in fulfilling their plans for annihilation. . . . Just as we are determined to abolish the murderers of all nations who participated directly or indirectly in the murder of the Jews—so too we support the complete annihilation of the murderers from within," stated the writer. These "partners of Satan" should not face vigilante justice, he cautioned, but rather be tried before "authorized institutions" that would determine their guilt.[13] *Iton Meyuhad* warned that the establishment of such an institution "must be done soon; otherwise the criminals may be able to conceal their acts of abomination." Any delay in establishing legal committees would result in more functionaries escaping justice, the writers feared. These "criminals" must pay for their actions against the nation.[14]

In the absence of a court to pronounce on allegations of collaboration, former inmates continued to take judgment into their own hands and to assault alleged collaborators. Indeed, some of the survivors faced trial for assaulting their former supervisors. On a Saturday afternoon in the summer of 1946, two survivors of the Gleiwitz labor camp, Rachel Luxemburg and Hella Honigman, together with Hella's brother David, were walking along the Yarkon River. They saw a couple rowing on the river, and identified the woman as their former camp supervisor Sarah Baumgarten, who was with her fiancé. When the couple docked, a scuffle developed. "You evil woman! You don't have the right to be here, in the Land of Israel," David Honigman shouted at Baumgarten, and slapped her face. In the eyes of Honigman and many like him, the Land of Israel was intended to give a new life to the true victims, not to the Nazi functionaries who had betrayed the nation. The skirmish continued, with a crowd watching, until police officers arrived and picked up the men and women.

The police did not recommend that the former kapo stand trial, but rather that Honigman, her brother, and Luxemburg be prosecuted for assault. In September 1946, their case came before the Tel Aviv Magistrates Court under Judge Max Kenneth (Kanterovitch), who would later try many of the cases against alleged collaborators brought by Israel's attorney general. It was probably the first time that a Holocaust-related story had been told in a courtroom in Mandatory Palestine. The

Honigman siblings admitted they had struck Baumgarten, but they also used the opportunity to confront Baumgarten with her actions in the camp. Six survivors described her harsh treatment of inmates. One survivor who came to support her friends sported a broken tooth, the result of Baumgarten's beatings. Judge Kenneth cleared Luxemburg of all charges for lack of evidence, but he convicted Hella and David Honigman of assault. However, he took into account the two siblings' suffering in Europe and imposed on them only the token fine of 50 Palestine mils.[15]

Rebels' Loathing of Collaborators

Upon their arrival in the Land of Israel, members of the Zionist youth movements who had rebelled and fought the Nazis in occupied Europe had the power to shape opinion within the Yishuv. One of the first to arrive in Haifa was Hayka Klinger, who had been a member of the Jewish underground in Bedzin. Even before the issue was raised in the Yishuv, Klinger voiced scathing criticism of the Jewish Councils in Europe. Members of these councils, she told a reporter in March 1944, managed social institutions "that had become tools of suppression in the hands of authorities." They played an "abject" role in the satanic Nazi plan. Initially, the council members did not know the fate of those whom the Nazis sent to forced labor camps. But later, Klinger said, expressing a belief commonly held by those associated with the rebel movement, "There were instances of clear knowledge . . . and they lied knowingly [to the deportees]." In contrast to these council members, members of the Zionist youth movements had exposed the truth about the Nazis' plans and struggled to open the eyes of the Jewish masses, to present the bitter truth "of mass killings, to disillusion [those who hoped to be] saved by the Germans' mercy, to bring those sentenced to death to take their fate into their own hands."[16] Klinger and other members of the rebel movement drew a stark contrast between their own heroic activities and those of the Jewish police and Judenrats that promoted the German cause, both attempting to shape what she described as a passive Jewish mass.

The black-haired, stern-faced Klinger also spoke to the leaders of various groups in the Yishuv.[17] She did not refrain from voicing her critical views even when speaking to men twice her age. From the executive board of the Histadrut (the general labor union), a dominant voice in Mandatory Palestine, she demanded an unflinching self-examination:

> One thing must be determined: [The] various Jewish communities [in Europe] were headed by members of the Zionist movement, and most of them understood that if [the Nazis] said A, they would need to carry on and [do] B. And after they began assisting the Germans in collecting gold and furniture from Jewish homes, they had no choice but to go on to help prepare lists of Jews for labor camps.... And precisely because those who stood at the head of most of the communities were Zionists, the psychological effect on the Jewish masses vis-à-vis the Zionist idea was devastating, and the hatred toward Zionism grew day by day.... One bright day we will need to try these people. We should not keep silent. It must be said clearly and publicly that many Zionists betrayed [their people].... Yes, one must judge Haim Molchadsky, the head of the JNF [Jewish National Fund] in Bedzin and later the head of the community, and [the same is true] with regard to many more.[18]

Members of the Zionist movement, Klinger believed, played a disproportionately large role in the leadership of European Jews under the Nazis. According to one postwar survey, two-thirds of such leaders were members of a Zionist party. As a result of their relatively greater numbers, Zionists also carried a greater burden of responsibility for the betrayal of their people, as many of them, she suggested, had collaborated with the Nazis. To achieve justice and prevent a public calamity to Zionism, she thought, it was necessary to judge the actions of the movement's members.[19]

Two years later, Zivia Lubetkin, a fighter in the Warsaw ghetto uprising and a legendary figure admired by many in the Yishuv, arrived in Mandatory Palestine. Of the few hundred thousand members of the Yishuv, 6,000 gathered at Kibbutz Yagur on June 8, 1946, to hear the account of this courageous woman, who had been mistakenly eulogized during the war after rumors spread that she had been killed by the Nazis. Lubetkin spoke for eight hours, and at one point she asked a question on the minds of many in the audience and beyond: "How did it happen that an entire nation, that millions of Jews, just went to their own slaughter?"

In her answer, Lubetkin focused on the Jewish Councils, ignoring their role in supporting and ordering Jewish society during difficult times and suggesting instead that they had led their flocks to their death: "Although there were people who went to work at the Jewish Council in good faith, from an objective viewpoint they, too, played a treacherous role against the Jewish nation, as they were obliged to follow German orders. The Germans issued decrees, and their despised work was carried out by Jews from the Jewish Council. . . . And in this way, each Jewish Council, without exception, in each and every town, played a treacherous part."[20]

Lubetkin added that the Germans used Jewish policemen to assemble the Jews, because it was easier for them to "persecute and crush the Jews by using the Jews themselves." These policemen first led their parents to the wagons, then their wives, and finally their children, she said. These people bore the responsibility for the Jews having gone like lambs to the slaughter. In Lubetkin's portrayal, the Jewish masses had no agency over their own lives. It was the Judenrat leadership that caused them to simply walk to their deaths, with no resistance. This was a double humiliation, she argued: not only did the Jews die passively, but they brought their own death upon themselves. "There were various people in the Jewish Council. Without exception, we will remember them all as traitors," Lubetkin said.[21]

Lubetkin was also critical of the head of the Warsaw ghetto Judenrat, Adam Czerniakow, who in response to the German order to participate in deporting Jews in the summer of 1942 had committed suicide. In life he had encircled himself with Jewish apostates and criminals, she said. And even though he killed himself, "the Jews who remained alive could not forgive him . . . why hadn't he warned them about the plans to destroy the ghetto?" A theme in this criticism was the idea that disaster came upon the Jews because of lack of information, information that their leaders, such as Czerniakow, had possessed but withheld from them. This motif of concealed information as a cause of the catastrophe would also surface as an argument in the trial of Rudolf Kastner ten years later. The question of what the masses of

Jews would have done, had they been exposed to such information, was hardly asked.[22]

The opinions of members of the rebel movement, including Lubetkin, overshadowed the few voices in Mandatory Palestine who up until then had attempted to express empathy toward leaders such as Czerniakow. The leader of one kibbutz movement, Ya'akov Hazan, stated in 1943, "I will not throw a stone at these leaders of Israel. Into the book of Jewish agony will be entered not only the blood of the ghetto rebels but also the poison drunk by Czerniakow and Zingelbaum, the faithful tears of the leaders who marched in their Sabbath clothes at the head of their communities toward death." In the years following the end of the war, critical voices such as those of Lubetkin and Klinger silenced empathetic voices such as Hazan's.[23]

Addressing the implications of Jewish betrayals during the war, Lubetkin pointed out that there were diametrically opposed ways of dealing with the situation. One could choose to ignore the animosity caused by betrayal and unite once again as one people, or one could admit the treachery within the Jewish nation and struggle as a fractured family. She opted for the latter, because "there are Jews who even today should be punished, there are Jews who must be excommunicated [from the Jewish community], and there are Jews with whom we shall not sit in [the same] organization."[24] The demand for judgment came not only from alleged collaborators and the media but also from many of the surviving rebels.

The Yishuv Leadership Response

During the war, the Jewish Agency, which was a quasi-governmental organization in the pre-state years, collected information on suspected war criminals. With the cooperation of the British Secret Intelligence Service (SIS), in 1943 the Agency established the Haifa Bureau of Investigations, also known by its code name, the Jewish Agency Statistics Office.[25] In this office, Gideon Rafael (Ruffer), who later became one of the key figures in Israel's Ministry of Foreign Affairs, and his team prepared lists of suspects associated with the Nazis. In addition to the names of 700 Nazi officers, the unit also had files on suspected war criminals among the Jewish communities of Greece, Slovakia,

Romania, Hungary, Bulgaria, Yugoslavia, Poland, Italy, Germany, France, and the Soviet Union. These Jews were suspected of having collaborated with the Nazis.[26]

In late December 1944, an employee of the Jewish Agency in Jerusalem presented a note to the Haifa Bureau of Investigations saying that a new immigrant named Jack Lebao "was an informer on Jews [in France] and [that] because of him many Jews were sent to concentration and death camps. A person from the [French] Resistance has arrived with orders to execute Jack Lebao."[27] The employee from Jerusalem asked Rafael to provide a photograph of the alleged collaborator to assist in the assassination, but no photograph was available.

Rafael was angered by the note requesting his assistance in the murder of Jack Lebao, and he wrote back to the Jewish Agency to express his grave concerns. How could they cooperate with the French Resistance in carrying out a murder with no thorough investigation of their own? Unknowingly, the Jewish Agency might be cooperating with vigilante justice. There could be a mistake in identification, he added, because no one acquainted with the alleged collaborator was available to identify him. Furthermore, Rafael wrote, they had to investigate the assassin. He warned his superiors to be cautious about trusting a member of the French Resistance, because that person might be associated with "dubious elements." Rafael wrote that the individual who had brought the note from Jerusalem had told him that a court had already conducted its own investigation and had issued a death verdict. "I am dismayed by these kinds of messages," he wrote. "If this is true, I should point out [that] I find it hard to understand how one can judge a person who has not yet been identified."[28]

The case of Jack Lebao, whose fate is unknown, led Rafael to demand that the heads of the Jewish Agency establish a central institution that would assess accusations of collaboration:

> My suggestion is to nominate a committee of judges made up of public figures who will have [the] authority to judge [alleged collaborators]. . . . There should be a prosecutor to bring the cases to the committee after a thorough investigation. The office [of the Haifa Bureau of Investigations] is willing to cooperate by conducting preliminary investigations into the cases and, most importantly, by selecting from among the many accusations. We have information

about the situation in the Diaspora that enables us to examine whether there is a basis for the accusation. . . . The time has come for this issue to be handled by a central committee, as we are currently the only nation that peacefully accepts quislings in its midst.[29]

Rafael suggested that the Jewish Agency establish a body like the committees of rehabilitation that had already been formed in other nations.

Rafael was not the only official who addressed the issue of collaboration. When the leadership of the Histadrut, convened in September 1945, one of its members brought up the issue of attempted lynchings. His name was Eliyahu Dobkin, and he was also a member of the Jewish Agency Board of Directors. "I want to speak about things that I am afraid to speak about," he stated hesitantly, as if he feared he was opening Pandora's box. "There is an optimistic assumption about the quality of the human character among those who survived. . . . [But] among those Jews who survived there are some, and thankfully only a fraction, whom survivors see as criminals, possibly even worse than Nazi Germans." The Nazis had acted out of loyalty to their nation, while the Jewish functionaries had betrayed their nation. Dobkin's words hinted at an idea prevalent in the Yishuv: that an "adverse selection" had taken place in the camps, whereby the worst sort of people survived while the better sort perished.[30]

Unlike Dobkin, David Ben-Gurion felt no need to apologize for the actions of Jewish collaborators. In late 1942 he learned from Stanislaw Kot, a member of the Polish government-in-exile, that the government had avoided publicizing the role of Jewish policemen in leading Jews to their deaths, for fear of the implications of such news. Responding to this report, Ben-Gurion, who rarely spoke about the topic of Jewish collaboration, stated that the Jewish nation was no different to any other nation. Just like other nations, the Jews too had their own "quislings and bastards," he said. Ben-Gurion accepted the fact that within any society there would be a variety of responses to repression, including collaboration.[31]

In a meeting of the Jewish National Council (the institution that governed the Yishuv), another leader, Izhak Ben-Zvi, ranked the different groups of collaborators. First he described how kapos, the worst in his eyes, had stolen other Jews' last piece of bread and "remained alive to this very day." Their lives, he believed, were lives of sin, saved through the deaths of others. He then turned to the second group, the Sonderkommando, who "in their service to the Germans brought death and annihilation upon thousands of Jews." Finally came the members of the Jewish Councils. "Of course, this all began under duress, but there were those who began under duress and ended up doing so willingly," Ben-Zvi said. While some of these Jews were innocent, he acknowledged, others had adopted the views and goals of the Germans in annihilating the Jews.[32]

One leader of the survivors told Dobkin that "three million Jews were murdered in Poland and seventy thousand Jews remain. It will not be such a tragedy if a few thousand fewer live on," indicating to Dobkin that he believed many of them deserved a death sentence. Dobkin was shocked at the idea of executing these Jews and thought that the survivor was exaggerating; Dobkin himself estimated the number of collaborators to be in the hundreds.[33] Ben-Zvi also saw estimates from the underground leader Antek Zuckerman, husband of Zivia Lubetkin, who presented him with a list of a thousand people who deserved to die. Alarmed, Ben-Zvi said, "Perhaps something should be done, to check, to isolate. It is not so simple. There are conspicuous figures who must be punished, but how far will these things go? These are serious issues that must be explored."[34]

Organizations such as the Jewish National Council and the Jewish Agency Board of Directors deliberated upon the question of how to confront this sensitive topic. In the Jewish National Council, Ben-Zvi warned that failing to deal with the issue would result in "complications." In September 1945, Dobkin stressed the need to establish a court. He added that trying these individuals was especially important in the Land of Israel, where Zionists wanted to create a new, pure society that did not incorporate any of the disloyal elements of exiled Jewry. However, he candidly admitted that he would not advise any of his friends to serve on such a panel.

Months later, at a meeting of the Agency's Board of Directors in 1946, Dobkin suggested the World Zionist Congress honor court (a court established in accordance with the organization's 1921 constitution) as the forum for such trials. The British controlled the criminal courts in Mandatory Palestine and the Yishuv had no such courts.

Dobkin's idea to bring the cases before a public communal court, as well as Rafael's suggestion to establish a committee of public figures to judge the accused, resembled the approach taken in the DP camps and European Jewish communities, which created communal courts focusing on the moral conduct of the defendant.[35]

But there was opposition to this approach at the highest levels of the Jewish Agency. When the head of the Agency's Political Department, Moshe Sharett (Shartok), learned of thirteen cases compiled against collaborators, he initially demanded that they be put on trial in a way that would result in "a harsh judgment."[36] Cases like these, he concluded shortly afterward, could not be judged in the World Zionist Congress honor court. The problem Shartok identified was that "if a person is found guilty, it might require punishment, and the punishment might be extremely harsh." The penalties for such actions, he indicated, needed to go beyond the social punishments available to communal courts. In the end, its lack of political independence and inability to pursue independent criminal justice prevented the Jewish Agency from establishing a court focused on cases of collaboration.[37]

Those held as collaborators continued to face accusations, but they had no institutional means or courts to turn to. The absence of any type of court or panel before which they could bring their cases frustrated both many accusers and some of the accused. The former wished to obtain retribution for their pain and suffering, while the later desired an opportunity to finally clear their sullied name.

A Judenrat Member's Defense

With neither an honor court nor a criminal court to determine the fate of alleged collaborators, bureaucrats took action on their own behalf and members of society spread rumors. In workplaces employers hesitated to hire alleged collaborators; in schools children castigated the offspring of suspected collaborators; in one children's newspaper the editor asked readers to weigh in on whether one should play with or exclude the child of a former kapo.[38] Members of Kibbutz Ein ha-Mifratz "had learned of collaborators who arrived here with the fortunes they received in return for abusing their victims, abuses committed not only out of duress, but out of pure greed. We have learned that there is a basis to the claim that these people have turned into legitimate citizens in the Yishuv thanks to their 'contributions.'"

Some of the same anti-Semitic tropes used by Germans against Jews were aimed at suspected collaborators by members of the Yishuv: collaborators had no moral check on how they made their money, and they were dishonest. The kibbutz assembly demanded action against "the Jewish collaborators with the Nazis who arrived with the new immigrants and live among us."[39]

One example of the arbitrary nature of the social judgments of alleged collaborators was the case of Menashe Hutschnecker. In mid-November 1944, after weeks of travel, Hutschnecker and his wife arrived in the Land of Israel and settled into their new home in Kiryat Bialik, a town near Haifa. Two years earlier, they had escaped from their hometown, Kolomyya, Ukraine, leaving behind their only daughter, whom they had sent to Lvov in late 1942 with Aryan papers and never heard from again.[40]

In search of a job, Hutschnecker turned to the offices of the Rescue Committee of the Jewish Agency (RCJA) in Haifa. In a community where ideological credentials mattered more than professional experience, his were first-rate. Before the war, Hutschnecker had served as secretary of the centrist General Zionists Party (Ha-Tzionim Ha-Klali'im) in his town, and as the secretary of the World Zionist Congress in his district. He was a member of the local B'nai B'rith organization and of Keren Hayesod, and for five years had served as president of the local chapter of the Jewish National Fund. In Haifa, the RCJA gave him a job in its new immigrants' home.[41]

Hutschnecker had been working in the home for just a few months when, in late April 1945, his employers summoned him to a meeting. They showed him a copy of an urgent letter sent by the offices of the Kolomyya *Landsmanschaft* in Tel Aviv to the management of the Jewish Agency in Jerusalem informing them of the recent arrival of Hutschnecker, "a Jew who had undermined the existence of the town's Jewish residents *and who was directly responsible for the death of more than one victim.*" The sole reason for Hutschnecker's collaboration, the writers continued, was financial benefit. "His hands are stained with

blood," they warned the Jewish Agency, and they urged the Agency to
"rid yourselves of this disgrace; otherwise we will be forced to turn to
the public opinion of the Yishuv." The heads of the Haifa immigrants'
home did not ask Hutschnecker for an explanation and terminated his
employment on the spot. With no central committee to examine such
unverified allegations, clerks in the Jewish Agency acted on their own
moral judgment.[42]

Hutschnecker turned to the secretary of the offices of the Kolomyya
Landsmanschaft, asking for an explanation of the letter charging him
with the murder of Jews. Within days the secretary replied, denying
ever having written such a letter of denunciation. Hutschnecker wrote
to the RCJA offices in Jerusalem, informing a member of the committee, Rafael Shefer, of the bogus letter and demanding that Shefer
reinstate him in his job.[43] Shefer refused.

On Shefer's table lay the secret Report 286 from February 1945, issued by the Haifa Bureau of Investigations. The report stated that
Hutschnecker had served as deputy head of the Jewish Council in Kolomyya during the war and, together with the head of the council, Mordechai Horowitz, had "executed the demands of the Gestapo with ex-
actitude and even exaggeration." In language that indicated willing
collaboration, the authors of the report wrote that in April 1942, the
Germans had "suggested" that the Kolomyya Jewish Council hand over
the town's old Jews and that the Jewish Council had "decided to accept their suggestion" to round up elderly Jews and deliver them to the
Nazis. The writers of the report clearly had no true understanding of
the context of Nazi duress in which Jewish leaders acted.[44]

"The members of the Jewish Council did not learn their lesson and
continued their activities," the investigators wrote. In another instance,
the council complied with the command of a Gestapo officer and
handed over 106 Jews. In a local slaughterhouse, in the presence of the
head of the Jewish Council, Horowitz, the Germans murdered all of
the assembled Jews. Shortly thereafter, Horowitz and his sister committed suicide. Hutschnecker, the report continued, replaced Horowitz
and continued to collaborate with the Nazis. "When they compre-
hended the nature of their work, some members of the Jewish Council
quit their jobs," but not Hutschnecker, who did not cease to serve the

Nazis, as the investigators implied they would have expected him to do. The possibility that such a resignation would leave the community leaderless in a time of crisis evidently had not crossed their mind. The report concluded by noting that "Hutschnecker, who before the war was not a man of means, amassed a considerable fortune."[45]

No one in the close-knit Yishuv wanted any association with a suspected Nazi collaborator, and Hutschnecker remained unemployed. After a month and a half with no job, he grew increasingly frustrated. He typed a four-page letter to Shefer at the RCJA. The place for the anonymous letter denouncing him "was, in truth, in the wastebasket," he wrote. In light of the terrible accusations, he added, "I wish to express my dismay that the [Jewish] Agency did not find it appropriate to first inform me of the content of this denunciation and thus allow me to express my view about it." In his letter, Hutschnecker, a former attorney, characterized those making the accusations as uneducated and morally dubious individuals who had indeed suffered in the ghetto but were "short-sighted people who misunderstood the tragic conditions of the Jewish community in the ghetto and, in searching for a scapegoat, chose those who were closest to them: the Jewish Council."[46]

Hutschnecker did not attempt to deny his past. "I served . . . as the deputy president of the Jewish Council of the Jewish community of Kolomyya from the end of September 1941 through October 1942. Later, from November to mid-December 1942, I served as the president of that council." The Germans had placed him in these positions, he asserted, and the fact that he had held these offices could not and should not be held against him. "We are too close to these events . . . to [allow us to] issue an objective verdict regarding whether or not membership in such a Jewish Council should be denounced." On the contrary, he wrote, with time history might come to the opposite conclusion, "that, in fact, membership in the Jewish Council in the time of occupation was fundamentally [an act of] defending Jewish interests in such difficult and dangerous times." In contrast to his pursuers, who viewed membership in the Jewish Council as a crime, Hutschnecker wrote, "I emphasize and reemphasize that one should not condemn membership of the Jewish Council in and of itself, but rather specific actions. And if there were members of the Jewish Council who did not attain the required standards—and sadly there were such members—we should not accuse the innocent, those whose hands are clean of wrongdoing and are of clear conscience. And your servant is one of that kind."[47] Hutschnecker advocated examining each case on its own merits, including the specific actions perpetrated, rather than issuing collective denunciations of all Judenrats. This was an argument that hardly registered in the Yishuv, where the collective label of "traitor" was used for anyone who had been a member of a Judenrat or the Jewish police, regardless of his or her actions.

Hutschnecker contributed one more argument against judging him and people like him, an argument that would gain traction only fifteen years later. Life in the ghetto had been like living with a 42°C fever, he wrote. One cannot condemn "the sick [for not acting] in a specific way." This was not a metaphor, added Hutschnecker. The context of the Holocaust would not allow anyone to judge another until he had stood in that person's place. In the circumstances of the ghetto, a person could not always make rational or moral decisions.[48]

On receipt of the letter, Shefer wrote back to Hutschnecker, informing him that if he wished to clear his name, he should locate the witnesses who had testified against him and have them sign an affidavit. Shefer added that Hutschnecker should know that the "testimonies of these two witnesses are very serious." Hutschnecker located the two witnesses and brought them to present their case before an attorney designated by the Jewish Agency. The two admitted that their allegations were all based on rumors, as frequently happened in such cases.[49]

In mid-September, five months after Hutschnecker was fired, the attorney Apolinary Hartglas, a prominent Zionist from Warsaw who escaped after the outbreak of World War II, wrote to inform Hutschnecker that "after investigating in your presence the two witnesses whose testimonies served as the basis for the rumors that besmirched your honor . . . we have come to the conclusion that there is insufficient information in their testimony to convict you."[50] The pursuit of a defenseless citizen by a bureaucrat, in the absence of a court process, was over, and Hutschnecker was reinstated in his job.

A Zionist Leader Defends an Alleged Collaborator

Rumors spiraling out of control affected not only the accused but also their relatives. Yitzhak Gruenbaum, the deputy head of the Jewish Agency under David Ben-Gurion, published an article in early 1945 accusing the leadership of the Polish Jews of being responsible for that community's demise. Under orders or of their own free will, he wrote, those leaders who joined the Jewish Council or enlisted in the Jewish police "became a tool in the [Germans'] hands. Most of them, to our huge regret, toed the line with the Nazis. Even if they did not cause harm, they [did not] help."[51] Gruenbaum concluded that the Jewish leadership in Europe had served as "self-executioners." Gruenbaum was known for his stark Zionist views, and for a long time during the war he refused to dedicate any funds for rescue work or help promote protests in the Yishuv against the Nazi killings of Jews, despite his role as the head of the RCJA. His argument was that "Zionism after all comes before everything," including the battle to save European Jewry.[52]

In August 1945, in bomb-shattered London, Gruenbaum attended the first Zionist Conference following the war. In the backrooms of this conference, as well as a year later in the Zionist Conference in Basel, disputes erupted regarding the alleged collaboration of members of the Zionist movement.[53] As Gruenbaum mingled with the delegates in London, the former leader of Polish Jewry, who before immigrating to the Land of Israel had, in the 1920s, headed the National Minorities Bloc in the Polish Sejm and was known in Poland as the "King of the Jews," felt that attendees were keeping their distance from him. It was as though a void surrounded him, he wrote to an acquaintance, "as if my friends, even those closest to me, are avoiding talking to me." Expecting to be embraced by members of the community he had led a decade earlier, he now felt that they were treating him like a pariah.[54]

The avoidance of Gruenbaum had nothing to do with his views or writings, however. The news had just arrived in London—although none of the delegates dared share it with Gruenbaum—that days earlier the French authorities had arrested his son Eliezer on suspicion of collaboration with the Nazis and that his son, too, was a "self-executioner."

Eliezer, Gruenbaum's second of three sons, was a staunch Communist and had remained behind in Europe when the rest of the family

Yitzhak Gruenbaum, father of a kapo and a leading Zionist figure, seated between Israel's president, Chaim Weizmann *(right)*, and Berl Locker, chairman of the Jewish Agency Board of Directors *(left)*, October 19, 1948.

moved to Jerusalem. Caught up in the war, he was deported in mid-1942 from France to Auschwitz, where he served as a kapo. The French authorities had arrested him on the basis of accusations made by former inmates that while in Auschwitz he had murdered Jews, beaten inmates, expressed anti-Semitic sentiments, and followed every SS directive he was given. In one instance, a witness testified, he kicked an elderly prisoner in the stomach; the man died hours later. Another inmate said he had heard Eliezer say, "Thousands of Jews have perished; so what? Less black market."[55]

Upon learning of his son's arrest, Gruenbaum immediately left London for Paris. Six years after father and son had bade farewell to each other in Geneva, they were reunited within the fenced compound of a French prison. The full-bearded Gruenbaum faced his bald-headed son and did not spare him any harsh questions: "How could you raise your rod against Jews? Are you not my son?"[56]

Eliezer then shared his story. For the smallest of infractions, the head of the barracks, Ludwik Konczal, had beaten inmates so harshly that some died. Other prisoners wanted Eliezer to serve as deputy head of the barracks. This way, they believed, he might shield inmates from

Konczal. To spare prisoners from Konczal's beatings, Eliezer had at times to hit them himself, but at least they did not die from his beatings. Hearing his son's account, Gruenbaum came to believe that he was innocent and that in the depths of Auschwitz he had acted courageously. As Gruenbaum left the prison that night, he resolved that he would go to any length to clear his son's name.[57] The elder Gruenbaum hired a leading defense attorney, André Ballot.[58]

Summer in the City of Light ended, fall came and went, and winter was nearing its end, but Eliezer remained behind bars. For months the deputy head of the Jewish Agency remained in Paris to support his son. Meanwhile, in Jerusalem, some people expressed dismay that a high-ranking figure such as Gruenbaum had abandoned his job to support someone they viewed as a collaborator. He should have disavowed such a son, some thought.

"I think it is not a secret that the son of one of the leading Zionist figures is included in that accusation [of collaborating with the Nazis]. I ache for the tragedy of this elderly father," said Dobkin.[59] In the Jewish National Council, Ben-Zvi reported that a Zionist activist in France, Marc Jarblum, had investigated a former kapo whose "name is difficult to mention because his father is too well-known among us." When asked why he had served the Germans, the kapo answered that he had wanted to keep Communist inmates alive at the expense of ordinary Jews. "And," Ben-Zvi concluded bitterly, "that is how he apologized."[60]

In March 1946, the French court dismissed Eliezer's case, stating that it had no jurisdiction over foreign nationals who had harmed other foreign citizens abroad. With no other state willing to take him in, Eliezer traveled via Cairo to Jerusalem with his father.

For years to come, accusations and rumors about Eliezer's conduct in Europe continued to haunt the Gruenbaums, as they haunted anyone in Israeli society who was labeled as a kapo or policeman. In a gathering of former residents of Bialystok in a Tel Aviv hall, one survivor, who had never met Eliezer, accused the latter of "thousands of Jews tortured and killed."[61] In another instance, a newspaper reader wrote to the editor of *Ha-Mashkif*, a publication associated with the Revisionist party, demanding justice. Somehow, after Eliezer's arrival in the Land of Israel, the reader complained, the accusations against him had all been framed as "a blood libel of a pure and innocent soul." The "liars" conveniently turned out to be the survivors, he wrote sarcastically. Changing tone, he went on to write that it was inappropriate for the son of a political leader to receive preferential treatment. The thought that a kapo might not be guilty of collaboration did not cross his mind.[62]

The ultra-Orthodox population also seized the opportunity to attack Gruenbaum, whom they had despised since before the war for his anti-religious views. Posters on Jerusalem walls declared misleadingly that Eliezer "was sentenced to death by a court in France." Only thanks to bribes from the coffers of the RCJA, the posters claimed, had this "murderer of tens of thousands of brothers and sisters" been saved from the noose.[63]

When the War of Independence broke out in May 1948, Eliezer volunteered to join the armed forces. The Haganah, the pre-independence Jewish paramilitary organization, ignored his previous military experience as a volunteer in a Jewish company in the Spanish Civil War and refused to allow him to enlist. The mere rumor that he had been a cruel kapo in Auschwitz meant that he had no place in the Haganah. Yitzhak Gruenbaum, who was one of the signatories of the Declaration of Independence and who had served as Israel's first minister of the interior, approached David Ben-Gurion, who ordered the Haganah to induct Eliezer. On May 22, a week after he was drafted, Eliezer's unit advanced from the south of Jerusalem to the rescue of Kibbutz Ramat Rachel, which was besieged by Jordanian forces. En route to the battle, Eliezer's armored vehicle was hit, and he was killed. The rumors about collaboration would stick to Eliezer even after his death: for years afterward, a false account circulated that a Holocaust survivor had assassinated Eliezer on the battlefield in revenge for his actions in Europe.[64]

And rumors were not confined to Eliezer Gruenbaum. On September 9, 1948, as the War of Independence continued, a thirty-eight-year-old man dressed in military uniform was hit by a car while crossing the street in Petah Tikva. Critically wounded, he was evacuated to Beilinson Hospital. Three days later, doctors informed the soldier's wife that her husband, Haim Molchadsky, the man on bus number 6 in Tel Aviv (who had since changed his name to Haim Aharoni, possibly to avoid identification), had died. Former residents of Bedzin held that the car accident that killed Molchadsky was no coincidence.[65]

Assassinating a Collaborator

On January 9, 1948, in the Nahalat Yitzhak Cemetery on the outskirts of Tel Aviv, a group of men stood above an open pit by the fence. A body wrapped in a plain white shroud lay on the ground as they whispered prayers. Under windswept trees they lowered the body into a sodden grave. Once mud had been tossed over the body and the grave filled, the funeral was over, and the secretary of the burial society went back to his office, where he registered the details of the deceased in the cemetery notebook: "Simcha Baumblat, 24. Next to the wall. An informer [*malshin*]." Burial at the edge of the cemetery was by Jewish tradition reserved for betrayers of the nation. No headstone has been placed at Baumblat's burial site to this day.[66]

Eight months before, in April 1947, Baumblat, a factory worker, had been walking down a Tel Aviv street when two sets of brothers, Joseph and Shami Koren and Mordechai and Moshe Kwelman, spotted and pursued him. They caught up with Baumblat, seized him, and handed him over to the British police, accusing the new immigrant of having exposed the hideouts of Jews in their hometown, Krasnik, in the Lublin uplands. The police transferred Baumblat to the custody of the British Criminal Investigation Department (CID), which shortly thereafter released him. Within days of Baumblat's release, the British arrested a Jewish underground member, Mordechai Laufer, as he was driving a truck loaded with illegal weapons near Baumblat's home. Some drew a connection between this arrest and the freed Baumblat. Then the British put Baumblat in the Latrun detention camp. Members of the Jewish underground incarcerated in the camp suspected that Baumblat was passing information to his new masters, the British.[67]

In January 1948, the British authorities released Baumblat, and he moved into an apartment in a central neighborhood of Ramat Gan, a town largely populated by supporters of the Revisionist party. Late one night, Baumblat heard loud knocking on his door. When he opened it, a group of men grabbed him and dragged him out to a local park, where they tied him to a bench. Four shots rang out. Baumblat, his liver and stomach punctured, was rushed by passersby to the hospital, where he died.[68]

Newspapers reported that the Revisionist IZL underground, headed by Menachem Begin, had conducted a trial before the assassination. Witnesses testified that Baumblat had disclosed a bunker of Jews to the Gestapo and that the Nazis had then murdered them. When he immigrated to Palestine, Baumblat brought with him 300 gold teeth he had extracted from his victims, witnesses said.[69] The IZL adjudicators concluded that he had served the Nazis, and now he was serving the British in exposing a member of the IZL. Once a traitor, always a traitor. The IZL condemned him to death.[70]

While most survivors saw functionaries as equivalent to Nazis, others viewed them as true Nazis themselves. They were accused of processing the bodies of victims to extract valuables. A survivor in the town of Lod claimed that a former Judenrat member had curtains adorned with a pattern of swastikas. One kapo "received for her birthday 23 roses from the SS men" and stood with Dr. Joseph Mengele selecting new arrivals at Auschwitz, testified one trial witness. Although all these reports are very likely false, they demonstrate how some survivors viewed these functionaries as people who completely identified with the Nazis.[71]

The First Case Comes Before a Zionist Honor Court

In 1949, the attorney general's office in the newly established State of Israel was asked if it would prosecute Julius Siegel. After being condemned by a court in an Italian DP camp as a betrayer of the nation (see Chapter 1), Siegel had moved to Israel in October 1948 with the specific goal of clearing his name. The attorney general's office determined that the state courts in Israel had no jurisdiction over the case, and referred it to the World Zionist Congress honor court. In the absence of appropriate legislation, this honor court was the only institution in Israel that offered a venue for prosecuting alleged collaborators. Siegel agreed to pay membership dues to the congress so that its honor court could hear his case.[72]

In the honor court, Siegel's attorney, Yitzhak Levi, called seven defense witnesses from Tel Aviv and Haifa and five witnesses who lived in Germany and Austria. Levi asked that the witness list remain confidential, "as my client (and I too) have well-justified concerns that irresponsible people will put unfair pressure on witnesses so that they don't dare testify in favor of the defendant and speak the truth."[73]

Levi's request was based on his personal experience. Days earlier, David Klein, a twenty-seven-year-old librarian from Ramat Gan, had arrived unbidden in Levi's Tel Aviv office, demanding to know how the lawyer dared to take on the case of a despicable person like Siegel. Levi informed the court of Klein's threats and claimed that Klein was hounding his client because of Siegel's political affiliation with the Revisionist party.[74]

On the stand, Klein testified about Siegel's brutal behavior in the Gross-Masselwitz concentration camp, portraying him as a German commander: If you opened his office door without knocking, he would strike you. If you did not stand at attention, he would strike you. If you smoked a cigarette, he would strike you. "This happened each and every day. He struck people every day. I saw it with my own eyes."[75]

Another witness, David Lieber, a member of the Jewish underground in Bedzin, branded the defendant as a collaborator "of the worst kind," adding that "Siegel fought within the Jewish community to receive public office. His psychological motivation was probably his lust for power and his inclination to glorify himself." Siegel, Lieber testified, was the first in the community to approach the Germans and offer to work for them. The Jewish underground had marked him for death.[76]

After only two days of testimony, the chair of the panel, Joseph Rufizen, died. At the recommendation of Moshe Smoira, the president of the Supreme Court, the administrators of the World Zionist Congress honor court wrote to Shmuel Eliashiv, the head of the Eastern European Department at the Ministry of Foreign Affairs, requesting that he replace the late Rufizen. Unaware of the position earlier taken by the attorney general's office that there was no way to try Nazi collaborators under current Israeli law, Eliashiv responded, "I am amazed that issues of collaboration with the Nazis are deliberated in an honor court."[77] In Eliashiv's view, much like in Moshe Sharett's three years earlier, issues of collaboration were too serious a matter to be left to a communal court. Now that the state had established criminal courts, Eliashiv believed, this kind of case should be heard by them. The trial

A wartime picture of policeman Julius Siegel (second from right, in light-colored jacket) marching Jews to slave labor in Bedzin, Poland. After the war, Siegel faced legal procedures five times in Europe and Israel.

in the honor court would not be resumed. Siegel had failed once again to clear his name. Two years later, after the passage of the Nazis and Nazi Collaborators Punishment Law, Siegel would again face the legal procedure of a preliminary investigation and a trial, this time before an Israeli criminal court.

CHAPTER THREE

THE NAZIS AND NAZI COLLABORATORS
PUNISHMENT LAW

IT WAS A HOT SUMMER'S day in July 1949 when a group of young Israel Defense Forces (IDF) soldiers stopped for refreshments at a small coffee shop in Ein Kerem, a neighborhood on the outskirts of Jerusalem. They sat down at a table, and the shop owner, Joseph Paal, came over to take their order. At the sight of the one-eyed Joseph, one of the soldiers, Staff Sgt. Yerachmiel Yanovsky, became agitated. He recognized the owner: "Blinder [Blind] Max" had been his *Blockältester* (barracks elder) in Block 10 of the Jaworzno concentration camp, an auxiliary camp of Auschwitz, and had beaten and tortured Yanovsky and his fellow prisoners. Yanovsky confronted Paal, who insisted that he had never heard of Jaworzno or of "Blinder Max." Paal's wife of three years, whom he had married after the Nazis murdered his first wife and children, was also present. She told the soldiers that now, in their new country, it was time to forget the past.[1]

Some survivors, such as Paal's wife, saw immigration to Israel as an opportunity to leave the past behind and start anew. But many survivors did not and could not forget their tormentors. A significant number of them believed that the new state should not be soiled by those who had collaborated with the Nazis—that it was a place for building a new and pure community.

The image of Blinder Max in Ein Kerem stuck in Yanovsky's mind. Four months later, in October 1949, Yanovsky met with another former inmate from Block 10, David Levi, and told him that he had seen Blinder Max. At Levi's prompting, the two went to a Jerusalem police station and filed a complaint. In February 1950, the police ordered Paal in for questioning. Paal remained adamant that he had never served as a *Blockältester* in Jaworzno.

The policeman called Yanovsky into the interrogation room and sat him across from Paal. When Paal continued to deny the accusations, Yanovsky screamed at him in Yiddish: "You don't know me? You didn't hit me? You don't know that I was one of the inmates in Block 10 in Jaworzno? You dare tell me that you are not Blinder Max?" Paal paled and answered, "Yes, I was in Jaworzno, and if I was there, does that make me a criminal?" The police released Paal shortly afterward, but not because they believed he was innocent. They could not continue to hold him since in the newly established Jewish state no law applied to alleged collaborators.[2]

Paal was not the only alleged collaborator released by the Israel Police for want of a law. In February 1949, the morning newspaper *Ha-Boker* published an open letter from a reader named Dov to the minister of justice, Pinchas Rosen. Dov described how a few days earlier he had been sitting at his desk in the civil registry when, to his amazement, a new immigrant whom he knew as the "commander of Jewish forced labor camps in upper Silesia" came into his office. This person, Dov wrote, had "helped the occupier arrange for the annihilation of Jews." Dov immediately filed a complaint, and two days later the police summoned both the accused and Dov himself.

The police questioned the suspect and decided to arrest him. At that moment, the man pulled out a document bearing a police letterhead and signed by Yerachmiel (Yaron) Lustig, head of the Israel Police Criminal Investigation Unit. The document stated that "one cannot prosecute a person in Israel for crimes conducted outside the State of Israel." After seeing the suspect walk free, Dov turned to the Polish consulate in Tel Aviv and demanded that the Polish authorities submit an extradition request to the State of Israel to have the accused sent back to stand trial in Poland. Dov ended his open letter to the minister of justice with a rebuke: "We, the survivors of the camps, see our persecutors from these very camps walking around the country with equal rights each and every day. We are forced to demand justice from the courts of foreign countries." It was time, Dov implied, that the State of Israel enact a law that would make it possible to prosecute these criminals in Israel.[3]

One Knesset member pointed out the "saddening and abnormal situation" that if "Goebbels and Göring, cursed be their names, were among us today, the hand of the law could not reach them." How could the State of Israel criticize other nations for not trying their collaborators, he asked, if it avoided prosecuting its own "war criminals"?[4]

In the first two years of Israel's existence as a state, 220,000 immigrants arrived from Europe, and the number of incidents involving former functionaries grew. The Rehovot police took into custody a woman whom residents at the new Kfar Bilu immigrants' camp accused of the deaths of several women in a Czechoslovak concentration camp.[5] A day laborer at Kibbutz Givat Brenner spotted a kapo from Auschwitz and summoned the police to arrest him.[6] A survivor confronted an IDF soldier sipping coffee at the Eisen Café on Allenby Street in Tel Aviv and accused her of being a member of the SS.[7] In Haifa, two police officers detained a Jew whom they identified as a functionary in the camps in Germany.[8] In the new immigrants' camp of Beit Lid the police arrested a twenty-nine-year-old woman, a former barracks commander in Auschwitz.[9]

"In the past two years there have been dozens and possibly even hundreds of such instances," the journalist Yaakov Gal wrote in the popular afternoon daily *Maariv*. The police would arrest suspects and then release them again within twenty-four hours. "Indeed, it seems that in our country there is no law with which one can bring these kinds of war criminals to trial," he wrote. His use of the phrase "war criminals" implied that he saw these Jewish functionaries and Axis war criminals as one and the same.

The term "war criminals" was commonly used in this period in reference to Jewish functionaries. But this usage ignored the difference between Jews and non-Jews under Nazi rule. Whereas Jews could not escape the Nazis' ultimate goal of destroying every Jew, non-Jewish collaborators frequently joined the Nazis out of ideological affinity and with the hope that Germany's victory would benefit them. Only after the Jungster trial (Chapter 6), which drew a distinction between Jews and non-Jews in relation to the Nazis and Nazi Collaborators Punishment Law, did the use of the term "war criminal" in reference to Jewish functionaries cease for the most part.[10]

Applying the term "war criminal" to Jewish functionaries not only drew an equivalence between Jewish and non-Jewish collaborators but also pointed to a common goal in Israel and Europe of removing soiled elements from society. An opinion writer in the morning daily *Davar* complained that Israel was a safe haven for the "Jewish criminals and crooks whom foreign states have ejected." The writer cited a man whom a foreign court had in absentia sentenced to death for murdering hundreds of thousands of Jews—and who was presently strolling Tel Aviv's sunny streets and enjoying his new job and home. This kind of criminal, the writer pointed out, was liable to bring "disaster upon our country, violating state order and the general wellbeing of its society." For this writer, as for others, the presence of these corrupt individuals threatened to blemish the new society, which strived to serve as a "light unto the nations."[11]

To deal with the functionaries, the police needed a tool that would allow it to respond to complaints against former functionaries and resolve its inability to arrest the suspects. Police Inspector Joseph Gorski wrote to Yerachmiel (Yaron) Lustig, head of the Israel Police Criminal Investigation Unit, and to Israel Police commissioner Sahar Yechezkel:

> Due to the lack of suitable laws in existing Israeli legislation, [criminals] are not being prosecuted here for crimes that they committed in Europe. On the contrary, the paradoxical situation is that many war criminals . . . are finding a safe haven in Israel. A large number of Jewish "kapos" and other "privileged" individuals are already in Israel, and the heads of security forces and the courts cannot prosecute them. I ask you, sirs, to take the necessary steps . . . to create suitable laws that will make it possible to bring these criminals to justice.[12]

In October 1949, the director-general of the Ministry of Police, Ram Salomon, replied to Gorski, saying, "I wish to inform you that the Ministry of Justice is preparing a bill related to war criminals and collaborators. It is hoped that this bill will be brought to the Knesset in its next parliamentary session."[13]

A Non-Jewish Militia Member Sighted in Israel

Before the Ministry of Justice presented the "war criminals bill" to the Knesset, some survivors spotted a non-Jewish Slovak whom they identified as a collaborator. On December 17, 1949, the Israeli Hungarian-language paper *Új Kelet* (The New East) reported that new immigrants from Slovakia had sighted "a notorious leader of the Hlinka Guard who had actively participated in the destruction of the Slovakian Jewry." An open letter from an unnamed reader to the minister of police, Bechor-Shalom Shitrit, described how this Slovak, Andrej Banik, had "participated in shoving Jews into train cars that took them to the death camps. He put my uncle and his family in a car and they never returned from that journey." Banik and his wife, Julia Mandel, a Jew who had converted to Christianity, were in Israel en route to Canada, the reader wrote, where "they hope to hide from suspicious eyes and continue their good life without interference while enjoying the property that they stole from murdered Jews." The letter writer ended with an appeal to the minister of police: "I ask your honor not to allow this murderer to continue fleeing the full weight of justice." Although no law existed in Israel to try war criminals, the editors added, "It is the duty of the legal authorities to arrest Banik. . . . The attorney general will find the appropriate clause by which to put Banik in the dock to be tried."[14]

The next day, in Beit Lid, a policeman named Tsvi Roth read the open letter in *Új Kelet* and inquired among the immigration camp inhabitants about Banik. They told him that Banik indeed lived in the immigration camp. On December 20, 1949, the police arrested him in tent 244 in the camp.[15] That same day, at around 10 A.M., Yitzhak Freiman, a man in his forties who was dressed in work clothes and had a scar above his eye, entered the police station.[16] Freiman told the commander, Sgt. Nathan Rabinowitz, and another policeman that in 1939 he had served as a translator in the 29th Battalion of the Hungarian army on the newly drawn border between Hungary and Slovakia, near Roznava. Banik, dressed in the uniform of the Hlinka Guard (Hlinkova garda), the Slovakian fascist militia, was patrolling the other side of the border.[17] Freiman, dressed in a Hungarian military uniform marked with a yellow star, watched as Banik abused Jews being deported to Slovakia. In one instance, he saw him stop a sixty-five-year-old attorney, Lajos Grossman, strip him, and take his gold wedding ring. Banik then noticed Grossman's gold teeth and pulled them out of his mouth. Freiman attempted to come to Grossman's rescue, telling the Slovak that no law required the killing of people. In response to these words, Banik pulled out a dagger and slashed Freiman above the eye.

It took him six weeks to recuperate, Freiman stated. Once back at his post, he again observed Banik abusing Jews. This time, a Roznava Jew named Jacob Gutelon arrived at the border crossing with his three-year-old grandchild in tow. Banik eyed a small backpack that the child was carrying, threw the child to the ground, and pressed his boot on the child's throat. The child choked to death. From the backpack Banik pulled out a small Torah scroll, two marriage certificates, and two death certificates. Freiman concluded his testimony by stating without further evidence that "I estimate that with his own hands Banik killed nearly 45 families."[18]

Over the next two weeks the police investigated Banik, first at the Beit Lid police outpost and then at the police headquarters in Tel Aviv. First the investigator, Sgt. Shmuel Menlas, listened to the suspect's account of his life. Banik said he had grown up in Lastovce, a small village near the Slovak-Hungarian border. Between September 1938 and March 1939 he had served in a Slovak militia, where he wrote propaganda pamphlets against the Hungarian forces and also served as a guard on the Slovakian border with Hungary. In words that seemed to indicate that he had indeed served as a member of the Hlinka Guard, Banik said, "Until March 1939 I worked on the border in civilian clothes, and I had a band with a special symbol. It was a blue band. [Following Slovak independence] in March we received military uniforms." After Hungary occupied parts of southern Slovakia in March 1939, Banik escaped to Michalovce. "I was not in the army, but we received a uniform and instruction in the use of arms, and we received a salary for guarding the border." A month later, after the redrawing of the border between Slovakia and Hungary, the army replaced them, and Banik quit his position in the militia. Then Banik joined the Hlinka political party as a clerk and eventually became a journalist.[19]

After Banik finished his account, the investigators questioned him. Had he been a member of the Slovakian fascist militia? "I was not a member of the Hlinka Guard," he responded, seemingly contradicting his earlier statements about his work on the border. Yes, Banik admitted, his father had paid 300,000 korunas for a textile shop in Secovce previously owned by Willey Klein, a Jew. After the war his father had voluntarily compensated Klein for his losses.

The police learned that en route to Israel from Czechoslovakia by way of Italy, Banik and his wife had attempted to leave the convoy of new immigrants. The heads of the convoy, however, refused to return his passport, and Banik had no choice but to come to Israel. The police seem to have suspected that Banik had joined the group of Jews immigrating to Israel only as a means of escaping Czechoslovakia. Asked to explain his attempt to leave the convoy, Banik responded that his wife had just wanted to enjoy the Italian scenery before traveling to the Holy Land. The investigator then asked Banik to explain his reasons for coming to Israel. Banik replied that, as a Catholic, he wanted to see the sacred sites of the Holy Land. He had also heard about the heroism of the Israelis during the War of Independence and wanted to observe it for himself, he said, seemingly trying to flatter his investigators' national pride.[20]

Banik was not the only non-Jewish suspect arrested by the Israeli police. Some survivors, betrayed in the past by their neighbors, suspected all non-Jews as having been collaborators. In one instance in November 1951, a new immigrant from Hungary identified Alfred Miller, a non-Jewish Hungarian waiter at the Passage Café in Tel Aviv, as the person who had handed him over to the Nazis. The police arrested Miller, who denied the accusations. Asked why he had come to the Jewish state, he answered that he wanted to live in a place where the land was not drenched in innocent blood. Members of the Tel Aviv–based association of Hungarian Jews came to his defense, testifying that Miller had in fact saved young children from the hands of the Nazis. Months later the police cleared his name.[21]

Rumors also circulated in the late 1940s that Adolf Eichmann and other Nazis had joined the Arab forces and were wandering the country. Another rumor held that Eichmann had mingled in the community of survivors "with a grown beard and *payot* [sidelocks], speaking with his victims in Yiddish or Hebrew." These rumors, as well as the arrest of Banik, would help influence at least one Knesset member to call for passage of the Nazis and Nazi Collaborators Punishment Law as a means not only to prosecute Jewish functionaries but also to prevent Nazis from coming to Israel.[22]

Two months after Banik's questioning, the police decided to drop the case against him, and notified the Czechoslovak consulate to prepare for his deportation from Israel. Israel's immigration minister, Moshe Shapira, signed the expulsion order.[23] Then, for unknown reasons, the police shifted course and confiscated Banik's passport. Despite strong suspicions, exacerbated by a report from "a friendly diplomatic source," that Banik's request to celebrate Christmas in a Jerusalem church with the Czechoslovak consul was a front for a planned escape across the border to Jordan, the police still had no legal basis to arrest him. But the police would not permit his exit from the country, either. Banik moved in with Salesian priests in Nazareth and worked in the church gardens.[24]

The Knesset Deliberates the Bill

In March 1950, the Ministry of Justice introduced the Nazis and Nazi Collaborators Punishment Law in the Knesset.[25] Just two days later the Knesset unanimously approved a related measure, the Crime of Genocide (Prevention and Punishment) Law, based on the Convention on the Prevention and Punishment of the Crime of Genocide approved by the UN Assembly in December of 1948. While the two statutes in front of the Knesset were closely related and complemented each other, the Crime of Genocide (Prevention and Punishment) Law aimed to prevent future "acts committed with intent to destroy, in whole or in part, a national, ethnical, racial or religious group," whereas the bill addressing Nazis and Nazi collaborators was a retroactive and extraterritorial measure that would allow Israeli courts to try individuals for events that had taken place between 1933 and 1945 in Nazi-occupied lands.[26]

In early discussions of the bill, some Knesset members raised the question of what kind of court would try the defendants. "The criminals cannot be judged in an ordinary court, because the crime is not ordinary and so the procedure cannot be ordinary," said Nahum Nir (Rafalkes), chair of the Knesset Law and Justice Committee. "I would suggest nominating five well-known people and giving them carte blanche, and I would tell them that they are not constrained by procedure and should judge according to their conscience, since this is not an ordinary trial." Knesset member Yona Kesse agreed: "If we wish to be true to this tragic phenomenon in our history, we must establish a court of jurors." Kesse added that the trials would have greater moral and symbolic significance if they were conducted in honor courts, as had been the procedure in the DP camps and in Jewish communities in Europe. In that view, moral judgment was more momentous than legal judgment.[27]

The minister of justice categorically rejected the idea of establishing a special court or a panel of jurors to try the collaborators. The existing state courts would hear the cases, Rosen determined. At a time when the government was laboring to move organizations from their fragmented pre-state status into a unified state system (*mamlakhtiyut*, "statism")—for example, by uniting the militant underground movements into the Israel Defense Forces (IDF) or the divergent educational systems run each by a different political party into one national system—it was unthinkable to suggest splitting the justice system into parallel systems of criminal and honor courts.[28] Also, members of the justice system, both policy-makers and prosecutors, seem to have sought harsh punishments. Honor courts and their social punishments did not suffice for the type of crime these functionaries had committed.[29]

While the name of the measure presented to the Knesset, the Nazis and Nazi Collaborators Punishment Law, implied that it targeted both Nazis and Nazi collaborators, Minister of Justice Pinchas Rosen, who introduced the bill, did not foresee any scenario in which a German perpetrator would face trial in Israel. "Nazi criminals who are guilty of the crimes listed in this law will not dare to come to Israel," the minister said. For him and for the majority of Knesset members, the law addressed the German Nazis only symbolically, pointing to the Jewish state's hostility to the regime that had annihilated millions of Jews. "In reality," Rosen said, "the law will apply less to Nazis than to their Jewish collaborators who are here in the State of Israel."[30]

A few Knesset members did, however, believe that Nazis might someday face trial in Israel. Knesset member Haim Rubin explained that while it was not currently feasible, it might be the case in the future that Israel would seek the extradition of Nazi criminals. Another Knesset member, Eri Jabotinsky, surmised that one day some Nazi might by chance fall into the hands of Israelis.[31] Knesset member Mordechai Nurock, who had lost his wife and two sons in the Holocaust, thought that Nazis had already penetrated Israel. During a June 1949 discussion he bemoaned, "On a daily basis former residents of Nazi concentration camps encounter Nazis and Jewish traitors who aided in the annihilation of members of the Jewish people, and the authorities can do nothing against them."[32] Rumors of non-Jews searching for refuge in the Jewish state were bolstered with the arrest of Banik in December 1949, but the majority of Knesset members saw the law as only symbolically aimed at German Nazis; practically, it would be used only in the case of Jewish functionaries.[33]

Knesset members took to the podium to express their views on the new bill. Yakov Gil, a former chief rabbi in the Jewish Brigade, expressed his bewilderment (shared by many other Knesset members) that this bill, the first to touch on the death of a third of the nation, lacked the word "Jew." The law seemed to adopt the spirit of the Nuremberg trials, which had almost completely avoided mentioning the unique fate of the Jews in the Holocaust. It was time, Gil said, for "the government of an independent Jewish state, after two thousand years of the absence of such a state, to assert itself and write: 'against Israel and humanity.'"[34]

In further discussions on the formulation of the law, the Knesset Constitution, Law, and Justice Committee decided to add to the law's first paragraph, which already spoke of "crimes against humanity" and "war crimes," the offense of "crimes against the Jewish people." Deputy Attorney General Haim Wilkenfeld, who drafted the law, had based it on the wording of the United Nations Convention on the Prevention and Punishment of the Crime of Genocide, substituting the word "Jews" wherever the convention used the phrase "members of the group" in its first five subclauses, as for example in the first subclause, where he replaced "killing members of the group" with "killing Jews." He also added to the offense of "crimes against the Jewish people" two new subclauses that focused on cultural genocide and anti-Semitism: "destroying or desecrating Jewish religious or cultural assets or values" and "inciting to hatred of Jews." The Knesset committee adopted the new clause specifying "crimes against the Jewish people" and after a short discussion decided to put it first, followed by "crimes against humanity" and "war crimes." The only justification for passing this unprecedented law, Knesset member Zerach Warhaftig reasoned, was that it pertained to Jewish victims, the prime target of the Nazi Final Solution.[35]

While the legislators agreed on specifying the unique offense of crimes against the Jewish people, which portrayed the Jews as victims, the majority refused to differentiate between a Jewish offender and a Nazi offender. The law speaks only of an offender as "a person," making no distinction between a Nazi SS man and a Jewish kapo. Wilkenfeld explained this choice by asking how one could legally distinguish collaborators from Nazis: "If there was a Nazi in the concentration camp who beat the people in the camp, and at the same camp there was a Jewish kapo who did the exact same thing, how could we apply a different clause to each of them?" One should consider only the act itself, not the person committing the act, he insisted in the face of criticism. The principle of equal justice under the law demanded that one should not allow the distinguishing of one group from another, he held—a position that disregarded the different historical status of Germans and Jews in the context of Nazi rule, and the fact that Jewish lives were illegal within Nazi Germany.[36]

Responding to a suggestion to permit exempting a person from criminal responsibility for his actions if he acted under duress or in self-defense, Knesset member Israel Bar-Yehuda (Idelsohn) of Mapam—a mining engineer by background who despite his lack of legal training was, according to another Knesset member who studied law, a brilliant legal mind—argued that such circumstances were irrelevant to the question of guilt or innocence. If a person was found guilty of acts of collaboration, only then could the court consider the circumstances of those actions in deciding whether to reduce or commute the offender's sentence.[37]

"I am opposed to . . . this kind of person being relieved [of legal responsibility] because he did what he did out of cowardice," Bar-Yehuda asserted. He continued: "If a person was told that if he did not kill another person, his daughter would be raped and killed, and, to save his daughter, he killed someone else, he is not, to my mind, relieved of criminal responsibility, even if he did all he could to prevent it."[38]

Behind this argument, in which Bar-Yehuda was joined by friends from his Mapam party, lay deeper cultural and political considerations. Mapam was closely associated with two of the youth movements, Ha-Shomer Ha-Tzair and Dror, that had played pivotal roles in the rebellions instigated against the Nazis in occupied Europe, including the most famous of them, the Warsaw ghetto uprising. During the war, members of these two leftist youth movements were strongly opposed to the Jewish Councils and Jewish police and regarded all who joined them as traitors. In the cultural milieu of Israel in the late 1940s and 1950s, Mapam positioned itself as the representative of these rebels and took a strong position against any conciliatory approach toward those it considered to be collaborators. In their view, anyone who served in the Jewish Council or police, and certainly kapos, had crossed the line of loyalty and joined the enemy side.[39]

Knesset members from other parties, including the governing party, Mapai, objected fiercely. Using the case of members of the Jewish Councils, Zerach Warhaftig of the Ha-Poel Ha-Mizrachi party, who had labored to save Jews in Lithuania during the war, accused Bar-Yehuda of both lack of knowledge and falsification of facts:

> There were instances in which a Jew accepted a position in the Jewish Council under duress after having been threatened, and there were instances in which individuals accepted such positions so as to do everything possible to lighten the burden on other Jews. It would be a crime on our part if we did not allow the court to relieve a person of criminal responsibility were it convinced that the defendant in question had accepted his appointment under duress and had done all he could have done to prevent the results of his actions.[40]

Knesset member Jacob Klivnov also rebuked Mapam members of the Constitution, Law, and Justice Committee:

> Whoever thinks of the situation of a Jew there, not with a biased perspective, but rather with a feeling of shared destiny, cannot but see that it was not betrayal, but often—and possibly in most cases—an act of courage and national loyalty on the part of those Jews who joined the Jewish Council. One could not have left those tens of thousands of Jews without any help or guidance. How can one say of a Jew who joined the Jewish Council that by his mere enlistment he became a collaborator with the Germans and cannot be forgiven? I protest against this view.[41]

The leader of Mapai, David Ben-Gurion, also refused to criticize Jews who had lived through the Holocaust, including members of the Jewish Councils. Furthermore, he opposed the view held by some, including members of Mapam, that failing to reprimand those who had served as members of the Jewish Councils would weaken Israeli society and especially its youth. In a letter sent in 1955 he wrote that "the young generation in the Land of Israel has grown up hearing the stories of the Shomer, the Haganah, and the IDF and there is no fear that the Jewish Councils . . . will influence our children."[42] To the contrary, members of Mapai feared that overstating the role of rebels in the Holocaust might overshadow the greater Zionist lesson to be gleaned from the Holocaust: namely, that the Jewish people in exile, unlike those in the Land of Israel, lived a passive life in which they could not defend themselves.[43]

In the end, the Knesset adopted a version of the law that allowed the court to exempt someone from criminal responsibility or reduce his sentence only in the rare instances in which that person acted under the immediate threat of death or, alternatively, "did or omitted to do the act with intent to avert consequences more serious than those that resulted from the act or omission, and actually averted them."[44]

Before final passage of the bill, however, members of Mapai and Mapam engaged in a debate about the proper way to treat policemen, kapos, and members of the Jewish Councils. Mapam's Bar-Yehuda thought the law should grant the court the authority to exempt from legal responsibility those who had been members of the underground as well as those who, through their actions, had sought to prevent more dire consequences.[45]

Joseph Lam, of the Mapai party, refused to accept the idea that only a representative of the underground or someone who acted to prevent more dire consequences would be exempted from legal responsibility. He, like the leader of his party, Ben-Gurion, took a conciliatory approach to European Jewry:

> Knesset Members, do not forget that this paragraph [no. 10] speaks of a persecuted person. We should not demand from a persecuted person—for the sole purpose of proving to history that the Jewish people is clean and kosher—that he should have behaved in a different way from the way we all would have behaved. If I fight for the rights of that victim, it is because in him I see all of us—how we might have behaved under those circumstances; for I refute [the argument] that you and I would have behaved any differently from many of those persecuted.

Lam's argument was supported by a majority of five committee members, and Bar-Yehuda's provision was turned down.[46]

Despite some opposition, the view that anyone who held office under the Nazis was incriminated, dominated among the leaders of the legal system as well. This new law, Minister of Justice Rosen told the Knesset, would provide accused survivors an opportunity "to prove their innocence and integrity in front of an authorized court." From this perspective, functionaries were guilty unless proven innocent. Rosen then cited a passage from the Hebrew Bible, "Therefore shall thy camp be holy" (Deut. 23:14), implying that the law would help purify Israeli society.[47]

With passage of the Nazis and Nazi Collaborators Punishment Law on August 1, 1950, the police and prosecutors had in their hands a tool with which they could charge former functionaries. It was now time to try Paal, Siegel, and Banik, along with a dozen others.

CHAPTER FOUR

PRELIMINARY COURT EXAMINATIONS

IN NOVEMBER 1950, three months after the Nazis and Nazi Collaborators Punishment Law went into effect, a forty-two-year-old woman entered a Tel Aviv police station and filed a complaint against Pinchas Pashititzky, a physician who had immigrated to Israel just two weeks earlier. The complainant, Rivka Nugelman (Ugnik), accused Pashititzky of killing her brother, husband, and three sons in the Wolanow labor camp.[1]

Nugelman was not the only one to lodge a complaint against a functionary. In the following fifteen months, some 350 Holocaust survivors did so.[2] In the city of Netanya, a member of Kibbutz Mishmar Ha-Sharon, Yerachmiel Barkai, filed a complaint against Herschel Shapshevsky, the kapo who had overseen him in the HASAG labor camp in Skarzysko and "whose job was to harass Jews, starve them, and send them to be killed."[3] Late one night in September 1950, two years after encountering her former *Blockältester* in a Tel Aviv shoe store, Tehila Amster went to a police station in Safed and filed a complaint against Miriam Goldberg for her mistreatment of inmates in Bergen-Belsen.[4]

To handle the investigation of complaints against functionaries for alleged collaboration, the head of the Israel Police Criminal Division, Shlomo Sofer, appointed a veteran police officer, First Inspector Michael Avatichi. More than a year earlier, both Sofer and Avatichi had been dismissed from the newly established Israel Police on suspicion of corruption and collaboration while serving in the British Palestine Police Force. As in the case of the Jewish policemen and kapos, suspicion dominated the image of those who had served the British Mandate authorities, as evidenced in the dismissal of a dozen and a half policemen. In this period of state establishment, the authorities searched for traitors and turncoats not only in the context of the Holocaust but also in relation to events that took place in Mandatory Palestine (and in one case even mistakenly executed an officer, Meir Tubianski, accused of assisting Arab enemy forces in bombarding facilities in Jerusalem). Together with sixteen other policemen, Sofer and Avatichi appealed to the Supreme Court. In their petition they evoked the Holocaust, saying that with the accusations "a sign of disgrace, a yellow badge, has been glued to our backs." The court ordered the police minister to rehire them all; the president of the court, Yitzhak Olshan, praised the men as loyal and worthy policemen and harshly criticized the purge.[5]

Now cleared of collaboration with the British, the two officers led the investigation of those suspected of collaboration with the Germans. In the Israel Police headquarters in south Tel Aviv, Avatichi, together with First Inspector Josef Singer and their team, assembled the evidence against the suspects. The team opened investigations based on complaints filed by survivors, who in some cases were anonymous. The team also received letters of complaint from survivors living abroad as well as from non-Jews.[6] They arrested several suspects but could not locate others, some of whom had fled as soon as the law was passed; as one newspaper reported, some individuals felt "the earth was burning under their feet" and left the country.[7]

Not all investigations followed from complaints by survivors. In late 1950, Moshe Puczyc applied for a job in a government ministry. The Shin Bet—Israel's internal security service—conducted a background check, which revealed that Puczyc had served as deputy of the Jewish police in Ostrowiec. It sent the Israel Police Criminal Division a photo and a list of witnesses and requested that an investigation be opened.[8] In another instance, the Tel Aviv Magistrates Court heard the case of Jacob Honigman, accused of mistreating inmates at the Grodziszcze and Faulbrück labor camps. On the stand, witnesses repeatedly mentioned the defendant's name in the same breath as that of another kapo, Yehezkel Jungster. "Is Jungster under investigation?" asked Judge Emanuel Matalon. The police contacted Jungster at Mishmar Ha-Shiv'a, an agricultural village, and called him in for questioning.[9]

The plaintiffs leveled harsh accusations against the suspects. Accusations against kapos focused mostly on physical abuse, and those against policemen included charges of handing Jews over to the Nazis in addition to physical abuse. Abraham Hendler described to police officers how he had been standing in the yard of the Sagan concentration camp when Mordechai Friedman, his kapo, approached him and without warning slapped his face multiple times.[10] Mordechai Goldstein, one complainant stated, had fiercely beaten many Jews while serving in a camp in Ostrowiec.[11] Leib Hass and his wife, Esther, described how the Jewish policeman Shimon Zuckerberg, together with SS men, exposed Jewish bunkers in their town. Hass also observed Zuckerberg standing beside an SS man after pulling Jews out of one house. "I heard how the German, Kuper, asked Shimon Zuckerberg if those were all the people that were hidden in that house, and Shimon answered that there must be one more in the house. And I saw Shimon Zuckerberg enter that house alone, and after a few moments he came out with a Jew." In this case, as in the others, the plaintiffs emphasized that the functionaries and policemen had acted in circumstances allowing free choice and were not under immediate duress.[12]

Another line of complaint focused on functionaries' financial gain. Witnesses described how, at the HASAG labor camp in Skarzysko, Tsvi Shapshevsky "would not distribute the food to those who deserved it but would sell the food to other people, and we starved." Shapsevsky also confiscated the belongings of a group of Jews who arrived at the camp from Majdanek, witnesses said. "From me," Genia Kempinski testified, "he took . . . 150 zlotys with which I could have bought ten loaves of bread and eased my life in camp." She concluded that "Shapshevsky was one of the worst kapos in camp."[13]

Some complainants described functionaries as cruel and sadistic. One described how in the camp Miriam Goldberg had treated an insane woman cruelly, reducing her food portion and beating her.[14] In October 1950, Hillel Itzkovitch, a twenty-two-year-old IDF solider, filed a complaint in the Ramle Police Station against one of his kapos in the camp, Abraham Fried, who was now a policeman at the station. One day the kapos in the camp caught a fourteen- or fifteen-year-old boy stealing soup from the kitchen pot. As punishment, lead kapo

Fried ordered the teenager to be thrown into a two-meter-deep pit half filled with freezing water, and Fried and the other kapos picked up frozen clods of earth and threw them at the youngster, eventually killing the boy. Fried, Itzkovitch continued, "beat and murdered many Jews and treated them cruelly . . . and he always used his [physical] strength and was the cruelest in camp."[15] While cruelty was mentioned in many complaints, it was not yet a key criterion by which one determined whether or not to charge a functionary, as it would become ten years later in the case of Hirsch Barenblat.

The suspects denied the accusers' portrayal of them as violent and selfish, asserting that they had helped and saved Jews and had paid a price for giving that help. Fried responded to the accusation of stoning the teenage boy by stating that "I helped Jews with food" and that for this the Germans had thrown him into solitary confinement. He also countered that the plaintiff, Itzkovitch, had himself collaborated with the Nazis. Itzkovitch had had endless supplies and was repeatedly rumored to be a German informer, Fried said.[16]

Not once in these investigations or in future trials did a functionary admit any wrongdoing. "It's all a lie, simply nonsense plucked from the air," responded Elimelech Rosenwald to the policeman who questioned him about the death of three inmates when he served as work inspector in a shoe factory in a camp.[17] Miriam Goldberg cast herself, not the plaintiffs, as the true victim. She categorically denied that she had ever beaten inmates at Bergen-Belsen. On the contrary, Goldberg stated, she was punished by the Germans because of the laziness of inmates who did not clean their barracks.[18]

While some denied ever having used force, others admitted the use of force but justified it as necessary to avoid harsher consequences. Mordechai Goldstein countered the accusations leveled against him by explaining that inmates laboring in a train factory stole rubber parts and that the Germans threatened that if the Jews in charge didn't stop this wave of thefts, all Jews, both those in charge and those who served as simple laborers, would be executed. "So I thought that in order to save the lives of Jews I must beat those who had done this." Whenever he beat someone it was in order to save them from being informed upon by the Poles or punished by the Germans, he claimed. "And I did all of this with good intentions and not with bad intentions and not because I wanted to serve the Nazis."[19]

A common defense was that functionaries had been attempting to ensure equitable distribution of resources such as food. An Auschwitz kapo, Elsa Trenk, said that when hungry inmates attempted to get a second portion of food, those who hadn't yet received any food fought for their share. To keep order, she beat those who had taken a second helping and so ensured that all received some food. "I was forced sometimes to raise my hand and hit," Trenk stated.[20]

Others claimed that the accusations against them were the result of present-day blackmail attempts. The previous summer, Jungster told Sergeant Nusblatt, an unfamiliar person had come to his village, Mishmar Ha-Shiv'a, and demanded 100 lira in exchange for not filing a complaint that Jungster had been a kapo. Jungster asserted that he had never served as a kapo: "I was just a foreman [*Vorarbeiter*]," he said, using the term "kapo" as a specific camp title and not in its generic meaning of anyone who served as a functionary under the Nazis. And besides, he stated, "if I did not have a clear conscience I would not have come to Israel." This was an argument repeated by several of the accused, who said that they were aware of survivors' hostility toward collaborators, and if they had had anything on their conscience they would not have chosen to immigrate to a state where more than half a million survivors lived. Their immigration proved their innocence and loyalty to the nation, they argued.[21]

In each of the cases, the policemen heard between five and thirty witnesses. After gathering an entire set of testimonies, Inspector Avatichi and his team assessed the evidence, checking mostly for consistencies or inconsistencies in the accounts. In those instances where they found the complaint merited it, they summoned the suspect again. In keeping with the spirit that dominated Israeli society, they treated those for whom they recommended charges as major criminals. In mid-August 1950, a police officer at the Israel Police headquarters in Tel Aviv declared to Trenk, "I, a sergeant in the Israel Police, accuse you, Elsa Trenk . . . of putting a national group in living conditions that could lead to its physical annihilation. . . . You participated in genocide." This set of charges, which was based on the Crime of Genocide

(Prevention and Punishment) Law, was shortly thereafter altered to draw on the Nazis and Nazi Collaborators Punishment Law. In the new set of charges, the actions Trenk was accused of, beating inmates and depriving them of food and clothing, were labeled "crimes against the Jewish people" and "crimes against humanity." Undoubtedly beating inmates in the camp was a harsh action, but the police officer attributed to Trenk no less than "an intention to annihilate the Jewish people." Here again, the police viewed alleged collaborators as true Nazis.[22]

In the first six months following passage of the legislation, from August 1950 until April 1951, police investigators handed over at least fifteen cases of alleged collaboration for consideration by the attorney general's office, all of which prosecutors would eventually pursue. The indictments included anywhere from four to twenty-one counts, with an average of ten counts. In each of these fifteen indictments, Israel's attorney general included the harshest accusation possible, charging the defendants with crimes against humanity. There was an average of five such crimes per indictment, and each of them could result in the death penalty. In their totality, the collection of indictments seemed to be asserting that these Jewish functionaries were partners to the Nazis in their war against the Jews.[23]

Preliminary Examination of a Slovak Mass Murderer

On August 24, 1950, the headline of the popular daily *Maariv* read: "First Trial in Israel Based on the Nazis and Nazi Collaborators Punishment Law—A Slovak Who Arrived as a New Immigrant Is on Trial on Charges of Annihilation of Jews."[24] The first case of collaboration with the Nazis would focus on the accused mass murderer Andrej Banik, and it was clearly chosen for the symbolic value of placing a non-Jew on trial for the persecution of Jews.

While all those indicted under this law were accused of having acted as Nazis, there was one difference between the Jewish functionaries and this non-Jew: Banik was also identified with Nazi ideology. In the indictment submitted to the magistrates court he is described as someone who "incited hatred of Jews" and "persecuted [Jews] for racial reasons," indicating an ideological association.[25] Newspaper accounts explicitly identified him as a Nazi, with headlines including "A Nazi Accused of Murdering Jews Was Arrested" and "A Nazi and Jew Murderer Will Face Trial."[26]

Ha-Dor, a daily newspaper affiliated with the political party of Prime Minister David Ben-Gurion, asserted, "It is possible that he [Banik] believes that the church has forgiven the entire Hlinka Guard and [thus has also forgiven him]. But the Jewish nation will not forgive him and his friends in the Hlinka Guard."[27] This writer saw the trial as much more than the trial of one individual facing a few of his victims. Banik was cast as an embodiment of the entire Hlinka Guard who was backed by "the church," while the few victims who confronted him represented "the Jewish nation." The writer celebrated the anticipated verdict for "one of the most typical hangmen of the Slovakian Jewry. . . . Under the new law, [he] is expected to receive the death penalty."[28] In this and similar newspaper accounts, journalists portrayed Banik as a central figure in the killing of Jews in Slovakia, an assertion that was far from true and was not even suggested by the accusations in the indictment. But for Israelis seeking revenge, this was the first and only "real" Nazi they had in hand, and his conviction would represent payback for all the dead Slovak Jews.

The legal preliminary examination in Banik's case began on September 10, 1950, in the Jerusalem Magistrates Court. The formal procedure of preliminary examination that existed in Israel in the 1950s was not intended to determine the guilt or innocence of the defendant, but rather was designed to consider the evidence and determine whether prosecutors could indict him in the district court, and if so on what charges.

Although the defendant lived in Beit Lid, halfway between Haifa and Tel Aviv, and the witnesses came mostly from Israel's coastal area, the prosecution insisted that the hearings take place in the country's capital, Jerusalem. The trial of an accused foreign mass murderer required close oversight by the heads of the Justice Ministry in Jerusalem. The attorney general, Haim Cohn, had put thirty-two-year-old Miriam Ben-Porat, a rising star in his office and a future Supreme Court justice, in charge of the case. Cohn himself was also involved in the matter and from time to time would take an active role in negotiations with defense attorneys.[29]

On the opening day, the public gallery of the courtroom was packed. The audience gathered there reflected the interest shown in the case by a variety of different groups. Catholic priests from the Salesian Church in Nazareth where the defendant now lived sat beside Holocaust survivors from Hungary and Slovakia, and representatives of the Czechoslovak consulate shared space with journalists and photographers from Israel and abroad.[30]

This would also be one of the first opportunities for Israelis to hear about the experiences of survivors in Europe. Only five years after the end of the war, "many have already forgotten what the Amalekites of our generation have done to the Jewish nation," reported A. Tovim in the newspaper *Yediot Aharonot*. This trial, he continued, would serve as a reminder. And indeed, as the survivors described life in the death camps, the audience sat "in a state of shock, listening attentively, and completely petrified . . . listening to the horror stories."[31]

The indictment submitted to the court included eleven counts, eight of which carried the death penalty. The prosecutor, Ben-Porat, who had lost most of her family in the killing fields of Lithuania, included in the counts incitement of hatred of Jews, racial persecution of Jews, and expulsion of Jews from their homes. Also included were the murder of a three-year-old Jewish boy and the slaying of an unknown number of Jews. While each of the eleven counts in the indictment focused on a specific context, the different counts echoed the larger Nazi Final Solution in all its stages, from anti-Semitic rhetoric through racial discrimination, plundering of goods, and expulsion to concentration camps, culminating with mass murder.[32]

The fourth and fifth counts of the indictment charged Banik with crimes against humanity, accusing him of causing "grave mental harm to unknown Jews in an attempt to destroy the Jewish people." Another count accused Banik of "murdering Jews on unknown dates between November 1938 and March 1940, whose number and name remain unknown." The word "unknown" would be repeated in many other counts in this and other indictments, pointing to a consistent attribute of kapo trials brought in front of Israeli courts: never in any of these cases did prosecutors present contemporaneous evidence, such as documents or proof produced in the camps or ghettos in the late 1930s or first half of the 1940s, instead relying on the recollections of witnesses.

WAR CRIMES CHARGES IN JERUSALEM

Andrei Banek of Czechoslovakia sitting between two policemen in the Magistrates Court in Jerusalem yesterday as he listened to charges of war crimes against Jews allegedly committed by him in Slovakia nearly ten years ago. Reading the charges at left is Mrs. M. Ben Porath, Assistant State Attorney.
                                                    Photo by Rubinger

Andrej Banik seated in a Jerusalem courtroom. Standing at left is the prosecutor, Miriam Ben-Porat.

Five to ten years after the war, however, survivors frequently could not recall full details of the events, and indictments reflected this in the use of the word "unknown." The use of this word also gave the impression that the charges had a greater scope than the specific contexts of the alleged events.[33]

This complete reliance on witnesses in the Israeli kapo trials stood in contrast to the role of witnesses in the International Military

Tribunal (IMT) Nuremberg trials. There, the American Supreme Court justice Robert Jackson, who served as prosecutor, chose "to put on no witnesses we could reasonably avoid." Indeed, only ninety-four witnesses testified in the IMT Nuremberg trials, two-thirds of them for the defense (and including in that number many of the twenty-four defendants themselves). Instead, the prosecution relied on the vast archival trail left behind by the Nazis. In the view of Nuremberg prosecutor Telford Taylor, it was preferable to use "clear and public proof, so that no one can ever doubt that they were fact and not fable." In the end, thanks to troves of documentation, the prosecution obtained convictions for nineteen of the defendants on trial in Nuremberg. But there was no option to use documentary evidence in the kapo trials, as almost no paper trail of significance recorded the actions of these purported Jewish collaborators. Witnesses would serve as the only means to present the cases against the defendants.[34]

After the counts in the indictment had been presented, Banik's defense attorney, Jacob Doron, rose to object, as nothing had been said about the specific type of mental harm allegedly caused. "Mental harm is a new kind of offense and one must give details of it," he asserted. Ben-Porat rejected his argument: "In the same way that it is difficult for the defense, it is also difficult for the prosecution. The witnesses that will appear on behalf of the prosecution have experienced a great deal, and basic facts are blurred in their minds," she said. This signaled a potential but crucial weakness in the prosecution's case: if the prosecutor proved that the witnesses on the stand had suffered "grave mental harm," that might disqualify the witnesses' testimony. Indeed, the precarious mental state of some witnesses would become evident as the trial unfolded. The prosecution would end up not using this count of mental harm in Banik's district court indictment, or in any of the other future kapo trials. "In light of the special circumstances of the trial [as a preliminary examination only]," Judge Moshe Perez responded to Doron's objection, "there is no need to demand further details from the prosecution."[35]

The prosecution scheduled the first witness to testify in early October. Yitzhak Freiman, the complainant who had come to the Beit Lid new immigrants' camp police to file a complaint against Banik, arrived at court twice on the wrong date. Then, on the correct date, he did not show up. The police searched the kibbutz registered as his home address but could not locate him. A month passed and Freiman was nowhere to be found. Hinting at a possible conspiracy, newspapers reported that "a key witness in the trial of Andrej Banik has disappeared."[36] If this key witness could not be found, the prosecution would be required to remove some of the weightiest charges from the indictment, including the count of murdering the three-year-old. In late November, after two months of searching for Freiman, the Czechoslovak consul in Jerusalem wrote to Attorney General Cohn requesting "that in light of the present circumstances, the question of [Banik's] release might be given earnest consideration."[37]

Meanwhile, a new piece of evidence emerged. The military censor intercepted a letter from the Hummene Local Council, Slovakia, responding to a letter from a priest, Professor Joseph Dobrovodsky at the Nazareth Salesian Church where Banik was presently staying, asking their assistance to prove Banik's innocence. The head of the Hummene committee wrote to Dobrovodsky:

> In response to your letter about the investigation of Andrej Banik from Lastovce, I dispute your argument that he is innocent and I am surprised that you support such a person . . . whose beastly actions took place from 1939 to March 1940. Indeed, your knowledge about his innocence is mistaken. . . . The aforementioned, who was at the time nineteen years old, participated in actions for which he was supposed to be hanged a long time ago and therefore we demand that you take a realistic view on this issue and not support a murderer, who is possibly the murderer of your fellow citizens. The aforementioned, as an enthusiastic member of the Hlinka Guard, walked in their uniform in the time of occupation and assisted the Germans in all of their brutal actions. . . . There is no other outcome for the brutal actions of a person such as the aforementioned, but the death penalty.[38]

The letter also listed the names of four individuals murdered by Banik.

On Ben-Porat's initiative, representatives of Israel's consulate in Prague traveled to Hummene to investigate more closely those who had sent this accusatory letter as well as the details mentioned in it. The representatives identified a few potential witnesses and had them submit affidavits.[39]

Informed about the letter, the defense attorney, Doron, turned to Attorney General Cohn and demanded that the prosecution not submit this piece of evidence, as it had been obtained in a dubious way. Cohn agreed, possibly because of ramifications for relations with Czechoslovakia, which viewed the charges against Banik and two other defendants who originated from Czechoslovakia, Elsa Trenk and Raya Hanes, as a diplomatic provocation. Nevertheless, Ben-Porat disregarded her superior's decision and decided to submit the letter as evidence. The law's fifteenth paragraph allowed "the court [to] deviate from the rules of evidence if it is satisfied that this will promote the ascertainment of the truth and the just handling of the case." Ben-Porat, who refused to let a fascist murderer slip out of her hands, wrote the legal advisor of the Israeli Ministry of Foreign Affairs that "this letter is currently a very important key to uncovering the truth about the most horrible actions of the defendant."[40]

Two months after he had been scheduled to testify, the police finally located Freiman. No one had kidnapped or assassinated him, as some might have suspected. He had moved to Tel Aviv, was working two jobs, and did not have the time to inquire about the new date on which he was scheduled to appear in court.

Now in court, Freiman testified in Hungarian—after refusing to respond to the defense attorney's questions in German, which he considered the language of the perpetrators—that in 1939 he was stationed on the Slovak side of the border with Hungary, near Betliar, not far from Roznava.[41] There he saw the defendant stop an older man attempting to cross the border with his three-year-old grandson. Although Freiman had previously told the police that he had seen the defendant choke the child with his boot, in court he testified that Banik had pushed the child to the ground and stepped on his belly: "I saw the belly of the child naked and covered in blood. I saw that one of the Jews took the boy and ran with him into the forest." Also contrary to his previous testimony, in which he had claimed that the boy had died, he now stated, "I do not know if the child was still alive." Asked to elaborate, he said that after the war he had heard that the mother could not find the boy, and so Freiman assumed that he had died.[42]

As this was only a preliminary examination, the inconsistencies in the witness's testimony and the fact that no other witnesses reported seeing the defendant in the area of Betliar and Roznava did not cause Judge Perez to remove the counts against Banik that were based on Freiman's testimony alone. In early January 1951, the judge handed down a decision that permitted the prosecution to file the indictment against Banik in the district court (a trial that will be discussed in detail in Chapter 5).[43]

Magistrates Courts' Definition of Crimes against Humanity

In late September 1950, newspapers reported on the forthcoming prosecution of two Auschwitz-Birkenau kapos with headlines such as "War Crimes Trial Begins Today in T.A. [Tel Aviv]" and "The Affair of Auschwitz Prisoners Abuse Unveiled Yesterday in Tel Aviv Courthouse." As in the case of Banik, these headlines gave the impression that the upcoming trials would uncover a slew of crimes that took place in Auschwitz, not only those by camp functionaries. While these headlines may have resulted from the wish to sell more newspapers, they also reflected a quest for revenge for the events that had unfolded in Europe. These trials, the newspapers seemed to indicate, represented a reckoning for what had occurred in Auschwitz specifically and in the Holocaust in general.[44]

On September 17, 1950, and shortly thereafter, on October 4, the attorney general's office in Tel Aviv charged two women, Elsa Trenk and Raya Hanes, both of whom had served as kapos in Auschwitz-Birkenau, with collaboration with the Nazis. In the first year following the enactment of the law, thirty cases would be presented to the magistrates court, mostly in Tel Aviv but also a few in Haifa and Jerusalem, for preliminary examination; seven of the cases involved women.[45] The choice to have two women among the first, if not *the* first, Jewish defendants in these trials may have resulted from the perception that their crime was especially abhorrent, because they had crossed two lines: they had not only betrayed the nation in collaborating with the Nazis but also shown "infidelity" to the image of a "proper" woman. Those women, in some people's opinion, had corrupted their inner innocent womanly self by serving as kapos. In dismissing the public outcry over how a woman could have collaborated with the Nazis, historian and survivor Mark Dvorzhetski indirectly confirmed the higher moral standard demanded of women: "So they have found a female Jewish traitor. Two female Jewish traitors. Three. Because of them—shall this clamoring sensation distort our view of the Hebraic woman in the days of the Holocaust . . . ?"[46]

Sexism around the issue of female kapos took several forms. For example, newspaper reports of the arrest of a male kapo did not focus on the suspect's gender, but when the suspect was female, that made the headlines, such as "A Woman Accused of Supporting the Nazis."[47] Other times it involved emphasizing sex-typical roles. Responding to the news of the upcoming Hanes hearings, David Ghiladi pointed out in *Maariv* that one could view female kapos in one of two extreme ways: as "impure vermin" or "as victims, who deserve great mercy." After these women had watched tens of thousands of humans murdered, he wrote, their emotions were blunted. "As they tortured their victims, they accused them: 'We were here when you danced at balls and had fun in night clubs and made love.' No human spark remained in them, except the animal instinct to live one more day and even at the expense of the lives of others. . . . Undoubtedly, were it not for the catastrophe of annihilation, these women would have stayed in their towns, would have married and borne children and continued their familial chain from one generation to another." The crime of the Nazis against these women was also twofold: causing them to collaborate and crippling their womanly attributes, which prevented them from fulfilling their familial duties.[48]

In the Tel Aviv Magistrates Court, prosecutor Eliezer Liebson, the Tel Aviv deputy district attorney in charge of Trenk's case, and prosecutor Max Chernobilski, who was in charge of Hanes's case, indicted the two women on similar charges. According to the indictment, the two had punished and harassed the prisoners under their supervision.

On the first day of testimony in Hanes's case before Judge Tsvi Waldman, Idit Leizerovich testified that in April 1944 a group of men was brought for a brief time into the women's camp. Among them, Leizerovich identified her father and ran to him. Hanes ran after her, caught her by the ear, pulled the shaven-headed woman to the ground, and beat her back and face, screaming at her that it was forbidden to go near men. For Leizerovich's transgression, Hanes ordered the entire block of 1,000 women to kneel for two hours.[49]

In their indictment, prosecutors contended that this action constituted a crime against humanity. They also accused Hanes of another crime against humanity for forcing a sick inmate, Rena Weiss, to stand holding a brick in the air for hours on end. These two charges exposed two different views of what constituted a crime against humanity. In the case of the 1,000 women who knelt for two hours it was cruelty against a group, whereas in the case of Rena Weiss it was cruelty against an individual. Even the case of a supervisor treating one woman cruelly, the prosecutors contended, should be viewed in the context of the concentration camps as a crime against humanity.[50]

The question of whether crimes against humanity should apply only to cruelty against a group or also to that against an individual (or individuals) was raised in Trenk's trial as well. Her indictment included a charge of crimes against humanity for an action taken against a group when she "abused inmates under her supervision. She woke them up three hours before the official 7 A.M. roll call and forced them to kneel until the start of the roll call."[51] The inmates clustered close to each other to warm up in the cold Polish dawn, but then Trenk ordered them to kneel on the soggy ground to prevent them from getting warm. "When anyone stood up from kneeling," Shoshana Bloch testified, "the defendant would beat her so harshly that the woman would collapse." At times "after the Germans went, only because the defendant wanted it, we would remain standing . . . for two hours, sometimes for three to four hours. We had to defecate right there."[52]

Witnesses described to magistrate court judge Mina Shamir how Trenk punished individual prisoners by ordering them to hold bricks in the air while kneeling. It was a cold dawn when Truda Lustig and her sister stood behind each other awaiting the morning roll call. The sister hugged Truda to help her warm up. "It was still dark, but Elsa [Trenk] noticed it. She came over and slapped Truda's sister," Berta Wosner testified. "The sister said that Truda is weak, that Elsa should allow her to warm up, but the defendant slapped Truda as well," she testified, highlighting the supervisor's lack of any empathy toward her subordinates. Then, Wosner continued, Trenk "chose a very deep puddle of water, and ordered Truda on her knees," forcing her to hold two bricks in the air. The witness could not recall how long Truda knelt in the puddle, but she knew that "when they seated her [there] it was dark and when they got her up it was light." She concluded that she "had never seen a single instance of kindheartedness toward inmates on the part of the defendant."[53]

When the preliminary examination concluded, Tel Aviv Magistrates Court judges Shamir and Waldman had to decide whether to indict the respective defendants in the district court on several counts of crimes against humanity in addition to other counts. In her decision, Shamir criticized the law, which "in its formulation and presentation is unlike any other law. Instead of clearly defined terms, here the legislator uses flowery words with a very broad meaning." She described her thinking about whether the charge of crimes against humanity was appropriate for Trenk's having ordered Truda Lustig to kneel in a puddle holding bricks in her hands: "One condition for constituting a crime against humanity is that the offense be against a group of people and not against individuals as such—the frequency or infrequency of the separate actions does not add or subtract, as long as each incident is a separate event with no connection between one event and another." A crime against humanity is only an action taken against a group as a group, she reiterated. Therefore, she rejected two of the counts of crimes against humanity, including the one for Trenk's punishment of Truda Lustig, and allowed Trenk to be tried for crimes against humanity only for ordering 800–1,000 women to kneel for hours.[54]

Judge Waldman, too, rejected the counts of crimes against humanity leveled against Hanes for her actions against individuals, and allowed the charges only in instances in which she had acted against a group.[55]

In a move that reflected the determination of prosecutors to try Jewish functionaries in the harshest possible way, the count of crimes against humanity against individuals that was rejected by the magistrates court at the preliminary examination was replaced with a count of war crimes in the district court indictments in Trenk's case, as well as in seven other cases. The prosecution refused to back down from the view that in their harsh treatment of individual inmates, these kapos had joined the Nazi forces in committing horrendous crimes—if not crimes against humanity, then war crimes.[56]

A Physician Faces Former Inmates

In November 1950, Pinchas Pashititzky emigrated with his wife and twelve-year-old son from Bratislava to Israel. They had survived the Holocaust and now moved to Israel with the hope of leaving behind their experiences in Europe and making a fresh start in a new place. At first things seemed to go well. The family moved into an apartment on Ben-Yehuda Street in central Tel Aviv. Within days, Pashititzky, a physician, found a job at the Hadassah Hospital in Sarona.[57]

Three weeks after his arrival, on December 5, 1950, the police turned up at forty-two-year-old Pashititzky's home carrying a warrant for his arrest. They took him to police headquarters, where First Inspector Michael Avatichi ushered him into an interrogation room. "I, First Inspector Michael Avatichi, accuse you, Pinchas Pashititzky, of the premeditated murder of a persecuted person. . . . On an unknown date in 1942 in the Wolanow concentration camp in Poland, a hostile country, you administered a lethal injection to Moshe Lindenbaum with the intention of killing him, and after an hour or two he died as a result of the injection." Avatichi continued to accuse Pashititzky: "On November 28, 1942, in the . . . Wolanow concentration camp, when you acted as the camp's physician, you selected 120 men and women, among them Abba Boymann and a child, Aharonic Boymann . . . knowing that they were going to be shot." He then charged him with crimes against humanity, stating that "when you acted as the camp's physician, you committed an inhuman act against a civilian population . . . when you sent the persecuted [people] in the winter to bathe in a public bath in Radom . . . and the people remained outside all night there, wet. As a result of that many of the people fell ill and died." Avatichi leveled a total of eleven charges at Pashititzky, and in a five-page summary report submitted to the attorney general's office, police sergeant Tsvi Nusblatt wrote that Pashititzky "was responsible for the death of many Jews interned in camp." These police officers and later the prosecutors portrayed Pashititzky as equivalent to a Nazi physician who had no concern for the health of Jews, selected them for life or death, and injected them with deadly substances.[58]

Pashititzky categorically denied all the accusations, saying, "I did not send any people to the public bath in Radom and wasn't even asked

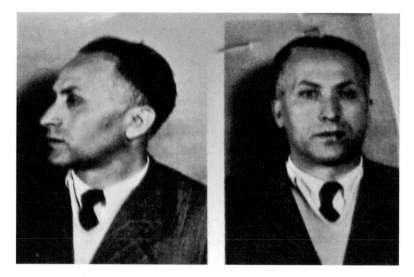

Pinchas Pashititzky, a defendant in the trials.

and I did not know anything of it." It was the German commanders of
the camp, Bargman and Wilhelm Rube, not Pashititzky, who selected
Jews for death, he said. To the contrary, when he diagnosed people with
typhus he always concealed it from the German commander, and only
listed them as having throat infection. In so doing he saved them from
execution. He admitted he had administered several injections in the
camp. He could not remember if he injected Moshe Lindenbaum,
"but I'm 100 percent sure that I gave no one an injection to kill." In
the difficult conditions of a labor camp, he did his best as a physician
to "ensure that nothing happened to any sick person because of the
Germans, and from a medical standpoint I always gave the best help
I could."[59]

One month later, Pashititzky's case came before Judge Waldman in
the Tel Aviv Magistrates Court for a preliminary examination. The indictment, which at the police station had included eleven counts, had
risen to sixteen counts, seven of which charged him with crimes against
humanity—one more than Adolf Eichmann would face a decade later.
Despite the rulings of Waldman and Shamir in the cases of Hanes and
Trenk that an individual who had committed a crime against one or

more individuals could not be charged with crimes against humanity, the prosecution refused to abandon its approach and indicted him for crimes against humanity against individual prisoners.[60]

The witness Shalom Lindenbaum related that he had called on Pashititzky to treat his ailing brother, Moshe. Recounting conduct that could match that of a Nazi physician, Lindenbaum described how Pashititzky injected his brother with a substance; minutes later, the sick man lay dead. "I found my brother dead; he was as black as if he had been electrocuted," the witness recalled.[61] In the camp sickroom, Esther Tugdman saw Pashititzky administer an injection to a patient and overheard an exchange between him and the sick person. "He [Pashititzky] said that within twenty-four hours he would feel better. The day after he came to the sick person and said, 'What a strong heart you have.' The sick person answered him, 'This time you did not suc-ceed.'"[62] Another witness peeked inside a barracks and saw Pashititzky inject a patient. "When he came out, he said to himself with a smirk, 'He won't laugh anymore.'" Many in the camp did not trust Pashititzky and avoided asking his advice, the witnesses said.[63]

Miriam Boymann reported other deadly actions on the part of the Nazi-like physician. Her mother had had dysentery, and Dr. Pashititzky prescribed eight pills that he told Boymann to give her mother all at once. Boymann feared giving such a large dose, and she dissolved only a portion of it in water. "My mother drank the solution and at 4:30 P.M. my mother told me that she wanted to sleep. She asked that I turn her around toward the wall because she was tired. I turned her. She did not speak to me again. My relatives arrived back from work. We saw that Mother had died. It was 4:45 P.M. Everyone said that the defendant had poisoned her."

Other witnesses in the Tel Aviv courtroom described the role of Pashititzky in the selection of Jews. At midday on November 28, 1942, the camp management ordered both men and women to assemble in the men's camp for a medical examination. There "the defendant and the German commander conducted a selection," Miriam Boymann testi-fied, describing Pashititzky as having colluded with the camp com-mander to send Jews to their execution. She and most of her family were sent to one side; her father and 120 others were sent to the other.

"I and my group ran toward the other camp and remained alive. My father and his group ran in the other direction. They were shot by the Ukrainians. They all died."[64]

Enhancing the portrayal of the defendant as a conspirator in the killing of camp inmates, Shalom Lindenbaum testified that the selection was "based on lists prepared by the management of the camp. The most active in preparing these lists was the defendant." In this account, the Jewish managers of the camp, of which the defendant was a member, were seen as the culprits responsible for selecting Jews for death. Another witness stated, "We would be horrified when we saw Dr. Pashititzky walking around camp with a list . . . as it was a sign that soon there would be a selection."[65]

Pashititzky was one of two physicians to face charges in the kapo trials. Witnesses also described the other physician, Joshua Sternberg, as a Nazi co-conspirator in selecting Jews for execution. During one selection in Auschwitz, a witness testified, he saw Sternberg standing by Joseph Mengele, and he overheard Sternberg tell Mengele that he should send the man to the crematorium. He had also heard from an attendant at the Auschwitz hospital that Sternberg administered lethal injections. Other witnesses recalled that Sternberg refused to give them medication, telling one of them that "you will die like a dog anyway, Jewish leper."[66]

On March 4, 1951, the last day of the hearings, after twenty-four prosecution witnesses had testified, the tension in the courtroom peaked as Pashititzky himself approached the stand. As was customary in preliminary examinations, the defense did not present its case, and the defendant did not take an oath, so as to avoid cross-examination that might incriminate him or her in any future proceeding in the district court. Pashititzky spoke in a quiet voice and in his final words declared, "I state that throughout the entire period of my work as a doctor and throughout the entire period of my work as the doctor in Wolanow I did not commit any act against humanity or against the Jewish people. I have never collaborated with the Nazis; and never did I act contrary to the Hippocratic Oath." In his view he had remained loyal to his moral conscience at all levels: as a human, as a Jew, and as a physician. In fact, he asserted, during his entire eight months in the camp a typhus epidemic had raged there, "and I as the only physician treated the sick with dedication and according to the best of my knowledge and conscience, and thanks to this the patients recovered." Only ten of the camp prisoners died due to complications, "which is less than the general statistics." He concluded by stating, "I wish to emphasize again that I have taken no acts against humanity or against the Jewish people, and that never did I collaborate with the Nazis and never did I act against medical ethics."[67]

In late March 1951, Judge Waldman pronounced his decision. Of the sixteen counts, he permitted the submission of eight to the Tel Aviv District Court. For lack of evidence he dismissed all counts of administering lethal injections and prescribing deadly doses of medication. He did permit the progression to the district court of two counts of crimes against humanity, one of them for selecting 120 Jews for death. Just as he had held six months earlier in the case of the Auschwitz supervisor Raya Hanes, Judge Waldman wrote that crimes against humanity can be committed only against a "population" and that most events described in the Pashititzky trial "did not constitute an act with respect to a 'civilian population.'" It would be nine months more, during which Pashititzky remained behind bars, before his trial opened in December 1951 in the Tel Aviv District Court (a trial discussed in detail in Chapter 6).[68]

CHAPTER FIVE

WEIGHING THE ACTIONS
OF JEWISH COLLABORATORS

ON MAY 14, 1951, just one day after the minister of foreign affairs, Moshe Sharett, announced Israel's demand for more than $1 billion in compensation from the German government for property Jews had lost in Europe, Attorney General Haim Cohn traveled from Jerusalem to Haifa to deliver the opening statement in the first trial to reach the district court level, that of the Slovak Andrej Banik. The trial opened on the third anniversary of the establishment of the Jewish state. It was as if the date had been selected to declare that the new, independent state of Israel now enabled Jews to hold Nazis and their associates accountable for murder.[1]

In his opening speech, Cohn, who played a central role in shaping Israel's fledgling legal system, spoke only briefly about Banik, describing him as "an evil person and an anti-Semite, a Jew-hater," and adding that he deserved the death penalty. This portrayal of Banik as an archetypal Nazi matched the image that came across in the preliminary examination (discussed in Chapter 4), but as it would later become clear, was surely not accurate.[2]

After a short focus on Banik, Cohn turned to educate the panel of three judges—Jacob Azulai, Dov Tobbin, and Moshe Etzioni—about the singular nature of the Nazis and Nazi Collaborators Punishment Law. Although at first glance the law might seem to be retroactive, he said, in reality it concerned actions that "are crimes by their very nature and always were crimes," and it was only as a result of the unprecedented atrocities committed by the Nazis that it had become necessary to codify such offenses in the law.[3]

Cohn, who had been devastated by the loss of his brother Leo, a member of the French Resistance whom the Nazis murdered, acknowledged to the court that some of the evidence in the trial would not be of the kind commonly accepted in ordinary legal procedures. In the coming days, he said, they would hear testimony from a woman who had been twelve years old at the time of the events. Furthermore, more than ten years had passed since those events; during that time she had been in several camps and encountered endless hardships. The judges should take this into account, he acknowledged, but they should also remember that "these people who appear before you as witnesses are not testifying about things or only about things that occurred in their presence, that their eyes saw or ears heard. Each and every one of them, Your Honors, is testifying about things that are fixed in their soul. A person's memory does not easily blur the face of an enemy, even if [the person] last saw that enemy in childhood or adolescence, . . . whose malicious actions changed the course of his life."[4] The horrific events of the Holocaust gave survivors' testimony a greater validity than that of ordinary witnesses, he argued. Even if witnesses were wrong on details, he believed, one should not discount their testimonies as lies but rather remember that they carried within them a core truth, one imprinted in their soul and memory by the trauma they had experienced.

In his statement Cohn assumed that early memories of an enemy are fixed in the soul of a witness, but he ignored other psychological factors that might skew the testimony of such traumatized people. The Banik proceedings exposed problems with survivors' testimonies, such as witnesses who combined disparate and unrelated occurrences into one account. In other cases, witnesses added unverified information to bolster testimonies that were truthful at their core. In future years, following the Kastner trial, Cohn would acknowledge the problems with some witnesses in the kapo trials and would come to change his mind about the quality of survivor accounts, viewing some of them with caution due to the "mental state" of the witnesses.[5]

The problematic mental state of some witnesses became evident with the first witness called to the stand in the Banik trial. In his testimony in the Haifa district court, Yitzhak Freiman focused on one day sometime between November 1939 and May 1940 at the Slovak-Hungarian border, where he was stationed as part of the 29th Regiment of the Hungarian army. There he saw the defendant brutalize a three-year-old Jewish boy:

> I saw with my own eyes how the defendant kicked the child's belly, and the child's intestines came out and I saw blood. The child lay with his intestines out, in blood, and the Jews collected the boy and fled. They entered the forest, they fled to the forest, because all were expelled there, and I don't know more. I know the child died because after liberation I heard from his mother who had returned that her son had died.[6]

As mentioned in Chapter 4, unlike Freiman's previous testimony to the police and in the preliminary examination in the Jerusalem magistrates court that he had seen Banik choking the boy with his boot or stepping on his belly, his testimony in the district court was that Banik had kicked the boy's belly. Most important, after declaring at the magistrates court that he did not know the fate of the child, he returned to what he had said in his initial statement to the police, that the child had been killed.[7]

In his cross-examination, the defense attorney asked Freiman where the child's mother had been on that fatal day. She did not witness the event, he responded. The Jewish men and women had been separated, he explained, an account that seemed more in keeping with his experience in Auschwitz than with his service at the Slovak-Hungarian border.[8]

Defense attorney Doron asked the court's permission to present an affidavit from the child's mother, Ibola Bokorova. Granted permission, he read it out: "I had only one son, Paul Vorosa, seven years old, who was always with me from his birth until May 19, 1944, . . . [in] the Auschwitz concentration camp, where my son was taken from me by the Germans and killed."[9]

Even as the affidavit exposed his error, Freiman stood by his account. "I am telling you," the witness said, "that I know better than the mother what happened to her son because at that time they separated husband from wife, wife from husband, and children from their parents. . . . What you read me now from the affidavit of the boy's mother is not in line with the truth." Freiman was insisting that he knew the truth better than anyone else, even the mother who lost her child in an Auschwitz selection; he would repeat this assertion in one form or another as his testimony unraveled.[10]

Doron pointed out to Freiman that in his testimony in the police station he had stated that Banik choked the child; now he was stating that Banik had kicked the child's belly open. In the preliminary examination he had stated that he saw the child bleeding but had said nothing about the child's intestines coming out. Previously he had stated that the child was only severely injured, but now he was claiming that he was killed. Which was correct? Irritated at the questioning, Freiman gulped water and wiped sweat off his forehead. He stood by his latest version of events, explaining that when he had signed the testimony at the police station, he had been less concerned with exact details than with indicating that the child was hurt and covered in blood.[11]

Doron shifted the focus to Freiman's testimony that Banik had punched the seventy-year-old attorney Lajos Grossman in the face and stolen his prosthesis of gold teeth. The defense attorney ignored some contradictions between Freiman's account to the police and his testimony in magistrates court and focused instead on the victim of the attack, asking Freiman if he knew Grossman's first name.

"As far as I can remember it was Louis or Lajos. . . . He was sixty-five to seventy years of age."

Was Grossman well known?

"He was a famous attorney in the northern part of Hungary. I knew him. Who did not know him? He was a famous attorney. His office was in Lucenec."

Was he an attorney or an intern?

"He was a famous attorney, not an intern."

Doron approached the bench and submitted as evidence a letter from Bratislava's attorneys' association declaring that no attorney named Grossman was registered in their books.[12]

"I am telling you that my whole story about the attorney Grossman is correct and not a lie as you are saying," Freiman insisted.

Next, Doron shifted from events that had taken place twelve years earlier to those that had occurred a year and a half earlier in Israel. He asked about the moment when Freiman had spotted Banik.

Freiman recounted that it had been in December 1949, while Freiman was standing guard at the residence of Israel's president in Rehovot. A bus stopped at a nearby station, and Freiman spotted Banik among the passengers disembarking. He neither called out for help nor assaulted Banik, but rather followed him as he got on and off another three buses. At the end of this journey, more than fifty kilometers north of Rehovot, Freiman entered the grounds of the Beit Lid new immigrants' camp. There he immediately sought out the camp's leadership and police and informed them about the presence in their midst of a Slovak war criminal.[13]

Doron approached the bench again and presented a letter from an adjutant at the president's residence, Lt. Col. R. Arnon. "To the best of my knowledge," Arnon wrote, at the time in question "there was no guard, soldier, or watchman named Yitzhak Freiman" serving at the president's residence.[14] As in earlier instances in which his testimony was discredited, here too Freiman stood by what seemed to be a false claim: "If you are telling me that in December of 1949 I did not work at all guarding the president's palace, I answer you that I did."[15]

The defense attorney did not press the point. His goal was no longer to attack Freiman's testimony, already discredited beyond repair, but rather to cast a stain on the conduct of the police in the investigation. In court, Freiman testified that "in Beit Lid there was a lineup. I entered the police station and there was a line of six to eight people. I was asked to find the defendant. I found him, but to be completely sure, I demanded that he remove his hat. I selected him two to three times and after my testimony was taken I was sent outside." The defense then pointed out that in the preliminary examination Freiman had said that he first saw the defendant in the police station corridor, near the reception desk. Once more Freiman stood by his account, denying that he had ever sat near the defendant in the police station's reception area and reiterating that he had identified the defendant in three police lineups.[16] Back in court a week later, the attorney presented a letter from the police stating that "there is no indication in the police station journal of any lineup related to the subject [Banik]."[17]

On the last day of trial testimonies, the defense called to the stand Sgt. Nathan Rabinowitz, the commander of the Beit Lid police station, who had taken down Freiman's testimony. "I am certain that there was no lineup with the defendant at any time," Rabinowitz told the court. Questioned again by the defense, he repeated his answer:

I am certain that there was no lineup in which the defendant stood between people to enable Freiman to identify him. There was nothing of that sort. At one point, Freiman and the defendant were brought together. . . . Freiman's response was amazing. He started screaming, shrieking, and truly wanted to attack the defendant. We were hardly able to calm him down and we pulled him out so he would not harm the defendant.[18]

Only because the policemen held Freiman back did he not assault the defendant. The police assumed that Freiman was seeking revenge on Banik because he knew him and his criminal actions. But as Freiman's testimony revealed, it is not at all clear that Freiman knew Banik during the war, and even if he did know him, there was no evidence that he saw him commit crimes. A few days later, before the summations began, Leni Rabinowitz, the Haifa district prosecutor, told the court, "To reduce the extent of the summations, I wish to inform the court that . . . the prosecution will not request the defendant's conviction on the first and fourth counts," which rested mostly on Freiman's testimony.[19]

In their verdict, the three judges wrote, "Our feeling, and we believe it is a sufficiently grounded feeling, is that this witness [Freiman] either lied intentionally or is suffering from hallucinations and imagines things that he may have experienced which he attributes to the defendant with no basis whatsoever."[20]

Besides the possibility that Freiman was "suffering from hallucinations," the court also mentioned the possibility that he had lied. But what might have motivated Freiman to lie? At one point during his testimony, when Doron had accused him of lying, Freiman had shouted: "Everything is true, the Hlinka Guard killed my three children." Freiman had never accused Banik of killing his children, but this outburst may reveal part of the motivation behind his testimony. By accusing Banik, who was reported in the media to be a member of the Hlinka Guard, he was getting back at the fascist militia that he viewed as responsible for the murder of his family members. The natural quest for revenge may have led him to lie, intentionally or unintentionally.[21]

When asked why he thought the witnesses were testifying against him, Banik offered a similar explanation. All the complainants, he said, had suffered so much that they lied "as a result of a mass psychosis."[22] Defense attorney Doron elaborated that witnesses such as Freiman had learned from a newspaper article about the defendant's presumed membership in the Hlinka Guard, thought about the young Hlinka Guard member in their village who mistreated them and against whom they sought revenge, inferred that the person facing trial was probably the same man, shortly thereafter became convinced of it, and came to give depositions against him.[23]

Both the judges and Banik attributed Freiman's and other witnesses' inaccurate testimonies to a possible mental issue. The court termed this disorder "hallucinations," while Banik called it "mass psychosis." In the accepted psychological framework of the 1950s, experiencing harsh events like the Holocaust could potentially trigger mental disorders in people from families with a prior disposition to such conditions. It was the individual and his family history that were viewed as responsible for the onset of mental problems after events such as the Holocaust. But following the Vietnam War, in which many soldiers with no such family disposition suffered from mental disorder, psychology adopted a new theory. Mental disorder was now seen as a result of witnessing difficult events and was no longer linked directly to a person's family background. Instead of hallucinations or psychosis, it was categorized as trauma.

One possible effect of trauma, clinical literature has pointed out, is an unstoppable desire to take revenge for one's suffering. It is thus plausible that Freiman, as well as a few other witnesses in the kapo trials, neither were directly impelled by trauma to lie nor lied deliberately, but rather as a result of trauma developed an obsession to take revenge, and as a result lied. The traumatized Freiman aimed to get revenge against a member of the Hlinka Guard for the killing of his children even if the person in front of him, Banik, had had nothing to do with their death.[24]

Freiman's was not the only case of problematic testimonies in the Banik trial. The next witness on the stand was Tova-Judith Greenberger (Shachner), a native of the village of Lastovce in Czechoslovakia and a neighbor of the Banik family. Her testimony, as well as that of some of her family members, demonstrates how an account that did not confuse reality and fiction can still be discredited for being motivated by anger and hatred deep enough to have tainted the truth.

Greenberger was twelve years old in 1938 when her half-brother Hugo, who was born in Hungary, returned home from serving in the Czechoslovak army. Banik, who served as the head of the fascist Hlinka Guard militia in Lastovce and Michalany, knocked on the door, she testified; he was wearing a cap, boots, and an armband. He had come not to greet Hugo on his return but rather to threaten that if the family did not pay him a bribe, he would deport Hugo to his native Hungary. "Of course my father gave him money," Greenberger said. But one payment did not satisfy Banik's appetite, and he reappeared time and again to demand money and belongings. In one instance he took the family's radio.[25]

Judge Moshe Etzioni asked Greenberger when she had last seen Banik, potentially opening a space to cast doubt on Greenberger's ability to identify a person she had last seen as a young girl. She answered that she had last laid eyes on him nine years earlier, in 1942 in Lastovce, when she was sixteen years old.[26]

The following day, the court heard the testimony of Greenberger's brother, Asher Lastovcy (formerly known as Arpad Schachner), who had come to know Banik in the summer of 1938 and had recommended him as an intern in the village secretary's office. "He came to our home in Lastovce in the evening hours, after sundown and before dark," Lastovcy recalled. In the room were his sister, Greenberger; his half-brother, Hugo; and their parents.

> The defendant turned to my brother [Hugo]. "I received an order to hand you over to the Hungarian border patrol."
>
> My brother answered, "I have Czechoslovak citizenship."
>
> The defendant answered, "I can't do a thing. I must hand you over to the border patrol."
>
> There was an argument in the house and the defendant sat with us. My mother started crying and turned to my father and said in Yiddish, "Give him some money; perhaps one can talk to him." Then they gave him some money. I can't remember who—my father or Hugo himself. I can't recall how much they gave him. Then the defendant was silent, sat a bit longer, and left.[27]

A year and a half earlier, in December 1949, Lastovcy had made no reference to this story at the police station, and instead told a distinctly different account. He had testified that in 1939 Banik walked around Lastovce with a blue armband bearing the red double cross of the Hlinka Guard. Near their village, Polish Jewish families with small children were stranded at the border between Hungary and Slovakia. It was in the middle of a freezing winter, and Banik came to Lastovcy's father demanding 500 korunas to allow those Polish Jews into Slovakia. Lastovcy's father consented. Then, every week following, the suspect threatened to deport the Jews to Hungary and demanded additional bribes. Lastovcy's father paid him 500 korunas again and again.

Like his sister, Lastovcy also testified in court that Banik "came to our house with a gendarme and they both entered and the defendant said, 'You have a radio. And you don't need a radio. You need a hanging tree and not a radio. I will take the radio.' And he took the radio, and we could not resist."[28]

Banik categorically denied all the accusations. "I never . . . demanded money from them. And I did not demand any other object, and did not take from them money or goods, or a radio or anything else."[29]

At the end of July, the court handed down its verdict. Greenberger, the court pointed out, had given a detailed account of the defendant. She mentioned that in 1939 he had switched from wearing civilian clothing to wearing a uniform; she knew his position as a commander of the local Hlinka Guard "who traveled all around Slovakia"; and she gave a detailed account of how he extorted money from her family. "These details are astounding and indicate very comprehensive knowledge," the judges wrote.

> No other witness gave a similar account. Nevertheless, we are not satisfied; she was only twelve years old, and it is hard to rationally believe that a girl of her age was able to acquire such knowledge. And therefore a doubt arises as to whether at the time that she testified before us she relied on her personal and independent knowledge alone and said what she said without the interference or influence of another source.[30]

The judges concluded that she had given her testimony with the aim of getting Banik convicted, and toward that end she conveyed minute details that she did not necessarily remember. In so doing she had tainted her entire testimony, because this effort indicated her entrenched hatred of the defendant, a feeling that did not allow her to report objectively to the court.

The court also found the testimony of Lastovcy, "who did not show as much knowledge as his sister," unreliable. In addition to his having changed his account of the extortion story between his police deposition and his court testimony, the judges also found mismatches between the stories of the two siblings. His sister's account did not support his, as she gave no detail of the emotional encounter, which the judges thought a twelve-year-old probably would have remembered. They wrote about Lastovcy, "We are under the impression that this witness came to testify with prejudice against the defendant. As justified as the loathing and bitterness may be, they must not make the witness insane and cause him to describe events that have no basis in reality and possibly are invented. The duty of the witness is to tell the truth, no matter who the defendant is."[31]

As we saw earlier in the case of Freiman, the quest to take revenge for their suffering on someone viewed as a member of a fascist militia, even if that person was only indirectly associated with their tormentors, motivated some of the witnesses in these trials. Toward this end, some witnesses tailored a testimony that they believed would ensure the defendant's conviction, including details and horrors that did not necessarily match what they really remembered or what had actually occurred. The court would not accept these blemished accounts.

One remaining count in the indictment, which the court characterized as "the linchpin of this entire procedure," accused Banik of having been "a member of the Hlinka Guard . . . one of the aims of which was to assist in carrying out an enemy regime's actions directed against persecuted persons."[32] Six witnesses, three who had lived in Lastovce in the late 1930s and three who in the early 1940s lived twenty kilometers to the north in the town of Secovce, testified that they had seen Banik dressed either in a Hlinka Guard uniform or with a blue armband associated with that militia tied around his arm. As we will see, while the court refused to rely on these six testimonies to convict Banik of membership in a hostile organization, this is one instance where there are grounds to believe that the court had come to the wrong conclusion.

Forty-eight-year-old bank manager Alexander Marko, described by the court as a cautious and reliable witness, testified that he had been walking through the streets of Secovce with his Jewish clients when they pointed out Banik. The clients related to Marko their fear that Banik "would come and demand more and more money." Marko observed Banik wearing a blue armband with a double red cross, the symbol of the Hlinka Guard.[33]

In his summation, defense attorney Doron questioned Marko's reliability as well as that of two other witnesses. Those witnesses admitted they had not known Banik well, but ten years later claimed that they recalled seeing him walking in the streets of Secovce in a Hlinka Guard uniform. Was it not essential in these circumstances, the attorney asked, that the police conduct a lineup to verify witness identification? Of the ten prosecution witnesses, the police had conducted a lineup only for Asher Lastovcy, the one witness in the trial who had grown up with the defendant and needed it least.[34]

The court accepted the attorney's criticism of the police's problematic choice to conduct only one lineup. It would violate the defendant's rights, the court held, if it relied on the testimony of the three witnesses who barely knew Banik but placed him in Secovce. The court also dismissed as unreliable the testimony of the three other witnesses who did not have the opportunity to identify Banik in a lineup and had placed him in Lastovce. Dismissing all six witnesses, the court determined that the prosecution had not proven beyond a reasonable doubt that the defendant was a member of the Hlinka Guard.

As noted earlier, the public saw the defendants in the kapo trials as guilty until proven innocent. With the opening of the trial, some newspapers wrote in what seems a gleeful manner that Banik "is expected to receive the death penalty."[35] Unlike the public, however, the court saw defendants as innocent unless proven guilty. Giving Banik the benefit of the doubt, the court acquitted him. Though the trial had begun as an effort to bring a real Nazi caught in Israel to justice, the proceeding turned out to be a legal blunder (which also helps explain why the trial has been completely forgotten in Israeli historical memory to this day).

Yet in his court testimony, the defendant repeated several times, "I did not wear the uniform of any organization or of the Hlinka Guard.

And I also did not wear any armband on my sleeve."[36] Why did Banik see a need to repeatedly deny having been a member of the Hlinka Guard and being dressed in their uniform? Was it only because six witnesses had testified about his membership in this hostile organization and about having seen him dressed in its clothing?

More than a year earlier, in his initial police investigation, Banik did state that he had "worked on the border until March 1939 in civilian clothes and . . . had a band with a special symbol. It was a blue band. In March we received a military uniform." He never repeated this account, and even here he did not explicitly admit membership in the Hlinka Guard, but this testimony does seem to indicate that he was a member of that organization, as he stated he wore a blue armband, the color of the Hlinka Guard armband, and especially as he says he began to dress in uniform in 1939, when Slovakia's status changed from that of an autonomous area to that of an independent state and the clothing worn by the militia changed as well.[37]

In a private letter from the Czechoslovak consulate in Jerusalem that was unknown to the Haifa court, Consul F. Necas reported to defense attorney Doron that an investigation of the Ministry of National Security in Prague had found that Banik had "joined the Hlinka Guard in 1943. He assisted in an action that made the business of a certain Mr. Kohn of Secovce become non-Jewish (a procedure called 'Aryanization'), but on the other hand he rescued Mr. Kohn from deportation." This letter confirmed the testimony of the six witnesses who said they had seen Banik in a Hlinka Guard uniform, as did also the letter intercepted from the head of the Hummene Local Council (see Chapter 4) and presented in the preliminary examination (but not in the district court procedure). All of these pieces of evidence combined with Banik's own partial admission about his dress indicate that he indeed was a member of the Hlinka Guard.

The letter from Necas to Doron also points out that Banik had participated in actions against Jews. The Czechoslovak consul informed Banik's defense attorney that the ministry had found that in the late 1930s Banik "ordered that radios belonging to people at Lastovce who were not trustworthy for the then existing regime, be confiscated," just as Greenberger and Lastovcy had testified.[38]

After the court dismissed some of the charges against Banik and acquitted him of the other, the media, which had initially anticipated the death penalty, now reported that Banik thanked his attorneys and commented, "The world ought to pay homage to Israel's justice." Shortly thereafter, the person who in all likelihood was a former Slovak militiaman left Israel for Canada, where his wife's family had settled, and opened a travel agency in Toronto.[39]

Auschwitz Kapos on Trial

Concurrently with and following the Banik case, trials began against Jewish defendants, proceedings that, in contrast with the acquittal of Banik, ended up with courts convicting two-thirds of the accused. In the Jerusalem district court, Judge Alfred Witkon found Joseph Paal guilty of hanging inmates from the barracks ceiling by their hands for ten to twenty minutes at a time and of beating prisoners until they bled. For his "sadistic" actions, wrote the judge, Paal deserved life in prison, but because these actions had occurred under the Nazi regime Witkon sentenced him to ten years, reduced later by the Supreme Court to five years.[40] In the Tel Aviv District Court, a panel of three judges headed by Max Kenneth found that Mordecai Friedman had beaten inmates who were slow in carrying out their jobs. The panel sentenced him to three years of imprisonment.[41] Kenneth, who sat alone on the trial of Miriam Goldberg, found her guilty of pouring soup on an inmate who during food distribution asked for another potato. In sentencing her he turned to the defendant and clarified that none of your "actions showed that you identified yourself with the Germans . . . and I have no doubt that you are not and you were not wicked. . . . I have no doubt that your actions resulted due to the concurrent circumstances of anger [and] disturbances from both sides," meaning both supervisors and subordinates. Kenneth sentenced Goldberg to the ten months she had already spent in detention awaiting trial.[42] While the prosecution requested the harshest punishments, the courts took a measured view of the actions of the defendants. Yet in their judgments the courts accepted the notion that a person could simultaneously be a victim and act as a criminal.

Some of the complexities of trying former inmates were evident in the trials of Raya Hanes and Elsa Trenk, who in March 1942 were among the first to arrive in what would become the largest concentration camp in the Third Reich's web of camps, Auschwitz-Birkenau. The trials of Trenk, eighteen at the time, and Hanes, twenty-one, who lived through similar experiences and served in closely related positions, one as *Blockältester* and one as *Lagerkapo*, pointed to the very different ways in which courts assessed the behaviors of camp functionaries. While the two seemed to have treated victims in the same manner, in one case the court believed the account of the prosecution witnesses and in the other it dismissed their testimony. While the courts refused to view Jewish functionaries as Nazis, they did not hesitate to view their actions in a critical manner and to convict and incarcerate them.

Elsa Trenk had been detained for fifteen months before her trial opened in November 1951 in front of a three-judge panel of Max Kenneth, Jacob Gavison, and Benjamin Cohn at the Tel Aviv District Court. She arrived in court in a bright-colored suit and lipstick, one newspaper reported, to face a twelve-count indictment that included one count of war crimes and one of crimes against humanity.[43] As noted in Chapter 4, after the magistrate courts repeatedly refused to charge defendants with crimes against humanity for acts committed against individuals, prosecutors would not back down and replaced the charge of crimes against humanity with that of war crimes. That prosecutors charged these Jewish functionaries with war crimes reveals their perception of these Jews as partners to the Nazis who in their actions sided with the enemy in committing egregious crimes against their co-religionists. In his summation in the Trenk trial, the prosecutor A. Dinari would point out that "in her actions the defendant identified with her German superiors."[44]

Seventeen prosecution witnesses, all women from Hungary and Czechoslovakia who had lived under Trenk's oversight, presented the case against her. They described how Trenk constantly struck them on their cheeks and ears. After a German supervisor who inspected the group of Jewish prisoners had left, Vera Schwartz turned to Trenk and asked permission to go to the bathroom. "You need to go to the bathroom?" asked the twenty-year-old *Blockältester*, and her fist landed on Schwartz's head. "She needed no reason to beat [someone]. She beat for no reason," Schwartz stated.[45] At roll call one morning, as the inmates awaited the Germans, "it was cold and we stood pressed together to warm up and then she struck all the girls who stood in line. . . . She said to all of us, 'You should die like dogs,'" Deborah Ashkenazi recalled.[46]

Hava Gottlieb also used the metaphor of being treated as animals when she described how upon awakening the women in the morning Trenk would beat them and treat them like "a trainer in a zoo."[47]

Following days of testimony by the prosecution witnesses, Trenk was sworn in, and the first sentence she uttered encapsulated her defense: "I have been accused of harsh offenses by people who arrived in camp in 1944, but those people can't imagine to themselves what the conditions were in 1942 when I was there." These latecomers to Auschwitz-Birkenau who remained there for only one month, she indicated, had suffered, but they did not live through the truly harsh conditions and experiences of those who had arrived first.[48] Whereas the 1944 arrivals slept under a roof and had water, she said, "when I came, there was no water and no barracks and no showers." This account of the harsher conditions in the early years of the camp is accurate: in testimony given in Germany in the 1964 Auschwitz trials, an SS officer named Joachim Caesar said that at first "the Birkenau camp was in an impossible state. . . . It had no paths or water. Throughout the area, not a well was found that was not contaminated with coli[form] bacteria, and not a puddle was not swarming with malaria-bearing anopheles mosquitoes."[49]

"Those in charge of us [in 1942] were prostitutes by profession," Trenk said of the German kapos who supervised her and her fellow inmates. In his writings Rudolf Höss, commander of Auschwitz-Birkenau, confirms this account when he describes a group of German prostitutes, criminals, and a few political internees brought in from Ravensbrück to serve as kapos in the women's barracks at the newly established Birkenau camp as "unfeeling, ruthless, base and corrupt."[50] When she arrived, Trenk testified, the German supervisors used dogs to manage inmates—and here Trenk pulled off her jacket to display scars from dog bites. In contrast to these German supervisors, Trenk continued in her testimony, Jewish *Blockälteste* who supervised the new arrivals near the war's end treated them less harshly.

Not only were the physical circumstances starkly different, but so too were the mental ones. When Trenk arrived in the camp, the Germans were conquering territory at a rapid rate and there seemed to be no hope that they could be stopped, while in 1944 the newcomers were aware of news that Allied forces were advancing on both the eastern and western fronts. "It is hard to describe the horror of that time," Trenk said. "We lived from one day to another and we saw how thousands of people are being led to the crematoria. And mothers saw how their children are being led to burning. The spell of death was over us all the time, I mean in the year 1942–1943." She added, "I wanted the court to have a picture from life [in Auschwitz-Birkenau in 1942–1943]. I wanted to prove to the court that in that period of 1944, the people who remained [in Auschwitz-Birkenau] for approximately one month were in paradise compared to what came earlier."

Having lived through such difficult hardships, she seemed to be saying, had shaped her mental state and her behavior. Her actions, she argued, should be seen as a consequence of her life experience and should be judged in relative terms. She had treated inmates "gently" compared to her own experience.[51]

Still, Trenk refused to take any responsibility for her actions. She testified that she ordered inmates to kneel, but contrary to witnesses' claims, she argued she had done so under orders from a German officer. In fact, she claimed she had no authority to do so on her own initiative. Apart from that, Trenk refuted all claims of harassment. "I did not hit on a regular basis but sometimes I struck a blow. My mother did not teach me how to hit. I did not hit the women on their ears. . . . I did not have enough strength to slap."[52]

Besides Trenk, three witnesses testified for the defense. None of the three had anything to say about Trenk's actions in Auschwitz-Birkenau, and one of them, Eirene Markowitz, related that Trenk had slapped her too: "I did not say that the defendant behaved nicely. . . . My luck was that she treated me better [than the others]."[53] It appears that Markowitz was not questioned by the defense prior to being called as a witness; had they done so, they would have realized that her account would not help Trenk. It may well be that the defense called these three women simply out of fear of having no witnesses testifying on her behalf. Similarly, in a few of the other kapo trials the defense had a difficult time finding witnesses to testify on the defendants' behalf, and there too they called on witnesses whose testimony would end up helping the prosecution.[54]

Nearly three weeks into the trial, before a packed court and a sobbing defendant, the judges issued their verdict. They found Trenk guilty of nine instances of striking inmates and ordering individuals to kneel, but cleared her of one count of assault and of the counts of war crimes and crimes against humanity. The judges determined Israeli law required that for an offense to be considered a war crime it must be a serious one, such as "murder, ill-treatment or deportation to forced labour or for any other purpose, of civilian population of or in occupied territory."[55] Trenk had not been found guilty of any serious crimes.

Furthermore, contrary to the prosecution's argument that several actions against individuals could constitute a war crime or a crime against humanity, the judges wrote that those actions for which the defendant was convicted, "even though they are not few, were carried out and intended to be carried out against individuals as individuals and not against a group as a group. . . . In addition, the actions were not carried out with a specific plan or predetermined conspiracy but rather with the intention of maintaining order." For all these reasons, the court would not convict Trenk for crimes against humanity or war crimes.[56]

In later rulings, two other district courts added one more basic condition for convicting a functionary of war crimes—namely, identification with the enemy and its actions. The common assumption made by the courts was that the actions of a member of a persecuted nation against his fellow citizens did not constitute a war crime. Yet it was theoretically possible, these courts added, that a member of the oppressed nation could identify with the oppressors and its actions against his own nation. To convict a member of the oppressed nation for war crimes one had to clearly prove that "he acted, knowingly, as the executioner of their orders, as their adjutant or as a partner . . . of the Nazi leadership, in their satanic plan to annihilate nations in general and that of the Jewish nation specifically." In none of the kapo trials did a court find a defendant guilty of war crimes.[57]

In determining Trenk's sentence, the judges took into account both the defendant's claim that the Nazis forced her to take the position of *Blockältester* as well as her harsh experiences in Auschwitz-Birkenau in the years 1942–1943.[58] They issued a relatively light sentence of two years' imprisonment, with credit for the time she had already spent in detention. This sentence was slightly lighter than the overall average of two years and two months that district courts imposed on those convicted in the kapo trials. (After appeals to the Supreme Court the average sentence went down to a year and a half.) This sentence was also relatively light given that Trenk was convicted on nine counts, the most of anyone tried as a kapo. The Prison Authority further reduced Trenk's sentence by a third for good behavior, and she was released a day after her sentencing.[59]

As the case of Trenk unfolded in the Tel Aviv District Court, another Auschwitz kapo sat in the detention center in Jaffa for four and a half months awaiting her trial. Despite the weighty accusations of crimes against humanity leveled at Raya Hanes, which required that she be held in detention until the end of the proceedings, in February 1951 the attorney general's office permitted her release because she was pregnant. Within weeks she gave birth to a baby girl.[60]

The indictment submitted eleven months later, in January 1952, to the Tel Aviv District Court did not include the count of crimes against humanity that had been approved by the magistrates court in the preliminary examination. After the birth of her daughter, the attorney general's office decided to remove this count, which could have resulted in her execution.[61]

The testimonies against Hanes seemed to echo those against Trenk. One witness, Miriam Tesler, stated that Hanes treated them like dogs "and with her stick she struck without caring whom. She put the entire camp, thousands, on its knees for days in a row. She just felt like it."[62] The witness added that "she was *Lagerkapo*, she beat me and others. She beat me when I was pregnant. She beat me with her hands." Miriam Meirovitch corroborated parts of Tesler's testimony that "there she killed people and beat them. She had a stick, she killed with it, even with [bare] hands. . . . Frequently, she took us out of the barracks, even at night, and we had to stand on our knees. We stood that way for hours."[63]

Testifying in Hanes's defense was Sarah Gross, but at first she too seemed to portray the defendant in the same way as many of the prosecution witnesses had: "The inmates said that she has a bad character. She always seemed angry and cruel."[64] But then Gross, who had served as Hanes's personal aide in Auschwitz-Birkenau, offered a surprising perspective on the defendant's behavior, one not frequently heard in the kapo trials. In Auschwitz-Birkenau it was essential for Hanes to have a reputation for being callous and harsh, Gross told the judge. She recounted that in the camp a friend of Gross's had fallen gravely ill, and that night Hanes sneaked into the hospital barracks and fetched medication. But "she prohibited me from telling this," Gross added, "because she did not want it to become known that she was helping, because it was dangerous for her if the Germans heard that she has a [good] character. But if [the prisoners] said she was cruel, it would be okay." In another instance, without their knowledge, Hanes obtained clothing for three of her subordinates, who cursed her constantly. When Gross wanted to tell the other subordinates who had provided the clothing, Hanes reproached her, saying that she was "stupid and it is better that they curse me."[65]

Issachar Blau, the only man to serve as a witness in this trial, testified that he had viewed Hanes's interaction with her inmates from the other side of the fence. "There was no significance to the inmates' cursing of the kapo," he said. "The more they cursed, the better it was for them, because the kapo needed to give the Germans the impression that she was loyal to them. Only then could she help inmates."[66] Blau, like Gross, indicated that inmates had only a limited and skewed understanding of their supervisor's true motivations and intentions. In the upside-down moral world of Auschwitz, the fact that the subordinates hated their supervisors and at times even suffered at their hands did not mean that these kapos had acted in inappropriate ways. In fact, it was essential that the inmates dislike their supervisors if the supervisors were to continue to act in a manner that assisted prisoners.

Further testimony revealed that Hanes had helped some prisoners, though not at any cost. Gross testified that she had begged Hanes to hide her elderly mother in the Lagerkapo's private room. Hanes refused at first. Only after Gross promised that if the Germans uncovered her mother she would swear that Hanes had nothing to do with it, did Hanes consent. The Germans entered the barracks and Hanes opened the door to her room and invited them in, but the Germans passed by. Gross's mother was saved and was now residing in Jerusalem.[67]

Hanes subverted German operations even before the Germans appointed her Lagerkapo. In October 1943, a transport of Dutch Jews arrived at the camp "hospital." Hanes, who worked there as a nurse, oversaw the newcomers. It was clear that within days all 800 Jews would end up in the crematorium. Hanes turned to her supervisor,

Dr. Anna Weiss, and with her consent smuggled six teenage girls out to a different camp. A Jewish secretary who learned about this operation informed on Hanes to the Germans. For unknown reasons the Nazis chose not to send Hanes to the gas chamber, instead giving her "only" six months' labor in a punishment camp (Straflager).

After Hanes completed her term in the punishment camp, the doctor in charge asked that she return to the hospital, but the German supervisor rejected his request. He wanted her with him as Lagerkapo. At first she refused, saying that after the time she had spent in the punishment camp she was too weak for the job. The supervisor would not take no for an answer. The next morning he placed her between two electrified fences. The space between the fences was so narrow that she could hardly move. Twelve hours later she still had not conceded. The following day she again was forced to crouch between the two fences. At the end of that day Hanes finally gave in. For the next few months, from June to September of 1944, she served as Lagerkapo in Birkenau camp B3. The group Hanes supervised, stated Elisheva Singer, a witness who also would testify in the Eichmann trial, was a very difficult one "because we were starving. We smelled the crematorium." Still, the witness continued, Hanes "behaved in B3 in a very humane manner."[68]

On January 18, 1952, the defense and prosecution completed their summations. Within hours, Judge Zeev Zeltner, a future recipient of the highest academic prize in the land, the Israel Prize, returned to the courtroom to pronounce his verdict. The prosecution witnesses surely believed the stories they had recounted, he noted, but they were confused. They may have described events that actually occurred, but they had not occurred under the supervision of Hanes.[69] The judge pointed out that under oath, one of the five prosecution witnesses stated that "to this very day, I'm not completely normal. . . . I suffer from headaches, and frequently my head can't comprehend many things. I'm forgetful."[70]

As in other trials, the judge wrote that some of the witnesses expressed deep animosity toward the defendant. One, for example, assailed the defense attorney for his willingness to represent the alleged collaborator, an action that resulted in the court jailing her for three hours. After so many years of torment, the judge wrote, this animosity was understandable, "but hatred blinds one . . . and one must treat this testimony very cautiously." From their vantage point the prosecution witnesses viewed Hanes as wicked and cruel and thus as fulfilling the demonic Nazi program. But, Zeltner concluded, many of the witnesses suffered from "a general psychosis"—in the spirit of 1950s psychology, he attributed a mental pathology to the witnesses.[71]

Next the judge assessed Hanes's personality, pointing out that she had saved six teenage girls as well as Gross's elderly mother. It was theoretically possible that even as she risked her life to save those individuals she also harassed others, but it would be hard to reconcile these two opposites in a single human being. "Why would the same person who risks herself for the benefit of the other, [put] herself at not a negligible risk, the risk of death, and not in the everyday world but in the circumstances of a concentration camp—why should this person behave at exactly the same time like a sadistic murderer?"[72]

Repeatedly in kapo trials, defense witnesses testified that a defendant had saved them. But Hanes's rescues were notably different from those of many others. Whereas in most other cases defendants helped prisoners only when the risk to themselves was minimal, Hanes had taken considerable risk to save others. Unlike other functionaries who frequently used their power to benefit their cronies and friends and protect themselves, Hanes acted out of altruistic motivations.

The defendant had a "strong personality," the judge wrote. Hanes served as a Lagerkapo, a position in which she could not "treat inmates gently, and if she had not taken control with an iron fist, she would have done them a disservice, because then the Nazis would have achieved with shots that which the defendant had achieved with shouts, with a sour face, and with shoves." The judge fully endorsed Hanes's behavior, including her physical actions, which to some of those who had lived in the camps and testified in court seemed to have crossed a line. These witnesses, the judge seemed to be saying, had only a limited grasp of the position in which Hanes had found herself.[73]

Furthermore, Zeltner went beyond merely justifying the defendant's behavior:

If I leave the slightest of blots on the defendant while she is in Israel, a formal acquittal by an Israeli judge will not help her. If I do only that, in a certain sense I will continue and perpetuate the Nazis' work, which strove to divide the inmates from their supervising inmates. I am convinced not only that the general prosecution has not proven that the defendant committed the crimes attributed to her but that the defendant in no way committed these crimes. I feel an obligation toward the defendant who lost her sister and husband in the concentration camp and feel an obligation to her children to determine this explicitly.

He concluded: "I therefore acquit the defendant."[74]

Public Reaction to the Trials

The opening of the kapo trials garnered significant public attention. At the Tel Aviv District Court, crowds amassed in the courtroom for the proceedings involving Elsa Trenk. Judge Max Kenneth, the head of the panel, ordered additional benches brought into the courtroom. Earlier one newspaper had reported that the preliminary examination had to be moved to a larger courtroom, as Trenk's case, the "first of its kind to be arbitrated in Tel Aviv, aroused great public interest, and from the morning a crowd gathered at the courthouse doors." Those who came to listen to the proceedings were mostly survivors, specifically members from the defendant's former community or inmates from the same camp on which the trial focused.[75]

Yet for a time the interest seemed to expand beyond those who were directly affected by the events during the Holocaust. Holocaust survivor Mark Dvorzhetski pointed out that after long public disregard of the annihilation in Europe, the trial of a woman accused of being a harsh kapo caused a spike in public attention to the Holocaust not only among survivors. He seemed unhappy with the public interest that resulted from the prosecution of Jews for their actions. Up until this trial, in Israel "there is no special interest in the period of the Holocaust, not in the agony nor even in the acts of heroism," he wrote. For lack of an audience, publishers rejected survivors' memoirs. But with these trials, Dvorzhetski continued, a curiosity had developed among non-survivors, probably as a result of "a harsh feeling, deeply hidden in the public soul, a feeling of unsatisfied vengeance." Not only Holocaust survivors but also Israelis who had not lived through the events in Europe sought a way to slake their thirst for revenge, and the trials satisfied some of that urge.[76]

With interest in the trials growing, some spectators protested what they viewed as the authorities' lack of action. One reader wrote a letter to the newspaper editor asserting, "From time to time we learn that one or two Nazis have infiltrated the State of Israel, instigating a court case against them." Unaware that there were more than a dozen trials pending, he declared that the few cases that had concluded were not enough. In Israel, he wrote, there resided at least 150 people who had "truly collaborated with the Hitlerites," again portraying the accused as if they had identified with the Nazis. "These kind of Jews, regrettably, are in the country," he continued, and nothing was being done to bring them to justice.[77]

This sudden attention to the deeds of former inmates intimidated some survivors. A Tel Aviv schoolteacher who had survived the Holocaust told friends that she feared that the parents of her students might view her, too, as a collaborator. How could she defend her honor? she asked. "A real psychosis has assailed the public as a result of that trial against a woman from Auschwitz," the teacher said, speaking of the Trenk trial.[78] When Ruth Bondy arrived in Israel, acquaintances asked the Prague-born writer, "'How did you remain alive? What did you have to do in order to survive?' And in their eyes there was a spark of suspicion: Kapo? Prostitute?"[79]

The prosecution's indictment of Jewish functionaries as Nazi collaborators carried with it implications not only for the defendants in the courthouse but also for their family members. Because of the charges of crimes against humanity and war crimes leveled at them, many of these former functionaries remained in detention for months on end, resulting in grave financial burdens on them and their families. From his jail cell, Abraham Fried wrote, "I am the father of a family, a wife and two children, aged four and two, and am their sole breadwinner. My arrest leaves them to starve." Addressing his letter to the justice minister, the attorney general, the state prosecutor's office, and the president of the Tel Aviv District Court, he requested an expedited trial. No one responded. Only after Fried turned to the Tel Aviv District Court secretary, Haim Matalon, did his trial begin. At the end of the proceedings, the court acquitted him and he was released after nine months' detention.[80]

Joseph Paal asked the president of the Jerusalem District Court, Benjamin Halevi, to help finance his defense at the preliminary investigation. "I am accused of having committed a crime against humanity, and on this basis I have been arrested," his letter began. "I am a new immigrant and I have no one to take an interest in me, except my wife. And she lacks money to live on, not to mention retaining an attorney who will represent me in the abovementioned trial on trumped-up charges. I therefore turn to your honor, the president of the court, with the request that you appoint an attorney who will represent me and disclose my innocence." Halevy rejected the request, explaining that the law did not allow such assistance at the preliminary examination. Paal, a cook with no legal education who could potentially face the death penalty, had to represent himself at that proceeding.[81]

* * *

The legal proceedings at the district court level exposed the views of prosecutors, witnesses, and many in the Israeli public, who saw functionaries not as victims but rather as associates who identified in their actions with the Nazi oppressors. Placing them on trial allowed many people to take revenge on the persecutors of the Jewish people. While some court rulings thwarted this quest, in other ways the legal actions did partly satisfy it by convicting some functionaries and sending them to jail.

CHAPTER SIX

DID JEWISH KAPOS COMMIT
CRIMES AGAINST HUMANITY?

In December 1951, the trial of Pinchas Pashititzky commenced at the Tel Aviv District Court. This trial pitted a successful physician against an unskilled laborer, a seamstress, a housewife, and a plumber, all of whom Pashititzky referred to during the trial as "riffraff." In his summation, Pashititzky's defense attorney, J. Hagler, would echo his client, evoking the "negative selection" theory in regard to the prosecution witnesses: he said that one must understand that "of the 3.5 million [Jews] who lived in Poland, 120,000 remained; not always the best material survived."[1]

The charges against Pashititzky no longer included serving as a physician responsible for selection under the Nazis at the Wolanow labor camp, which had been one of the central focuses of the preliminary examination. The district court indictment included eight counts: six counts for murder, one for surrendering Jews, and one for war crimes for the combination of all previous counts.[2] While the legal proceedings focused on these counts, in between the accusations and counteraccusations heard in the courtroom could be perceived a social gap between the high-status physician and the powerless inmates. The prosecution witness Rivka Nugelman described this relation when she stated that "in camp one hated the defendant. He lived separately in the white room. He had better clothing. People were jealous of him since he was a physician and we were simple people."[3]

Even Pashititzky himself acknowledged the social distance between himself and the other inmates. "There was jealousy against me because I lived with my family in a special place. The house was called the White House. . . . The public thought I was living in a magnificent palace. . . . I dressed in good clothes and I did not use food from the kitchen but bought food with my money from the Poles. . . . Hatred developed toward me."[4] Another physician tried as a kapo, Joshua Sternberg, said something similar about the prosecution witnesses: "Possibly they are all angry at me [because] I had maybe a little bit more soup."[5] The social differences among inmates and functionaries during the war created resentment and anger that played a role in the postwar trials.

To pay for his better life, witnesses contended, Pashititzky extorted exorbitant amounts of money from camp inmates. Pinchas Berkowitz described how when his wife fell ill he called in Dr. Pashititzky. "I paid [Pashititzky] at least 500 zloty per visit," he testified, but in comparison, "after the outbreak of the war, a Christian doctor received 100 zloty or more: [maybe] 150 zloty."[6] Two of the sons of dental technician Joseph Lindenbaum developed fevers. "I paid 10–20 zloty to the defendant and this was for the treatment of both of my sons," Lindenbaum testified. "I did not have any money then and I gave him my [dental] machines to sell and receive money for them." Then his wife fell ill. Because Lindenbaum had no money left, Pashititzky ignored his requests to come and treat her. He only transferred her into a broken shack isolated from other camp residents. Not only would he refuse to treat those who could not pay, but they ran the risk that he would put them on the sick list, which would put them at risk of being deported to a death camp.[7]

Pashititzky disputed accounts that he had charged patients for treatment. "I never took money from people if not for medication. Lindenbaum paid me either for medications or for the execution of a special medical treatment, such as using my syringe, the boiling of the syringe, breaking of the thermometer, or the use of special equipment. For my work I did not receive any payment."[8] The prosecutor, A. Dinari, questioned this argument: "Who would believe a defendant who said he took money only for a broken syringe or something similar?"[9]

None of the charges in the indictment dealt with Pashititzky's charging money for medical treatment, but during the course of the proceedings the question arose whether, in the conditions of a labor camp, it had been morally permissible for Dr. Pashititzky to receive money. The prosecution, led by Dinari, held that "the defendant is cloaking himself in pretensions of professional ethics although in at least one of these cases he demanded money for medical treatment. Demanding money and accepting money in those conditions of starving people is a huge moral crime."[10]

Defense attorney Hagler responded to Dinari, "It's not morality that is on trial here but rather the defendant and the charges that appear in the indictment." Still, Hagler went on to admit that "this is the only thing he did that might not have been correct." And he reminded the judges that "Pashititzky, too, had to make a living, and if he received money, it was for his livelihood."[11]

In their eighteen-page verdict, Judges Kenneth, Gavison, and Cohn went beyond their role as factfinders to assess the defendant's personality and moral behavior:

> This is the place to point out two failed attempts, one by the defense and the other by the prosecution. The prosecution labored to convince us that the defendant oppressed the camp inhabitants on his own initiative, as a kind of conscious, cruel, and bloodthirsty collaborator, while the defense labored to convince us that the defendant had the moral personality of an exalted physician who fulfills his dangerous job for the benefit of the public. And we are convinced that neither is the defendant's character. We believe the defendant is a selfish, average person who hoped to better his situation and save his skin, and that, without hesitation, he demanded payment from each and every patient he thought could pay. And naturally he paid more attention to those patients that paid than those that didn't.

The judges dismissed the view of Pashititzky as a Jewish incarnation of a Nazi physician. He was not, they wrote, a "bloodthirsty collaborator." But they found Pashititzky's moral conduct questionable and placed a blot on his name for charging money to treat the ill. Here, as had happened with the earlier trials, the court had again dismissed the view of functionaries as Nazi-like, but it was willing to call into question the moral behavior of victims. However, a court whose authority was based on the criminal code, unlike an honor court, could not sentence him for his moral transgressions, and at the end of the proceedings, after Pashititzky had been detained for more than a year, the police released him.

In exiting the courthouse, Pashititzky praised the judicial system in Israel and told a reporter that he planned to return to his work in the internal medicine department of Hadassah Hospital in Tel Aviv, as he indeed did. Interestingly, the courts acquitted all three medical people in the kapo trials, the physicians Pashititzky and Sternberg and the nurse Raya Hanes, the most educated people who faced legal proceedings.[12]

The Trial of Two Cruel Kapos

"I don't want to talk here in favor of the Germans, but I must tell the truth," said the witness Meir Ziskovich in the trial of Jacob Honigman, a kapo from the Grodziszcze and Faulbrück camps. When German craftsmen at the two neighboring camps tried to hand food to inmates, Jewish kapos dissuaded them from doing so.[13] "The Aryan Germans attempted and succeeded in supplying us with a little bit of food," concurred Hertzkopf Gleitman. "I cannot recall a case of a Jew being murdered by a German," he continued. "On the contrary, a German saved me from the accused. There were among the Nazis those who saved Jews, and I was one of them." After a kapo beat him, a German craftsman shielded him from the Jewish kapos and helped him recuperate.[14]

Repeatedly in these trials witnesses described Jewish functionaries as having behaved as badly as or worse than the Nazi Germans. In one trial a witness went so far as to say that "one feared the defendant like Hitler."[15] Some witnesses portrayed kapos as Nazis with the aim of urging the courts to judge them harshly; others really had suffered more beatings and harassment from Jewish kapos than from Germans. In the camps, many witnesses had only seen their direct Jewish supervisors and could not see beyond them to the Nazis who stood above. For them the Germans did not beat; the Jewish functionaries did. For them the Jewish functionaries were worse than the Germans.

The defendant in the 1951 trial was twenty-eight-year-old Jacob Honigman, who had been a *Vorarbeiter* responsible for waking up the inmates in the Grodziszcze and Faulbrück subcamps of the Gross-Rosen concentration camp, located in southwestern Poland, not far from the town of Swidnica. The two camps belonged to the Schmelt organization, which enjoyed financial benefits from using Jewish forced labor in nearby German factories.

Running almost simultaneously with Honigman's trial was the trial of his colleague Yehezkel Jungster, a locksmith who had also served as a kapo in these two largely self-administered camps. Wehrmacht soldiers patrolled outside the fence, while a few dozen Jewish kapos managed life from within, a practice that grew more common as the war progressed and the Germans suffered from manpower shortages. "The [German] camp commander [of the Grodziszcze camp] entered sometimes, not every day, when food was distributed," reported Abba Moshenberg. "There were days in which I did not see a German in the camp."[16]

Honigman and Jungster were among the handful of kapos, out of a total of fifty to sixty kapos in camp, whom the inmates dubbed "the malicious kapos" for the brutal way they treated others. Honigman, a butcher by profession, "beat [inmates] so frequently that I do not have enough hair on my head to count the number of times he beat people," Ziskovich testified. Furthermore, he testified, Honigman was not forced to beat others; rather, "he chose to beat."[17] "Already on my first day at work the defendant punched me and broke two of my teeth," Yehuda Holtzman testified about Jungster.[18] "If a person did not jump from his bed with the required speed, he struck him with his stick. If he found a bed not made exactly as it should be, he would hit him with his stick. . . . If he found a pair of shoes not lined up precisely—he would strike," added the witness David Levkovitch, ascribing to Jungster characteristics of punctuality and orderliness that usually were stereotypically attributed to Germans.[19]

Witnesses addressed not only the physical suffering inflicted by the defendants but also the consequences of the abuse for the prisoners' morale. "In Faulbrück," one witness asserted, Jungster "beat innocent people and would strike anywhere and everywhere; and people whose existence rested solely on the hope that the day of liberation would come, because they were beaten at a time when they were already extremely weak physically, lost their morale and died."[20] Another witness estimated that through their effect on prisoners' spirits, kapos such as Honigman and Jungster had brought about the death of "one hundred, hundreds or thousands" of inmates.[21]

Faulbrück's estimated 2,000 inmates marched out of the camp every day and then traveled by train to their workplaces. There, watched by

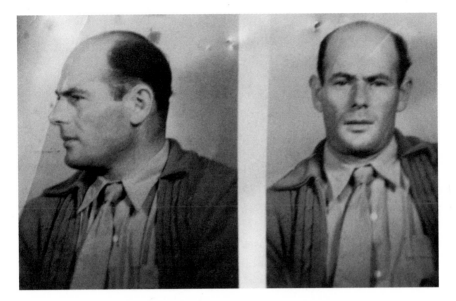

Yehezkel Jungster, a defendant in the trials.

German inspectors, the group of malicious kapos did not dare harm inmates. At times, Moshenberg testified, Jungster—who had no authority in the workplace—would come to inmates and "comment that they were not working fast enough, but would avoid hitting because he could not behave that way in the workplace in the presence of German craftsmen."[22]

Kapos' Brutal Murder of Inmates

Defense attorneys responded with several different strategies to this very stark portrayal of the kapos as just as bad as or worse than Germans. One tactic was to present an alternative interpretation of events—for example, that a beating resulted not from the kapo's cruelty but from his or her goal of avoiding harsher treatment by Germans. Another was for the defense to choose complete denial. Part of this strategy meant attacking the prosecution witnesses. "You're lying," Honigman's defense attorney, I. Hake, accused the witness Abraham Lehrer. "You never worked under Honigman's supervision!" Grilled for hours on end, the witness could at last tolerate the humiliation no longer and snapped, just as the defense had hoped. He moved from behind the witness stand and slammed his fist on the prosecution table. Two policemen jumped to their feet and blocked him from moving any closer to the defendant. The witness cried out at the defendant, "Deny that I worked for you!" District court president Judge Bar-Zakai interjected, warning the witness to control his anger. "After all I suffered in all kinds of camps, I have become nervous," Lehrer explained. "But I am telling the truth."[23]

Challenging witnesses to the point where they lost their equanimity was part of Hake's strategy. In the preliminary examination, Hake castigated a witness, asking him, "In what world were you living there in the camp, just in your world of soup? You were willing to murder to get soup?" The prosecutor protested; such a statement was offensive to all those who had been in the camps, he said. The judge rebuked the defense attorney. Unlike the Eichmann trial ten years later, in which witnesses served as storytellers whose accounts were hardly challenged, in the kapo trials the defense at times challenged witnesses, characterizing them as mistaken or as liars.[24]

Similarly, Hake asked Ziskovich whether he had seen with his own eyes the events he described. The witness erupted in anger: "Leave me alone. I'm sorry that you did not witness the defendant's acts in the concentration camps. Jews were murdered for money and you are defending the accused for money." In this witness's eyes, Hake was acting like one of the anti-Semites in Europe, attacking Jews for money.[25]

One especially horrific event dominated the trials of both Honigman and Jungster. Witnesses, some of whom testified in both proceedings, accused the two of taking part in the murder of eight Jews (by some accounts ten or twelve) at the Grodziszcze camp.[26] One evening in 1943 the prisoners returned to camp to find a small group of men leaning against each other by the camp's gate. Some recognized acquaintances among them. For an unknown reason the Germans had transferred the group from the nearby Gadenfrei camp to Grodziszcze. A few witnesses recalled the men as being gravely ill; others remembered them as healthy.[27]

The Grodziszcze prisoners continued their march to the camp dining hall as the small group remained by the gate. Ordinarily in the evening there was time between dinner and sleep, but on this night a loud whistle ordered them to their beds immediately after dinner. All rushed up the stairs of the three-story wheat mill that now served as their barracks. The kapos verified that all the inmates were inside the building. Then half a dozen kapos exited the building.[28]

From a corridor window, Moshenberg observed a handful of the Grodziszcze kapos gathering below in the camp yard. Then he saw one kapo holding onto the leg of one of the Jews they had seen earlier by the camp's gate and dragging him fifty meters across the yard to the washroom entrance. Next he saw Honigman grasping another yelping and screaming newcomer, pulling him to the washroom as well.[29]

From a window hatch by his bed, Holtzman too observed the events in the yard below. Honigman and five or six other kapos beat the new inmates and forced them into the washroom.[30] Loud screams came from the direction of the washroom. A voice called out in Yiddish, "Let me go, I have a wife and child!"[31] Moshenberg "heard the cries of a man being beaten."[32] None of the witnesses, however, observed the events inside the washroom. A few said they had observed German soldiers in the courtyard; most denied such a presence. Some heard shots; others did not.[33]

An hour after the men were dragged to the washroom, an eerie silence fell over the camp and the kapos returned to their barracks. One entered the room where Jacob Schweitzer lay, climbed into bed, and wept. Schweitzer turned to the kapo, whose name was Wasserberg, and asked what had happened. "Get lost," was the response. Schweitzer got out of bed and came across a second kapo, named Sibel. "Leave me alone," Sibel told him.[34] Another prisoner, Jacob Neufeld, witnessed two teenage servants bring their kapo masters meat, bread, and butter, a token of gratitude from the German commanders of the camp.[35]

Around midnight, a few inmates went out of the barracks to the washroom, where they found a pile covered in blankets. Moshenberg peeked under the blankets and saw naked, disfigured corpses bearing signs of beating. They had been beaten with metal rods, he reckoned. He could not detect bullet wounds.[36]

Late at night someone woke Holtzman, a member of the camp's Hevrah Kadisha (burial society), and ordered him to bury the murdered men.[37] Holtzman observed that the dead had been "beaten and were bleeding . . . so much so that I could not look at them." He added, "The heads were full of holes and not from gunshots," which suggested that the killers were the Jewish kapos and not Germans, who would simply have shot them. Together with other members of the burial society he loaded the bodies onto a carriage and rolled them one kilometer away from the camp, where they dug graves and buried the men. At the end of this night it was clear to many of the prisoners in camp that a group of Jewish kapos had murdered a group of inmates.[38]

Jungster and Honigman denied all the accusations leveled at them. "It's not true that I was cruel to inmates. On the contrary. Whenever I could, I always helped," Honigman declared.[39] Jungster asserted, "I did not torture people, I myself was persecuted [by the Germans]."[40] He felt that the prisoners who worked for him did a good job, "and they were happy with me."[41] Both Jungster and Honigman, not wishing to be associated with the title "kapo," used after the war for collaborators, stated they had held a different title.[42] Honigman emphasized that he had never served as kapo, only as *Vorarbeiter* (foreman). To one witness who had referred to him in the past as a kapo, Honigman responded, "If you use the word 'kapo' once more, I will kill you."[43] And both of the accused said the Germans had forced them to assume that role. When Jungster wanted to quit, the German commander informed him, "We decide that, not you."[44]

Jungster remembered the arrival of the group of men from Gadenfrei at Grodziszcze but declared that he had had nothing to do with their killing. After dinner and a shower he had just gone to sleep, he said. When he woke up in the morning he heard about the horrific killing. "It never happened that a Jew was beaten and killed by another Jew," Honigman stated, completely denying any part in the murder.[45] Jungster refuted the claim that he had repeatedly beaten inmates, saying, "Everything that the witnesses described . . . is a lie." Jungster, who had lost his wife in Auschwitz and did not know the fate of his child, said that the witnesses sought someone to blame for their suffering and "I am the victim."[46] Honigman concluded his testimony by stating, "When I beat someone it was essential for work. . . . I'm innocent. My conscience is clean."[47]

The Testimony of a "Good Kapo"

In early December 1951 the prosecution rested its case, and Jungster's defense attorney presented his key witness, Tsvi Schlimmer, who had served as a kapo in Grodziszcze and was one of a group that witnesses identified as the "good kapos." Here was an opportunity for the court to go beyond the limited viewpoint of the victims and hear the perspective of a former functionary on his experience of being positioned between the German masters and the Jewish inmates.

Schlimmer admitted that he had chosen to work for the Germans "because I knew that a *Vorarbeiter* does not need to work, and that was splendid for me." He added, "If I had wished not to take the job, I could have [refused, but] I do not know of any case in which a person turned down the offer to become a kapo. . . . A kapo's life was more comfortable. He did not need to work, received an additional portion of food, and had greater freedom to move about." In these words Schlimmer reflected the reality that many Jews sought positions as policemen or kapos in order to secure their own well-being and sometimes also that of their families.[48] Schlimmer countered Jungster's earlier argument, one also repeated in Honigman's trial, that the Germans had left him no choice but to accept the position of kapo.[49]

Schlimmer, who had never been indicted by any legal authorities, acknowledged that he too had beaten inmates. He slapped people on the face and even hit them with a stick. But unlike Jungster and Honigman, who mostly beat inmates in the Jewish-administered Grodziszcze barracks, Schlimmer punished them only at the German-overseen workplace, and he did so only when he feared that a German guard would inflict a harsher punishment. "And I was elated if a day passed and I was not obliged to beat someone. If I was obliged to do so, I would take the person into the hut, hit the table, and order him to scream."[50]

Schlimmer's subordinates appreciated his treatment, and back at Grodziszcze they obeyed his orders for the most part. When he commanded inmates to sleep, "they would urge each other to climb into bed so everything would be okay." In the instances when this did not happen, Schlimmer continued, "I would roar so loudly the entire camp shook, and that would be enough."[51] Indeed, Ziskovich had testified earlier that the "good kapo" Schlimmer "was a devil in his roars but [he] did not hit."[52] This kapo even assisted people in carrying out prohibited food transactions with non-Jews. Schlimmer's example of being a "good kapo" highlighted that the "malicious kapos," like Jungster and Honigman, could have chosen to behave differently but did not.[53]

Schlimmer saw Jungster and other kapos constantly beat inmates in the barracks. "When I [say] that in Grodziszcze people were beaten all the time, I see the defendant among those beating," he stated. In his view, "the defendant belonged to the bad kapos, but there were worse than him."[54] This testimony by a "good kapo" hardly served to support Jungster's defense. Jungster had a difficult time finding witnesses to testify in his favor. Against the fifteen witnesses of the prosecution, the defense called, in addition to Jungster himself and Schlimmer, three other witnesses, one of whom had not been a prisoner in Grodziszcze and Faulbrück, one who had been incarcerated in the camp after Jungster was sent to a different camp, and one who was an inmate under the defendant but for only four or five weeks and did not see him beat anyone. Much as with Trenk, it seems as if the defense chose to present these witnesses merely to have someone to speak for Jungster, almost regardless of the content of their testimony.

In his closing argument, Honigman's attorney painted a scene in which "Jews [are] attempting to put forward a version of events as if Jews themselves are responsible for their suffering in the camps . . . as if the kapo alone is guilty for everything." Hake's argument was that the kapo trials portrayed Jews, not Germans, as bearing responsibility for aspects of the Holocaust. Only a handful of Nazis had paid a price for their conduct, he asserted, and even they were being released from prisons in Europe. But in the Jewish state former kapos were being tried and going to jail as if they were worse than the Germans.[55]

In Hake's argument, the view that kapos bore responsibility for the beating of inmates was based on a mistaken assumption about the relationship between a German commander and his subordinate kapo. "One tends to place the entire blame on the subordinate, especially in those abnormal conditions." In a situation in which one person is responsible for thousands of people, "all the anger is directed against the supervisor . . . , and all that remains in [the victims'] memory is the memory of the kapo." Hake also argued that the memory of a victim represents only a limited vantage point.

"I ask [the court] to reject out of hand the argument . . . that each and every kapo—by virtue of being a kapo—was surely a murderer," he went on. He urged the court to reject the view that the law intended to punish "any Jew who gave a slap on the face as though, in that act, he became a 'helper' to the Nazi." Through his criticism of those interpreting the law Hake presented a veiled criticism of the law itself, suggesting that it allowed even the slightest of transgressions to be characterized as an act that linked the Jewish functionary to the Nazi. His point seemed to be that a perspective in which any use of force in camp was criminal failed to take into account the historical circumstances of the camp, and so was not socially beneficial.[56]

"I request that the accused be exonerated," the attorney pleaded. "What public benefit is there in punishing the defendant? Whom do we need to deter from these kinds of actions?" he said, trying to characterize the goal of the law as deterrence.[57] However, as the deliberations in the Knesset before passage of the bill demonstrated, that was not the dominant view. In a trial more than two years later a judge commented, "This law has almost no intention of deterrence, not in regard to the defendant or any another person. I see the rationale of the law . . . in payback." For his bad deeds the convicted functionary deserved a punishment proportional to his actions, this judge held.[58]

However, continuing his argument as if the law did in fact aim at deterrence, Hake said, "The tragedy is over. The Nazis are being released from prisons and all we shall remain with is the story of the Jews who misbehaved in the camps. Especially after so many years have passed! I ask that [the defendant] be fully rehabilitated for the sake of the rehabilitation of the entire Jewish people who were accused of this annihilation." Not only had the Allies not put the killing of the Jews on the agenda of the Nuremberg tribunal, but Hake was claiming that the kapo trials in Israel portrayed the Jews as responsible for their own killing.[59]

In January 1952, the panels of judges issued their verdicts in the cases of Jungster and Honigman. The murder of the Jewish men in the washroom of the Grodziszcze camp appeared only in the district court indictment of Honigman, but conflicting witness accounts, a lack of

valid proof of death, and a lack of direct testimony regarding the beatings in the washroom had instilled doubt in the minds of the judges,
and they dismissed the murder charges. For the same reasons they also
dismissed the nine other counts of murder in Honigman's indictment.[60]
In no kapo trial was there enough legal evidence to convict any defendant of killing a fellow prisoner, but from a historical perspective it is
clear that these functionaries did murder their fellow inmates. The
many witness accounts are convincing in themselves and corroborate
each other to such a degree that one can conclude with a high degree
of confidence that at least in Grodziszcze camp a group of kapos had
indeed murdered inmates under their supervision.

As with Pashititzky's trial, had the cases against Honigman and
Jungster taken place in an honor court, where judgment is based on
moral law, there would have been a greater chance of convicting these
murderers. Indeed, given the difficulty of proving in criminal court
that a murder took place in a concentration camp in Europe, an honor
court would have been a more appropriate venue to hear these cases.
But, as we have seen, Israeli authorities refused to adopt that model and
opted for criminal courts.

The judges who absolved Honigman of the most serious charges did
not spare him a harsh assessment. In Grodziszcze and Faulbrück,
Judges Natan Bar-Zakai, Yitzhak Kister, and Yitzhak Zundelovitch
wrote, inmates did not see Germans as malicious, but "many of the
inmates saw the Jewish policeman—be his title *Stubenalteste, Vorarbeiter, Uber,* or *Kapo*—as the enemy and source of evil." While the
judges acknowledged the defense argument that the perspective of prisoners was limited, as they most often saw their immediate Jewish
supervisors, not the German commanders, this limited purview did
not in the judges' eyes lift the Jewish functionaries' responsibility for
their cruel and malicious behavior. The court added its moral assessment that "there were among the Jewish policemen not a few who,
feeling a sense of power and authority in their hands, did not spare their
imprisoned brethren, or did not spare them sufficiently, and oppressed
their brethren, for a reason and also for no reason."[61]

Honigman's behavior, the three judges concluded, was "evil and
cruel; he tortured inmates and loutishly abused them, adding cheap

curses and swear words like an omnipotent tyrant. Moreover, [he] struck the frail inmates in camp with his whip—his baton of authority—in a horrific and exaggerated and unforgivable manner. He would also kick them in the belly, the genitalia, and would tread on them. . . . He would for no reason strike in all directions, for no reason whatsoever, just for sadistic pleasure." While the judges had not convicted him of murder, they portrayed his personality as that of a true sadist, possibly even capable of murder.[62]

Similarly, Judges Pinchas Avishar, Yisrael Levin, and Josef Lam found that when the exhausted and starving inmates returned to the camp after a day's hard labor, Jungster greeted them with a stick or a fist.[63] Yet both courts dismissed the charges of war crimes. In the case of Jungster, the judges explained that "one cannot convict a person for a war crime when both he and his victims are members of the same persecuted people." Although there possibly could be exceptions to this rule, for example, if the defendant had ideologically identified with the occupier, the judges concluded that "in this case, that is not the situation."[64]

Jungster and Honigman had also been accused of committing crimes against humanity. In Honigman's case, the judges dismissed those counts because they believed that to convict a person for crimes against humanity one needed to show that he identified with the oppressor in his actions and that he committed them against a population and not against individuals. Still, the judges in Honigman's case concluded that the defendant had "acted as a cruel, vicious and brutal Jew against his brethren who were in jeopardy and distress." The judges found him guilty of fourteen separate counts of "common assault" and "assault causing actual body harm" to individual inmates, sentencing him to eight and a half years' imprisonment, which was reduced upon appeal to six and a half years, the longest sentence handed down by the Supreme Court in the kapo trials.[65]

In the case of Jungster, however, the judges were divided over whether to convict him on the count of crimes against humanity. Judges Avishar and Levin distinguished between war crimes, for which the accused had to identify with the goals of the perpetrator, and crimes against humanity, which in their view did not require such an identification but did require two other elements: "the action has to be of a severe nature that might make a person miserable, humiliate him, and inflict on him grave physical or mental torments," and "the action must be committed against civilians in a wide-scale and systematic manner . . . [and] in a way that arouses a revolt of conscience and of human emotion."[66]

In his repeated acts of beating inmates, the two judges concluded, Jungster had committed a crime against humanity. Although the acts had been against individuals, they had been committed on a wide scale and thus qualified as a crime against humanity. "The defendant had allowed himself to be used as a tool in the hands of the barbaric Nazi regime [to carry out] its plan to annihilate the Jewish people, and because his actions took place under the Nazi regime in an enemy country, he committed a crime against humanity as defined in the first paragraph of the law." This judicial opinion confirmed the prosecution's interpretation of crimes against humanity. In this case, the attorney general's office persistence in charging defendants with crimes against humanity had achieved the desired result.[67]

Judge Josef Lam, who was a survivor of Dachau and before resigning his post was one of the Knesset members who had formulated the law at issue, dissented. On the basis of the Convention on the Prevention and Punishment of the Crime of Genocide (1950), which was adopted into law by the Knesset, he determined that "for the defendant to be convicted of a crime against humanity his actions must be: (a) aimed at annihilating a population, in its entirety or in part. . . . (b) inhuman actions." These conditions did not apply to Jungster, he determined. Most of his actions could not be considered "inhuman," and he surely had not *aimed* to annihilate the Jewish population.[68]

After two of the three judges convicted Jungster of crimes against humanity, the court faced the question of whether the law required the imposition of a death sentence. In his opening statement at the Banik trial, Attorney General Cohn stated his view that merely being convicted of a crime described in paragraph 1 of the Nazis and Nazi Collaborators Punishment Law did not mean that the death penalty had to be imposed; it was only a maximum sentence. Others, including one senior legal figure, took a different approach, criticizing the law. In a newspaper report that did not specify the name of this legal figure, he was quoted as saying, "The Knesset presented the judges . . . with a difficult choice. Those convicted [of a crime outlined in the first paragraph of the law] can only be sentenced to death, and those exonerated can only be sentenced for release. There is no middle ground." Had he been a Knesset member, the speaker professed, he would have allowed for a third option for judges who believed a person was guilty but were uncertain as to how anyone would have acted in such circumstances. This approach had been raised by a minority in the discussions of the Knesset Law and Justice Committee, suggesting the option of convicting a person but relieving him or her of legal responsibility.[69]

The panel of judges split again in determining the sentence. Judge Lam cited paragraph 11 of the law, on extenuating circumstances, which allowed a court to consider "as grounds for mitigating the punishment . . . that the offence was committed with an intent to avert, and was indeed calculated to avert, consequences more serious than those that resulted from the offence." Because Jungster was convicted of crimes against humanity on the basis of several individual cases of beating and harassment, there was a possibility that at least in some instances Jungster had administered the beatings in an attempt to avert harsher consequences, Lam wrote. Consequently, he felt, one could not sentence him to death. Lam proposed a sentence of ten years.[70]

The other two judges, Avishar and Levin, did not share Lam's view. "We approach the sentencing in this case with dread," they wrote. Signaling their unhappiness with the law and its meaning, they went on to explain that "it is quite clear that it is not the same [to order the death penalty] in the case of a Nazi criminal who identified as a Nazi or identified with the barbaric Nazi regime and in the case of this defendant, who himself was a persecuted person and lived in inhuman conditions like his victims." Unlike many of the witnesses who saw no distinction between the Jewish collaborators and Nazis, the judges in this as well as all other courts clearly distinguished between the two. But the law, Avishar and Levin believed, left them no options. "As we come to issue the sentence in this trial our heart trembles. . . . Since we convicted the defendant of crimes against humanity the law does not leave any choice but to sentence the defendant to death. This result is to our discontentment."[71]

Although Jungster's appeal to the Supreme Court would overturn his conviction of committing crimes against humanity, the initial outcome of this case caused other prosecutors to make a distinction between Jewish functionaries and Nazi perpetrators, determining that Jewish functionaries would no longer be indicted for war crimes or crimes against humanity.

CHAPTER SEVEN

THE FIRST DOUBTS
ABOUT THE KAPO TRIALS

A FEW WEEKS BEFORE the Jungster verdict in late November 1951, a well-dressed man, age seventy-four, sat in an SAS airliner en route from Karachi to Copenhagen with his wife, thirty years younger, beside him. As the plane descended for a fueling stopover at Lod International Airport outside Tel Aviv, the woman became visibly nervous, while the man struggled to maintain his composure.

The aircraft touched down and taxied to the airport terminal. Passengers disembarked and proceeded to the transit area. The two sat down in the terminal's coffee shop and ordered breakfast. A few workers, immigrants from Germany, spotted the man and congregated around him. The man finished his coffee, and the coffee shop owner approached and asked him if he would be kind enough to sign the airport's VIP book. The man agreed and inscribed his name—Hjalmar Schacht.[1]

Twenty years earlier, in the early 1930s, Schacht had ensured the support of the heads of Germany's industrial sector for the Nazi Party and its rising political star, Adolf Hitler. In return for his help, Hitler appointed Schacht to head the Reichsbank and later nominated him as the Reich's finance minister. At the end of the war, the Allied forces put him among the defendants at the International Military Tribunal at Nuremberg alongside people like Rudolf Hess, Hermann Göring, and Alfred Rosenberg. That court narrowly acquitted Schacht, but a Stuttgart denazification court sentenced him to eight years' imprisonment, only to have a higher court overturn the verdict.[2]

Under ordinary circumstances Schacht never would have set foot in Israel. But he had mistakenly booked a flight that stopped over there. Three journalists—from the dailies *Maariv* and *Davar* and from the United Press news agency—who were awaiting the arrival of the chairperson of the Dead Sea Works, Lord Glenconner, noticed the commotion in the airport coffee shop and spotted Schacht. Heading over to his table, they conducted an impromptu news conference. Did West Germany plan to pay reparations to the Jewish state, and was it capable of doing so? one journalist asked. Ever since it had been revealed earlier that year that representatives of Israel and West Germany had been holding secret negotiations on possible reparation payments, the issue had created a deep divide in Israeli society. The former head of the German economy responded diplomatically, "Germany will pay if it is able to do so." He added, "From what I see in the airport and according to what I read in the newspapers, you are progressing greatly and I believe that this country will continue to develop."[3]

The plane finished refueling, Schacht reboarded, and the plane took off and disappeared into the sky. But that afternoon *Maariv* broke a story with the headline "Dr. Schacht, Hitler's Adviser, Visited Israel." And in Jerusalem, Knesset member Aryeh Ben-Eliezer, of the opposition, interrupted the session to demand that the government explain how one of the architects of Hitler's rise in Germany had "arrived today in Lod without being arrested under the law existing in the State of Israel that requires prosecution of war criminals and murderers of a nation and a race."[4]

Two days later, the Knesset discussed the topic again. Another stunned opposition member, Yochanan Bader, asked how it could have happened that Schacht, Hitler's associate, "the man who supplied him with the means for his crimes, the person who collected in the Reichsbank gold from the teeth of tens of thousands to serve as tools of murder, a person whom a denazification court in German identified as a Nazi," had not been arrested and in fact had been permitted to leave the country. How was it, he continued, that not one of the many armed guards at the airport had assassinated Schacht? Bader answered his own question: the attitude associated with the reparation negotiations was responsible for such complacency. The negotiations with West Germany, he declared, had led people to believe there was no reason to go on hating the Germans for their murderous actions.[5] The greed of the country's leaders had blinded them to the crimes committed by Schacht, wrote journalist Josef Vinizky.[6]

Another writer wondered who had come up with the policy of arresting and trying the "small (and miserable) fry" from the camps "who were nothing but tools in the hands of the gestapo . . . who mostly wanted nothing but to save themselves from the fire." The true focus should be on the perpetrators, who "planned the fire [and are] enjoyably touring our country." Members of the Jewish public, he added, had lost their sense of national dignity. In Israel "there is no pride, no honor, no nationalism and no ethics." This writer distinguished between the "planners" and their "tools," between Nazi architects of the crime such as Schacht and their instruments such as the Jewish functionaries. But still, for the first year and a half of the implementation of the Nazis and Nazi Collaborators Punishment Law, most people made no distinction between the two groups.[7]

Overturning a Death Verdict

On January 7, 1952, thousands of demonstrators congregated in downtown Jerusalem to protest what they saw as the national humiliation of the reparation negotiations, a topic that the Knesset would deliberate that day. The leader of the opposition party Herut, Menachem Begin, delivered a stirring speech that many saw as a direct incitement to civil war. Standing on a balcony at a hotel in Zion Square, he proclaimed that if the Knesset approved the reparation negotiations with West Germany, he would order his men in the IZL paramilitary organization to open hostilities. He accused David Ben-Gurion and his associates of besmirching the nation's honor. "And now you have come, despotic profiteers, you have come to demolish all that was achieved with our blood. And again the nation will be turned into mud, [a victim of] the sword of pogrom and annihilation." Signing the agreement would be an international humiliation, he contended. "How will we be seen in the eyes of the nations when our humiliation is made public, when we approach the murderers of our fathers to receive blood money?"[8]

The demonstrators marched on the Knesset, hurling stones through the windows and injuring a few Knesset members. More than a hundred police officers and demonstrators were hurt in the clashes. The military joined the police in its efforts to control the crowds.[9]

It was not only the right-wing nationalists in the Knesset, such as Herut, who opposed the agreement; the far left parties, such as Mapam and the Communists, were against it as well. They likened accepting the agreement to betraying the nation and collaborating with its worst enemies—the Nazis and their heirs. Members of Mapam, who, as noted in Chapter 3, saw themselves as the preservers of the Jewish rebel legacy, viewed Israel's ties with West Germany and other countries as part of a new Western fascist-capitalist coalition standing in opposition to the Soviet Union. One of its representatives, Abraham Berman, a member of the Warsaw ghetto rebel movement, told the Knesset:

> No, not for this did the ghetto fighters raise the flag of the revolt, so that but a few years later, representatives of the Jewish people would sit with those who drowned the ghetto in blood, those who burnt it in fire! . . . I am pained to say that the deliberations I hear [now] in the Knesset are not new to me. I heard the [same] spirit and the [same] arguments in the Warsaw ghetto. There a harsh internal struggle ensued between the fighters of the underground and the defenders of "realpolitik," . . . those [who believed one must] make peace with the Nazis and negotiate with them. And there were many such people, not only in the Jewish Councils. . . . We all know to where these people's fatalistic views lead: only to disgrace and shame, to betrayal and national humiliation. . . . Do not bring upon our people and state this humiliation![10]

Berman saw Ben-Gurion's negotiations with West Germany as equivalent to the actions of the Jewish Councils and other "practical" people who had advocated working with the Nazis, not against them. Collaboration had not ceased with the end of World War II, he held; it continued in Ben-Gurion's negotiations with the West Germans.

Three days before the demonstration, the Tel Aviv District Court had issued its death sentence in the case of Yehezkel Jungster. In the controversy surrounding the reparation negotiations and the upcoming vote on the reparation agreement in the Knesset as well as the violent demonstration that followed the Knesset's approval of the negotiations, the newspapers and public largely ignored the death sentence meted out to the former kapo.

The harsh verdict in Jungster's trial, however, did not go unnoticed by the attorney general's office. Faced with the consequences of its choice to charge alleged collaborators with crimes against humanity and war crimes—that is, the specter of the Jewish state putting Jews to death—the office hastily altered open indictments against other defendants.

Miriam Goldberg, a former kapo in Bergen-Belsen, faced one count of war crimes and another of crimes against humanity. Months earlier, in October 1951, prior to the opening of her trial at the district court level, her attorney sent a five-page letter to the attorney general requesting the immediate release of his client, at least on bail, as she had been detained for ten months at that point and was the mother of a two-year-old. But the attorney general turned down the request, as the law stipulated that suspects who faced charges that potentially could result in capital punishment had to remain behind bars until the completion of their trial.[11]

Following Jungster's death sentence, however, the prosecution unilaterally removed both counts from Goldberg's indictment.[12] With only minor exceptions, after the Jungster verdict prosecutors avoided charging Jewish defendants with crimes against humanity or war crimes. This move marked a first major shift in the kapo trials, one that established a distinction between functionaries and Nazis. The harshest charges allowed under the Nazis and Nazi Collaborators Punishment Law would no longer be applicable to Jewish defendants, only to non-Jewish ones.[13]

This alteration in policy did not diminish the sense of mission that drove prosecutors in their quest to convict and sentence functionaries. Arguing years later for sentencing a defendant to jail time, one prosecutor explained that the court had to consider what kind of punishment the victims would have wished as payback from their oppressors. He added another justification for a severe sentence: that it would help "to enhance the public's trust in the justice done by the court" and "would help prevent victims from punishing the Nazis' helpers with their own hands."[14]

These arguments did not persuade Judge Yitzhak Raveh, who would go on to serve on the panel of judges at the Eichmann trial. He was concerned that problems with witnesses' memories, confusion, and a desire for revenge tainted their testimony, and so he imposed a sentence of just one month and then suspended it. The prosecutor was enraged at the judge's failure to put the defendant behind bars: "I'm shocked

[by] what happened to Raveh in this case! Of nine prosecution witnesses who all testified to the cruelty of the defendant, Raveh believes
only one. . . . I believe we must appeal. It is not enough for a judge to
say that he doubts the credibility of the prosecution witnesses. The
doubt must be reasonable and rational, which is not the case here."[15]

In this case, as in many of the kapo trials, the defense appealed district court verdicts. But in Jungster's, the death sentence triggered an
automatic appeal to the Supreme Court. Without publishing an
opinion—a rare occurrence—the justices vacated Jungster's conviction
on the count of crimes against humanity but left standing the conviction for assault, an offense that carried a two-year sentence.[16] Jungster
began serving his time at the Tel Mond correctional facility, but two
months into his term, his health deteriorated. The police minister,
Bechor-Shalom Shitrit, signed a release order. Two weeks later, on
July 10, 1952, Jungster died of natural causes.[17]

Following the Supreme Court's setting aside of the Jungster verdict,
the editor-in-chief of *Yediot Aharonot*, Herzl Rosenblum, wrote an editorial praising the high court's decision and drawing a line between
the punishment of Nazis and the punishment of Jews. "No German
swine," he contended, had been executed primarily for the mass murder
of Jews, and so it would be unfair "to hang the few Jewish helpers in
these circumstances—who did what they did under the most unbear-
able pressure." Furthermore, the prominent journalist argued, no one
who had not experienced the hell of the camps could ever comprehend
that reality. "To judge here those who were there—and precisely by our
common laws, that are normal here according to *our* everyday logic—
that is difficult!" Putting a few survivors on trial, he concluded, might
result in casting a moral shadow on all survivors. He added that it was
said with regard to most survivors that they survived "not necessarily
in ways that would make them eligible for the position of chief rabbi. . . .
Indeed, different moral laws reigned there. For everyone! Also for
us—had we been there!"[18]

The view that the Holocaust took place in a different moral uni-
verse applied not only in cases in which judges issued death sentences
but also in all kapo trials involving lesser offenses. Yet neither Rosenblum nor others questioned the overall legitimacy of trying Jewish
functionaries, and the trials continued.

A Convicted Collaborator's Changing Image

In March 1953, the fifth legal proceeding against Julius Siegel opened in Tel Aviv District Court. In 1946, two honor courts in Italy had examined accusations leveled at him by residents of Bedzin and Sosnowiec regarding his actions as a Judenrat member and as *Judenältester* and *Lagerältester* in several labor camps. After the first honor court procedure was terminated by a higher court for administrative reasons, the next honor court proceeding found that he had acted out of "loyalty to the Germans" and barred him from filling any public position in the Jewish community.[19] In 1948, after he immigrated to Israel, the World Zionist Congress honor court heard his case, but the lead judge died midway through the trial, and the proceedings were halted. The fourth proceeding took place in April 1952, a preliminary examination in Tel Aviv Magistrates Court that cleared the way for his fifth indictment, in Tel Aviv District Court. At the end of this process, Siegel was portrayed in the criminal courts very differently from the way he had been characterized in the honor court proceedings.[20]

The presiding district court judge, Max Kenneth, administered the oath, and Siegel swore to speak the truth, the whole truth, and nothing but the truth. He refuted the accusation that he was responsible for handing over Jews to the Germans for forced labor, saying, "I received orders [to do so] from the community [council, the Judenrat]."[21] He maintained that when he worked in the Judenrat he was not in charge of the lists of deportees; he was just one of ten people who compiled those lists. Long forgotten were Siegel's boastful statements in his previous trials that the Germans had admired his organizational abilities in managing "his Jews" and that thanks to his achievements he "was famous throughout Europe."[22]

In the Tel Aviv courtroom, Siegel recounted that he had failed to provide the Germans with 1,200 men. Accusing him of sabotage, the agitated German commander pulled out his pistol, aimed it at Siegel, and ordered him to literally run on ice. Then the German locked him up in a local jail.[23] But in 1946, in Italy, Siegel had testified that when he headed the employment office of the Judenrat he won the Germans' appreciation after he delivered to them 600 Jews they had demanded.[24]

Two counts in Siegel's indictment were for beating inmates. "I did not beat or torture Jews," he told Judge Kenneth. Only in one exceptional instance, he continued, had he lost his temper and struck a person. "In Auschwitz it happened that I struck [someone]. I found there a Jew who traded gold dental crowns in the black market. . . . My [deceased] wife and daughter also had gold teeth, and when I saw this I could not restrain myself and I struck him."[25] Yes, Siegel admitted on cross-examination, he carried a small stick in the camp, but "I carried it just for the heck of it, not to prove my authority."[26] No, he repeatedly stated, he had never struck anyone. No remnant remained of the remorseful Siegel who, while testifying in 1946, admitted that he had treated Jews harshly and beaten them. "In retrospect I always regretted this," he had said then.[27]

Before the honor court in Milan he had also described another assignment he had carried out for the Germans, the mission of selecting Jews. "When I worked at the [Bedzin Rossner] workshop, a few times during screening events [selections], I took out [and saved] several dozen Jews who were destined for Auschwitz, that is, for death." He never took bribes to save people during these selections, he emphasized. "It was not my way to take money for these kinds of things. I pulled out [from among those destined for death] the people who had relatives at the Rossner workshop, where uniforms for the Wehrmacht were sewed. In this way, about 1,000 of those ordered were handed over to the Germans for transfer."[28] Facing an accusation in the Tel Aviv District Court of surrendering Jews to the Germans, he again denied any wrongdoing. "I never informed on or handed over any Jew and I did not help the Germans search for Jews. I tried my best to save Jews."[29]

Unlike Siegel's accounts, which had changed drastically between Italy and Israel, those of the prosecution witnesses remained largely consistent. They accused him of having served as a close collaborator of the Germans, informing on the Jews who worked at the Rossner workshop.[30] "He collaborated with the Germans from [the time of] their entry [to Bedzin] until the end [of the war]," one witness reported. In Auschwitz, this witness continued, "I saw that Siegel beat Jews for minor things."[31] Another witness stated, "The defendant sent people to work [in labor camps] and whatever he said transpired."[32]

In his verdict, Judge Kenneth cleared Siegel of the charge of surrendering Jews to the Germans. He wrote that "in fact, the testimonies point only at suspicions, and none of the witnesses testified about
any concrete fact on the basis of which I can convict the defendant."
This was something that even the prosecution conceded in its
summation.[33]

In examining the accusation that Siegel had systematically beaten
inmates, Kenneth first analyzed the defendant's personality. "The accused seems to me," Kenneth wrote of the former Austrian army officer, "like a principled person when it comes to order and discipline.
He required order and cleanliness wherever he took a position. It does
not seem at all that he wanted to abuse people."[34] This assessment was
very different from the one made by the honor court in Italy, which
had found that Siegel was loyal to the Germans, acting on his own initiative in abusing Jews, and caring only about his own prestige and
power. Judge Kenneth viewed him in a positive light, as acting with
people's best interests in mind.[35]

Kenneth accepted, however, the testimony of one witness, Dov, who
related that when he was standing in line for food in one of the camps,
the defendant struck him twice. Kenneth concluded that Siegel struck
Dov in the belief that "it was justified and in the interest of his people"
but that Siegel's belief was wrong. While the judge seemed to have
taken a liking to Siegel, who had studied engineering in a polytechnic
institution, on this charge he did not exonerate him, the way other educated defendants had been exonerated (see Chapter 6), but rather convicted him of beating Dov. The judge also credited the defendant for
voluntarily coming to Israel and subjecting himself to trial, assuming
that it pointed to an inner conviction of innocence. He sentenced Siegel
to a month in prison or ten days' imprisonment and a 100-lira fine, one
of the lightest sentences in the kapo trials.[36]

Portraying Kapos on the Stage

In late 1950, journalist Z. Klinov expressed an uncommon feeling of
empathy with the alleged Jewish collaborators. Was it possible to compare a Jewish and a non-Jewish collaborator? he asked. "Did the collaborators among the Christians . . . see their families annihilated, see

millions of their brethren being led into the gas chambers, and therefore fail the moral test and lend a hand to the Nazis?" How could one judge these people? Could anyone who lived in a ghetto or camp withstand the difficulties and not become a policeman or kapo if given the opportunity? Then Klinov explained that he was not attempting "to give any justification for a Jew, an individual Jew, who had collaborated with the Nazis. . . . I'm not intending to argue against punishing the criminals, specifically the Jewish criminals, but all I want is to express the background on which the tragedy of the Jewish individual who failed took place."[37]

While Klinov was one of the few journalists who expressed a mitigated empathy toward kapos, a focused exploration of the justice of trying survivors would first arise in the realm of imagination. In 1954, during the week commemorating the eleventh anniversary of the Warsaw ghetto uprising, the Cameri, a leading Tel Aviv theater, premiered the play *Heshbon hadash* (New account), by a young and aspiring Israeli writer, Nathan Shaham. In the play, Ami, an idealistic young Israeli employed at the Dead Sea Works, learns that the plant manager and engineer, Auerbach, served as a kapo in Auschwitz. Shaken by the revelation, Ami determines to take revenge and comes up with a plan to assassinate Auerbach. He confides in a fellow worker, an Auschwitz survivor, who dismisses the idea. "The old account is finished," the survivor tells Ami. "There is a new account." The choice for those who served the Nazis in Europe, says the survivor, is between being "a human being in Sodom or a dog on Lilienblum Street," the location of Israel's black market. By choosing to help build the new state in a desolate outpost such as Sodom, the plant manager and former kapo had changed his ways and become human. "A new account has been opened," the survivor repeats.[38]

However, the naive young Israeli rejects this view and seeks revenge in the name of the nation. On a dark night, Ami, whose name literally means "my nation," breaks into Auerbach's home. With his pistol aimed at Auerbach, he speaks in the name of Israeli youth: "The government has proved its powerlessness in punishing the guilty and in combating those who are contaminating our country's air. We have taken that job upon ourselves." Legal procedures with their due process, Ami seems to believe, are not the appropriate way of dealing with collaborators. Operative actions such as executions, he thinks, are the right way to act.

Startled, Auerbach orders him to place the pistol on the table, but Ami continues to aim the gun at him, the exile and the native-born pitted against each other. Auerbach responds, "You think you can understand everything? Kapo, not a kapo. Do you know what a concentration camp is? You are too young to judge me. . . . You want to judge me? What right do you have to do so?"[39]

The playwright questions what Israeli society and its legal system took for granted—namely, that Israelis have the right to try those who transgressed during the Holocaust. In his oversimplified answer that rebuilding the state compensates for past transgressions, Shaham ignores the complexities of the relations between past and present and evaluates the kapo's behavior solely on the basis of his current actions and contribution to the national project. He ignores the ways the past penetrates and shapes present societies, the manner in which humans treat each other based on memories of the past. "The past is dead. A new account begins now," one of the protagonists utters for the third time. Yet Shaham's mere questioning of the legitimacy of the trials is significant.[40]

Watching the premiere of this play in the Cameri Theater was the former Warsaw ghetto rebel Yisrael Gutman, who could not accept Shaham's erasure of the past. Gutman, who would go on to become a famous historian and a leading figure at Yad Vashem, wrote an angry op-ed:

> In the agonizing paths of Majdanek and Auschwitz I came to know Jewish kapos. I saw them carry out their despised work of beasts of prey, hated by all. Devoured by sadism and free of any inhibitions, they were obedient tools in the hands of the murderers. We cannot invent any social or public motive that forced them to accept the "position." All they saw was the contemptible goal of assuring themselves an hour of life and entertaining themselves with the illusion of "authority," at the price of the lives of others.

Gutman continued to view the functionaries as people who had acted for selfish reasons and ignored the collective national goals. For him and his rebel friends, he wrote, there are crimes for which there is no forgiveness and for which one is prohibited from introducing the idea of pardon and absolution. Someone who served as a kapo has removed himself from the public, and his place is outside organized society. One shouldn't erase the mark of Cain from a kapo's forehead, and even if he goes on living physically, we will consider him dead.

Unlike some members of Israel's cultural elite who expressed dissenting views about judging functionaries, Gutman and others who had been there rejected any expression of forgiveness for collaborators, even in a play depicting an imaginary figure.[41]

The Kastner Trial

In 1954, when the filing of indictments against functionaries had tapered down to almost zero, another proceeding began in a Jerusalem courtroom that touched on the alleged collaboration of a Jew with the Nazis during the Holocaust. Yet this trial, which ostensibly was about defamation, stood out starkly from all the kapo criminal trials that preceded it and was not part of that set of trials. Unlike the kapo trials, which focused on the brutality of alleged collaborators toward an individual or a group of a few thousand at most, in this case the Jerusalem defendant, a man branded by one attorney as a collaborator worse than the French general Philippe Pétain, was accused of having taken part knowingly in the Nazi plan to rid Hungary of half a million Jews. From the moment the audience rose upon the first entrance of Judge Benjamin Halevi to the final knock of the gavel in the hand of Supreme Court chief justice Yitzhak Olshan, this trial lasted four years and shook Israeli society. For the first time, the issue of collaboration in the Holocaust became a major public and political topic.[42]

The events that led up to the trial began to unfold in the summer of 1952, weeks after Jungster's death sentence was overturned and with the controversy surrounding the reparation negotiations with Germany still raging. Malkiel Gruenwald, a seventy-year-old Jerusalemite who had lost his son, a member of the IZL, during the Israeli War of Independence, mailed a few hundred copies of issue no. 17 of his *Letters to Friends*, a pamphlet that regularly lambasted Israeli political figures in vicious language. Possibly inspired by the death penalty issued to Jungster, Gruenwald wrote, "The stench of a carcass is irritating my nostrils! This will be the finest funeral yet! Dr. Rudolf Kastner must be liquidated!"[43]

Ten years earlier, in 1944, Rudolf (Rezso) Kastner had been one of the heads of a Zionist organization, the Rescue Committee, in Budapest. In this position, Kastner had a role in the "blood for goods" negotiations with Adolf Eichmann, in which Eichmann offered to "sell" all the Jews of Hungary in exchange for 10,000 trucks and additional merchandise. When this negotiation failed, the Jewish leadership in Budapest attempted to find another way to save some of the Jews from being deported to the death camps. One of Eichmann's top aids, Hermann Krumey, suggested that in exchange for money and other valuables the Nazis would release a group of six hundred Jews to any Allied country (except Mandatory Palestine). Eichmann accepted the idea and ordered the release of a train, the "Kastner Train," which ended up being loaded with 1,685 passengers, including friends and fifty-two members of Kastner's family. The train departed Budapest on the night between June 30 and July 1, 1944, with the passengers not knowing what their destiny was, if to death in an Auschwitz crematorium or to freedom in an Allied country. After a ten-day journey the train arrived in Bergen Belsen, where the passengers lived in a separate section of the camp. After a few months of internment, those on the Kastner Train would eventually arrive safely in Switzerland.[44]

Prior to the war, the Hungarian-born Gruenwald lived in Vienna. The Nazis offered him the opportunity to collaborate with them, but he refused, and in 1938 he emigrated from Vienna to Mandatory Palestine. During the war, fifty-two members of his family perished. Gruenwald was obsessed. "How did the events in Hungary unfold?" he asked. "What happened to my brethren who were led in the last train from Hungary to Auschwitz?"[45]

From the bits of information and quasi rumors he gathered, Gruenwald surmised that Kastner had known about the killing fields and the death camps and did not want to inform Hungary's half million Jews about the danger they faced. According to Gruenwald, Kastner feared that if he informed the Hungarian Jews, they might escape to Romania, hide among non-Jews, refuse to board the trains, or even revolt, any of which might have hindered the exit of the train loaded with his cronies. To ensure his train's safe departure, Gruenwald continued, Kastner kept the Hungarian Jews in the dark about their fate. "Because of his criminal machinations and his collaboration with the Nazis," Gruenwald wrote, "I regard him as implicated in the murder of my dear brethren." The amateur journalist concluded that Hungarian Jewry's leadership, headed by Kastner, had enabled and assisted the Nazis in executing members of Gruenwald's family and their community. In his view it was not that the Jewish victims had reacted passively to the Nazis but rather that their leadership had misled them into "going like sheep to the slaughter."[46]

To this weighty accusation Gruenwald added another: after the war, Kastner enjoyed a good life in Switzerland, living off money that he and Kurt Becher, an SS officer on the team responsible for the destruction of Hungary's Jews, had looted from Jews. (In reality, Kastner lived an impoverished life in Switzerland.) To prevent the exposure of this robbery, Gruenwald concluded, Kastner submitted an affidavit in support of Becher to the U.S. military tribunals prosecuting war crimes at Nuremberg, testimony that saved Becher from facing justice.[47]

Letters to Friends no. 17, with its incendiary accusations, landed on the desk of Attorney General Haim Cohn. After he read it, he became convinced action had to be taken, and he mailed a confidential letter to the minister of trade and industry, Dov Yosef, for whom Kastner served as spokesperson. "It is my view that we cannot remain silent about this publication," wrote Cohn. "If there is an iota of truth in the accusations that appear in this article against Dr. Kastner, it is incumbent upon us to investigate them and draw conclusions; if, as I presume, there is no truth in these accusations, the man printing them should be prosecuted."[48]

In a meeting with Kastner, Cohn informed him of his intention to file a criminal libel suit against Gruenwald for defamation of a high-ranking government official. Kastner hesitated; Justice Minister Pinchas Rosen as well as Kastner's boss, Yosef, who was also an attorney, both advised against such a move. However, Cohn insisted and informed Kastner that if he did not agree to participate in the libel suit, the attorney general's office would have no choice but to charge him

Haim Cohn, the attorney general who managed the kapo trials and later, as a Supreme Court justice, helped bring them to an end. He also initiated the Kastner trial.

under the Nazis and Nazi Collaborators Punishment Law as a collaborator. Kastner consulted with family members and eventually consented to the attorney general filing a criminal libel suit against Gruenwald.[49]

In the courtroom, Gruenwald's maverick defense lawyer, Shmuel Tamir, turned the trial on its head. From *Attorney General v. Malkiel Gruenwald* to a case that became known to the public as the Kastner trial, the proceeding saw Kastner, officially neither accused nor accuser, become the de facto defendant. Tamir manipulated the trial so that it targeted not only the former head of the Rescue Committee in Budapest but also current political leaders in Israel. Thirty-one-year-old Tamir, who had been born in the Land of Israel and who was until 1953 a member of the Revisionist party before leaving it because of what he viewed as its failure to oppose the reparations agreement with West Germany, held in deep disdain the old guard of exile-born Mapai leaders who controlled the state, for he viewed them as having taken over the reins of leadership illegitimately instead of passing them to the members of the underground who had fought and risked their lives to create the State of Israel. This trial was his chance to implicate them in the destruction of European Jewry during the Second World War.

On the stand Tamir questioned Kastner:

> Q: Is it right that the Joint and the Jewish Agency did not publicize the Holocaust and silenced it in America both before and during 1944?
> PROSECUTOR TAL: Objection. Not relevant.
> Q: Kastner actively and knowingly participated in the silencing conspiracy.
> JUDGE HALEVI: I will allow the question.[50]

In Tamir's view, just as Kastner had kept the Jews of Hungary in the dark about the deportations to Auschwitz, so too the heads of Mapai and the Jewish Agency had avoided informing world Jewry about the catastrophe of the Holocaust as it unfolded. While Kastner had collaborated with the Nazis to benefit his cronies, the heads of Mapai collaborated with the British in silencing news of the Holocaust in order to secure power in Mandatory Palestine. In suppressing the story of the Holocaust in the media, especially in the United States, they had assisted the Germans, though with no intention to destroy European Jewry.[51]

Tamir's dispute with the heads of Mapai was not solely ideological; he also bore a personal grudge against the party and its members. In 1946, when he had been deputy head of the IZL underground in Jerusalem, he had been arrested by the British. In previous years, members of the Haganah's paramilitary organization, which was closely affiliated with Mapai, had collaborated with the British, surrendering members of the IZL. The British deported Tamir to Kenya, where he remained until May 1948. While there, he served as the prosecutor in a mock trial for collaboration of Jacob Gens, head of the Judenrat in the Vilna ghetto, who had died in the Holocaust. Now, he argued, it was time to try the true criminals from the Judenrat "who had been tools in the hands of the Nazis as part of their annihilation program." He framed the historical event to the court as a binary choice in which one served either as part of a heroic revolt or in cowardly collaboration, a structure that fit well with the prevalent Zionist ideology and one that also matched the courts' binary option of conviction or acquittal. There was no place, in his view, for negotiation as a saving tactic.[52]

To divert attention from the crimes of Mapai and the Jewish Agency's leadership, Tamir held,

> this learned attorney general has prosecuted dozens of people, and they have been sentenced to death, to life sentences, and to decades of imprisonment. And who has been sentenced? Small kapos, a kapo who to save his own life beat a woman in a concentration camp, a barracks commander, people with only a limited role. All the power of the state has been mobilized against them. . . . Is it so, your honor, that in this country laws are created in such a way that only small fry will be caught in the net? Are large holes left [in the net] to allow the whales [to escape]?[53]

"The whales" were national leaders like Kastner, who had run for the first and second Knesset at the bottom of the Mapai list. They had silenced the masses and in doing so prevented them from organizing a rebellion, which caused them "to go like sheep to slaughter." In Tamir's view, Kastner—and Mapai's heads, who had covered up his actions—had kept half a million Jews in the dark about their fate.[54]

To prove Gruenwald guilty of defamation, Attorney General Cohn attempted to refute the notion that Kastner had collaborated with the Nazis. He began by addressing Kastner's intention. "From the first moment to the last moment of his activity," Cohn declared, "Dr. Kastner had but one sole aim in mind: to serve his people." Unlike members of Herut and Mapam, Cohn and members of Mapai believed that securing the freedom of some Jews via negotiations had been a legitimate tactic. They argued that Kastner should be viewed not as someone who had saved 1,685 relatives and friends at the expense of half a million others, but rather as one who had saved 1,685 people from among half a million doomed men and women.[55]

Kastner and the Rescue Committee might have made wrong choices, Cohn told the court, but how could they be judged for those choices? "With all due respect, I am telling the court that it has no right to judge and [it] cannot set itself up as the judge of whether they did good or did evil, whether they were right or wrong, whether they weighed seriously or decided hastily, or whether they did what they did out of panic and fear or as part of a well-considered policy. We are unable to judge. This is a matter between them and heaven." For the first time, Cohn admitted the limitations of the binary nature of legal justice, with its verdict of either innocent or guilty, in grappling with the complexities of actions taken by Jewish leadership during the Holocaust. The tragic reality that the Jewish leadership faced of saving one person at the expense of another was too complicated for the legal justice system to pass simple judgments of guilt or innocence.[56]

These words coming from Israel's prosecution's most powerful legal figure represented a major shift in his view of alleged collaborators. Just four years earlier, in the Knesset Law and Justice Committee, Cohn had firmly asserted that anyone who had assisted the Nazis must be prosecuted. Now he took a "who are we to judge" approach with regard to Kastner. This approach did not fully apply to ordinary kapos, however; his office continued to prosecute them, though, as we will see, in a more restricted manner. For Cohn it would take this gradual change of mind and a move from the prosecutor's chair to the justice's bench to lead him to the conclusion that one should completely refrain from trying those who had lived under such extreme circumstances.[57]

In the years since the 1950 enactment of the Nazis and Nazi Collaborators Punishment Law, Cohn had also altered his views on the veracity of survivors' testimony. In the Banik trial he had stated that witnesses who saw life-changing events in the Holocaust were trustworthy because they are "testifying about things that are fixed in their soul. A person's memory does not easily blur the face of an enemy."[58] Now, three years later, in the Kastner trial he admitted that he had been mistaken in the Banik trial and that the Haifa District Court's dismissal of testimonies such as that of Yitzhak Freiman, who had

imagined Banik tearing open the belly of a three-year-old boy, was justified. Cohn told Judge Halevi that "in general the court should be
very cautious in accepting the testimony of witnesses who are testifying about events that took place ten years ago. Not only because of
the long time that has passed since then, but also and especially because
of the mental state of these witnesses."[59] But Cohn's change of mind
about the quality of witness testimony in the kapo trials had not yet
translated into a policy change regarding the trials of ordinary kapos,
whom the attorney general's office continued to indict.

Seven hours into his closing argument defending Kastner's actions,
Cohn paused for a minute. Turning to Judge Halevi, he read aloud a
letter written by a rabbi in the depths of the Holocaust. "My Jewish
brethren, have you gone mad? Don't you know what kind of hell we
are living in? Who has given you permission to ask him for a reckoning?" Facing Judge Halevi, Cohn asked, "Have we gone mad, your
honor? Who are they who have come here to heap their obscenities
upon people who have given their blood?" With these words he concluded his summation in defense of Kastner and sat down.[60]

Tamir rose to deliver his closing argument. When Kastner served as
the head of the Rescue Committee in Budapest, Tamir asserted, he had
done so "as an agent of the Nazi gang"; he was "their confidant, their
ally, one of them." The judge should not only clear Gruenwald of the
libel charges but must "also recommend that this Dr. Kastner be prosecuted under the Nazis and Nazi Collaborators (Punishment) Law."
The Attorney General's Office, Tamir insisted, must indict Kastner for
crimes against humanity and for delivering persecuted persons to the
enemy.[61]

The trial arguments concluded in October 1954, and for nine months
Judge Halevi studied the detailed transcripts. On June 22, 1955, with
the entire nation awaiting his words, the judge read out his 274-page
verdict. What had caused the Jews of Hungary to board the trains obediently and not resist? asked Halevi, voicing a question that many Israelis shared. It was their ignorance about the destiny of their trip, an
absence of knowledge that Kastner could have remedied but failed
to do. Had Kastner informed Hungary's Jews, the judge continued, they
would have either escaped or resisted—though with what means they
would have resisted or how they would have escaped en masse, he did

not explain. Kastner's collaboration in the annihilation of Hungarian Jewry, the judge determined, was criminal "in the full sense of the word."[62] "Kastner had sold his soul to the devil," Halevi declared, a sentence that would reverberate in newspapers and households for years to come. He cleared Gruenwald of libel in all but one minor issue and sentenced Gruenwald to a symbolic fine of one lira.[63]

Some, mostly opponents of the ruling Mapai party from both the right and the left of the Israeli political spectrum, commended the ruling. The political party Herut published a statement that linked Kastner's political affiliation to his criminal actions. "The court ruled: A devotee of Mapai in the Rescue Committee and its candidate for the Knesset, R. Kastner, had sold his soul to Satan and was a quisling."[64] In its editorial, the Communist newspaper *Kol ha-Am* expressed relief that at last the verdict had revealed to the relatives of the deceased the role Jewish leaders had played in the murder of their loved ones. The editors then added that "with the publication of the verdict, the episode has not come to an end. *First of all, one must arrest and prosecute Kastner and all those who, together with him, are responsible for collaboration with the Nazis and for indirectly murdering half a million Hungarian Jews.*" The attorney general's office, some held, should file criminal charges against Kastner as a Nazi collaborator.[65] Instead, the attorney general's office immediately filed an appeal of Halevi's ruling to the Supreme Court, thereby delaying any possible criminal prosecution of Kastner.

Angered by the trial, in 1954 the acclaimed poet Nathan Alterman, who was closely associated with the Mapai Party, published a controversial poem, "Between Two Paths" *(Al shete derakhim).* During the Holocaust and during the 1948 War of Independence, he had written some of the nation's most iconic poems praising the heroism and valor of the fighters. In this new poem he questioned the sharp line drawn by members of Mapam and the left-wing party Ahdut ha-Avoda between the path of the rebels and that of the Jewish Councils. "'There were two paths,'—so we are used to saying—two divided and separated paths," he wrote. "Is that so? When and where? What is the distinction between one path and the other?" Those leaders labeled as collaborators, he wrote, had also done their utmost to save lives. The critics who reproached those who negotiated with the Nazis were basing their views on hindsight. During the Holocaust, he pointed out, even the rebels had postponed instigating the revolt until the last possible moment. In some of the ghettos, such as Bialystok, he added, the Jewish Councils and rebellion movements had even cooperated with each other.[66]

Half a year earlier, on the April 30, 1954, anniversary of the Warsaw ghetto uprising, he had published the poem "Memorial Day and the Rebels" (*Yom ha-Zikaron ve-ha-mordim*), which questioned the practice, common among organizers of commemorative events, of distinguishing between the rebels and the masses, between those who fought courageously and those who did not. In his poem, the rebels choose to blend in with the massacred masses and not stand out as venerated icons, and the dead rebels demand veneration also of "Jewish fathers who said, 'the underground will bring a catastrophe upon us,' and also of that boy or girl . . . who left behind nothing but a small white sock." Those who supported the memory of the rebels, he argued, neglected to appreciate the memory of ordinary deceased small children and failed to empathize with a parent's efforts to preserve his child's life as long as possible.[67]

Alterman refused to view all Jewish Councils, their leaders, and their members in the same light. At least in some instances, he asserted, their opposition to battling the Germans stemmed from the goal of preserving lives. Yet he held that some individual collaborators did not deserve any empathy or understanding whatsoever. For "those beasts of prey among these 'collaborators,' their helpers, who follow their commands," there could be no forgiveness, he wrote. "There are acts and occurrences that a sane human being must not 'understand.'" In his writing, Alterman no longer considered the collective guilt of collaborators but rather distinguished between individuals and their specific actions.[68]

A few went further than Alterman and refused to question the morality not only of the actions of the Judenräte and the Jewish police but also of the actions of the kapos, whom Alterman did not address specifically. In the daily *Maariv*, writer Avigdor Hameiri asked, "Are we permitted to judge?" Hameiri believed that the Kastner trial was a "historic crime for which there is no atonement and no forgiveness." In that context, what would permit anyone to judge Kastner and others like him? he asked. No law can apply to people who sought "to live, to live, to live." Under those circumstances, he wrote, one cannot judge anyone, not even a kapo.[69]

Members of Mapam and Ahdut ha-Avoda, who, as we have seen, had closely linked themselves to the rebel movement in Europe, strongly opposed the perspective taken by Alterman, the most prominent literary figure associated with the Mapai party. In May 1954 Abba Kovner and his wife, Vitka, both members of the Jewish revolt in Europe, traveled from northern Israel to Tel Aviv to meet with Nathan Alterman. They expressed their revulsion about his poem "Memorial Day and the Rebels." The members of the Judenräte who opposed the revolt, said Kovner and Vitka, had been morally decrepit and aimed to save their own lives at the expense of others. In a newspaper associated with Ahdut ha-Avoda, one writer, Mati Meged, wrote that the question of collaboration was not an issue of the past; rather, "our treatment today of a phenomenon such as this still determines and may continue to constitute real precedents in political circumstances and national morals, in educating the public and educating individuals, in shaping the nation in its state and in shaping the image of its citizens. . . . The one who forgives and forgets—he may determine, and already determines, the way in which the present and future citizen in Israel will be educated."[70]

But Alterman, who between 1939 and 1945 had lived in Tel Aviv, refused to accept this generalization. Even if the Judenräte opposed the revolt, he held, often they had done so in order to save the lives of others, and not only for selfish reasons. Furthermore, one should not alter history for the sake of contemporary educational goals.[71] Unlike Alterman, however, the common view was that there was not only a right but an obligation to judge the betrayers of the nation. And some issued their own verdicts.

While Kastner was waiting to hear the result of his appeal to the Supreme Court, he returned home a few minutes after midnight on March 4, 1957, after working in the editorial office of the Hungarian newspaper *Új Kelet*. He parked his car outside the Tel Aviv apartment building where he lived with his wife and their only child, a daughter. As he turned the car key in the lock, a man jumped off a Jeep and approached him. "Are you Dr. Kastner?" he asked. When Kastner said yes, the man pulled out a pistol. Kastner ran for his life. Three shots rang out. Kastner fell down, gravely wounded. In the hospital, he gave the police details about his attacker. Ten days later, he died.[72]

The night of the shooting, Israel's Shin Bet, which had just a few weeks earlier withdrawn the bodyguards it had assigned to protect Kastner, arrested three suspects: Yosef Menkes, Dan Shemer, and Ze'ev Eckstein. Within days, Eckstein admitted that he had shot Kastner. The other two had served as accomplices. All three were members of a right-wing underground cell that aimed to reestablish the Kingdom of Israel from the Mediterranean Sea to the Euphrates River. The court sentenced them to life in prison, but they served only five years.[73]

In January 1958, nine months after the murder of Kastner and two and a half years after Halevi's harsh verdict in which he acquitted Gruenwald of the criminal libel suit, the Supreme Court ruled on the attorney general's appeal. The justices held that Cohn had been wrong in deciding to indict Gruenwald. In a statement never made in any of the kapo trials, Justice Shimon Agranat wrote in his opinion that the court lacked the ability to put itself in the position and context in which the historical protagonists had acted in Hungary ten years earlier. A committee made up of professional historians would have had more access to historical sources and a better chance to uncover the truth, he stated. This was a first acknowledgment by the court of the impossibility of trying certain people who had lived and decided within the circumstances of the war years.[74]

Given that the case had come to the Supreme Court on appeal, however, the justices had no choice but to issue a ruling. All five justices criticized Halevi for mishandling the proceedings. He had treated rumors as facts and permitted witnesses to veer off topic and give testimony unrelated to the issues under consideration.[75] Four of the justices cleared Kastner of the allegation of collaboration; one justice, Moshe Zilberg, upheld Halevi's verdict.

In determining whether someone collaborated or not, Justice Agranat wrote, the defendant's intent is crucial. Even if a person knew that some of his actions would benefit the Nazis but his overall motivation was morally justified, one could not label him a collaborator. Kastner had clearly acted with the larger motivation of saving the Jews of Hungary.[76] Agranat wrote:

First, we should not jump to the conclusion that if a certain person who lived under harsh Nazi rule had taken an action that gave the latter a specific benefit—he had indeed seen this benefit as his main or final goal; that assisting the Nazis was the *motivation* that caused him to act as he acted. Second—and this is the key issue I wish to highlight—we should not cast a blot on such a person just because he had taken knowingly an act that might assist the Nazis' goals when it became clear [to us] that his motivations were kosher and are not morally questionable; in other words, Heaven forbid that we shall name this person "collaborator."[77]

In other words, Agranat held that in the context of Nazi rule a person could have legitimately taken short-term actions that benefited the Nazis if his overall goal was to assist and save Jews. And Justice Shneur Zalman Cheshin pointed out that the results of Kastner's actions "are miraculous. He saved not one person but . . . at least 1,700 Jews."

As for Gruenwald, the high court sentenced him to one year of probation and a 200-lira fine.[78]

A Shift in the Kapo Trials

For Cohn personally, the Kastner trial was an illuminating experience, one that taught him about the complexities of life and moral choices faced by victims of the Holocaust. Having learned about the events that unfolded in Hungary in 1944, Cohn wrote years later, "[I came] to believe that those of us who did not experience the Holocaust ourselves, have no ability or the right to try a person for his actions, intentions and constraints when he [was trapped in] that Hell."[79] While Cohn's office did continue to file charges against alleged collaborators, it did so to only a limited extent. The three years between 1955 and 1957 saw no indictments, and the years 1958–1959 saw five district court indictments.[80]

Almost two years after the Supreme Court issued the Kastner verdict, in September 1959 Attorney General Cohn would rely on that decision to alter the course of a case before the Tel Aviv Magistrates Court. This would mark a new stage in the kapo trials: the attorney general's office would place additional restrictions on who could be placed on trial, beyond the already existing restriction that the first paragraph of the Nazis and Nazi Collaborators Punishment Law no longer applied to Jews.

The current case focused on Eliezer Landau. During the war, Landau, his wife, and their three young children escaped the Polish town of Bochnia for Bucharest and from there sailed to Mandatory Palestine. Upon his arrival in Haifa in August 1944, rumors circulated that Landau, who had had close relations with leading SS men in Bochnia, had extorted money from Jews in that town in exchange for promises to save them from deportation. "Landau, who before the war was penniless, arrived in Bucharest with substantial amounts of money" and now in Mandatory Palestine had at his disposal hundreds of liras, investigators from the Haifa Bureau of Investigations wrote in a secret 1945 report. In Landau's position as the Jewish community's contact with the Germans, they wrote, "it seems that he took [for himself] a significant percentage of the money given to him [by Jews] as ransom for the Gestapo."[81]

Learning of the allegations against him, Landau turned to the chief rabbi of the Land of Israel, Isaac Halevi Herzog, and demanded a public hearing. Nothing came of that request, but more than a decade later, in 1959, the police arrested the Tel Aviv–based wholesaler on charges that he had revealed to the Germans the location of one family's jewelry cache, and that he had assisted the Nazis in ways that resulted in many Jews being sent to unknown locations.[82]

In the preliminary process, the Tel Aviv Magistrates Court heard testimony from dozens of people saved by Landau's actions, including influential rabbis, who organized and approached Attorney General Cohn demanding he withdraw the indictment. In the face of this outpouring of support, Cohn took a step back. In a lengthy letter to the court, described in one newspaper as "daring," he explained that the Kastner ruling had taught that intention was crucial for determining whether a person's actions fell under the Nazis and Nazi Collaborators Punishment Law:

> If the defendant thought that in order to gain or maintain the goodwill of the Nazis (which he needed for the sake of his actions of help and rescuing) it was necessary to reveal the hiding places of Jewish

money, then even if, objectively, he was mistaken, and even if handing
the money over to the Nazis was a bad action, the fact that he revealed these hiding places to the Nazis does not prove . . . that he
intended to assist the Nazis in a manner such that the Nazi collaboration laws would apply to him.[83]

That is, if a person acted with the motivation of saving and assisting
victims but, to maintain good connections with the Nazis, took actions that resulted in negative consequences, that person should not
be prosecuted, according to Cohn's new interpretation of the ruling and
the law.[84]

Cohn drew a distinction between Landau, who had aligned himself with the Nazis' goals so as to save or assist Jews, building up a connection with the Nazis for that purpose, and those whose intent was
"to align themselves with the Nazis to achieve their own goals."

This signaled that a third stage in the kapo trials had begun. From
this point forward, the attorney general's office would file charges only
against those seen as having aligned themselves with the Nazis' goals
for selfish purposes.[85]

Doubting the Necessity of Trials

The shift in the kapo prosecutions was influenced not only by the
Kastner trial and the attorney general's change in attitude but also by
social and cultural transformations that had begun to take place in
Israeli society during the second half of the 1950s. With the distance
of time from the catastrophic era of the Holocaust growing, for the first
time some survivors began to doubt the need to pursue alleged collaborators, believing it was time to put the controversies of "those days"
behind. Others did not change their view and continued to believe it
was essential to pursue figures from the past.

We can discern this shift in attitude among some survivors from
the case of Aryeh Praport, which took place in the final months of 1957.
Moshe Yavlonsky took the witness stand in Tel Aviv Magistrates Court
and was describing how in 1941 the Nazis had uncovered a hideout in
his apartment in the Pabianice ghetto and captured seven women, including two of his sisters, when District Attorney Itamar Pilpel interrupted him with a question: was Yavlonsky certain he was speaking

the truth? Coming from the prosecutor, this question was surprising, not least because Yavlonsky was a prosecution witness.

Ten days earlier at the police station, Yavlonsky had described to the investigator how the Jewish policeman Praport had arrived with a group of Gestapo men at an apartment building owned by his father on 5 Warszawska Street to search for young women. They searched all the building's apartments, including his own, but found nothing. Minutes later, Yavlonsky told the police, Praport returned alone to the building. He walked directly to Yavlonsky's apartment and searched it high and low, stopping for only a moment to call in Gestapo men and sniffer dogs. In the apartment, Yavlonsky watched as Praport "moved the closet that hid a double wall and uncovered the seven girls," including Sheindel and Dina, his two sisters. Yavlonsky stressed to the police that Praport was "the one that enabled the Gestapo to take the girls and kill them."[86]

On the stand in the magistrates court, Yavlonsky altered his account in dramatic and suspicious ways. Just as in his police account, he recalled the first search in the building's various apartments, from which the Gestapo came away empty-handed. But in this later account, Yavlonsky said that Praport and the Gestapo left, only to return "a few minutes later . . . [and] they went directly to my apartment. I stayed on the ground floor [in his parents' apartment] because I was afraid to go up. . . . Later I saw the Gestapo people leading the girls down. The Gestapo people gave orders and the defendant went with them." Unlike his account to the police, Yavlonsky's testimony in court was that Praport had only followed the Germans' orders; he had not summoned the Gestapo to search for the young women. Yavlonsky also stated in court that he had not been present in his apartment during the search and did not see Praport move the closet to uncover the women's hiding place, as he had said in his police deposition.[87]

Yavlonsky's wife, Tziral, who in her deposition to the police had corroborated her husband's account, now also confirmed his altered court testimony. In the time between the two searches, she told the court, she was in the building courtyard. She saw the Germans assemble girls from different buildings, including the daughter of Mrs. Krotoschinsky, a neighbor of theirs. "Mrs. Krotoschinsky stood [in the yard] shouting—not shouting, but crying and shaking. She went up to the Jewish policeman and told him, 'In fact, at Yavlonsky's [apartment] there are two strong girls; if you don't go up there, I will tell the Gestapo people." It was Mrs. Krotoschinsky, Tziral told the court, who had been responsible for exposing the girls' hiding place. Mrs. Krotoschinsky had even apologized later for revealing the hideout, saying she had been unaware that not two girls but seven were hidden there. To the best of her recollection, Tziral added, the Germans had ordered Praport to move the closet. It was not his own initiative.[88]

At the request of the prosecutor in this trial, the judge declared both Moshe and Tziral Yavlonsky hostile witnesses. This trial was the first and possibly the only one of the kapo trials to be heard behind closed doors—because both the defense lawyer and the prosecutor agreed that publication of the defendant's name "might tarnish him before he was found guilty." For the first time, there was a sensitivity on both sides of the case to the public image of the accused collaborators.[89]

Asked in both the magistrates court and the district court to explain their altered accounts, the Yavlonskys fingered the complainant in the case, Mendel Bogonsky, a forty-five-year-old tailor. Bogonsky had sought revenge against Praport for surrendering the seven girls, one of whom was Bogonsky's seventeen-year-old "beautiful fiancée," Dina Yavlonsky. In the seventeen years since her capture, Bogonsky had never married. He repeatedly referred to Yavlonsky as "my brother-in-law" when in fact they were never brothers-in-law. From his home in New York, he searched continuously for Aryeh Praport. And when he learned that Praport lived in a town south of Tel Aviv and worked as a truck driver, he boarded a ship and came to Israel.[90]

According to the Yavlonskys, Bogonsky had pressured them into filing a false account with the police. If they did not file incriminating testimony against Praport, Bogonsky threatened, he would tell their relatives in the United States to stop sending them money. When they met Bogonsky at the police station, he warned them not to talk about Mrs. Krotoschinsky's having revealed the hiding place—"otherwise I will be considered a liar." "And when I saw the defendant," Tziral went on, "we again saw the past, and the horror was before us again and we did not know what we were saying. We were terrified by Bogonsky's screams." Moshe Yavlonsky testified, "Bogonsky told me what to say; after all, I did not remember everything."[91]

In the ten days that elapsed between the police investigation and their court appearance, both Tziral and Moshe Yavlonsky recalled the true events and the role their neighbor Mrs. Krotoschinsky had played in surrendering the girls. Tziral still harbored deep hatred toward Jewish policemen like Praport for handing over her family members; those who had served in the police, she declared, "are not worth a penny." Still, at one point she acknowledged, "So many years have passed, what do we need this for?" With these words she expressed the sentiment shared by some survivors that it was time to move on and put the past to rest. A decade and a half had passed since these events had taken place, and while these survivors had deep reservations about the actions of these policemen and kapos, they no longer believed it was wise to prosecute them.[92]

The panel of judges cleared Praport on the ground that the testimony of all the witnesses was flawed and so they could not determine which account was true, Bogonsky's or Yavlonsky's.[93] But a year later, Israel's attorney general's office filed charges against Moshe and Tziral Yavlonsky for their false testimony—for being "willing, in exchange for financial benefit, to sell their soul to the devil." Unlike in the Kastner trial, where the devil was Eichmann and his men, here the devil was the Jewish policeman and collaborator Praport.[94]

The Yavlonskys called to the stand as a defense witness Antek Zuckerman, a leader of the underground movement in the Warsaw ghetto, to explain the instinctive reaction that had led them to provide false testimony criminalizing a Jewish policeman. Zuckerman had strongly opposed poet Nathan Alterman's call to blur the lines between rebels and collaborators and was one of the survivors who refused to forgive the policemen and kapos for their past actions. "Only in the lines of Nathan Alterman's poem do the Judenrat men and the fighters live in peace. [Only] in the dead letters. But in [real] life there was a bitter fight, there was a battle, there were victims."[95] The sight of Praport awoke in Moshe and Tziral "a primitive response, certainly a spontaneous one, of a desire for revenge," Zuckerman explained to the judge. To that very day, Zuckerman added, he refused to shake the hand of former policemen.[96]

"The Jewish police is a hostile organization and is an institution that bears guilt with regard to the Jewish people," Zuckerman went on. "Of course there are exceptions, [but] I would say in general that anyone who served in the Jewish police must prove his innocence, because he did despicable jobs." Zuckerman's testimony helped clear the Yavlonskys.[97] The question of whether the Jewish police had indeed been a hostile organization would lie at the heart of a trial that would begin a few years later, the trial of a former head of a Jewish police force. That trial would take place shortly after the trial of a very different commander, the head of the department of Jewish affairs and evacuation in the Reich's main security office—Adolf Eichmann.

[CHAPTER EIGHT]

JUDGING A NAZI AND REFRAMING COLLABORATION

IN THE SPRING OF 1961, before a Jerusalem courtroom packed with 700 spectators, Gideon Hausner, who had been appointed attorney general less than a year earlier, delivered his opening statement in case 40/61, *The State of Israel v. Adolf Eichmann.* Clad in a black robe, Hausner raised his arm to point at the person seated inside the glass-walled dock. "When I stand before you here, judges of Israel, to lead the prosecution of Adolf Eichmann, I am not standing alone," he declared. "With me are six million accusers. But they cannot rise to their feet and point an accusing finger at him who sits in the dock and cry 'I accuse.'"[1]

A few minutes later, Hausner spoke briefly about Jewish functionaries who had served under the Nazis. "We shall find Jews among those carrying out Nazi orders, in the Jewish police, in the ghettos, and in the Councils of Elders. Even at the entrance of the gas chambers there were Jews." Those Jews, he pointed out, had served the Nazi death machine but would not be incriminated during the proceedings. "In this trial we shall not deal with the Jews who carried out orders, either the 'kapos' or the members of the Councils of Elders. This is not the trial of the victims, but the trial of the destroyer," he told the court. Hausner portrayed all "Nazi helpers" as people who were forced to carry out Nazi orders and ignored the small minority who at times had acted not under duress but of their own volition.[2]

Throughout the next 120 days of this closely watched trial, Hausner attempted to silence any account that cast moral doubt on the behavior of any Jew during the Holocaust. He would not deal with hard questions about the motivations, deeds, or behavior of those who served as functionaries of the Nazi regime. His framing of the trial juxtaposed pure Jewish victims with brutal Nazi perpetrators and minimized the role of those whose actions fell within the gray zone. In so doing, one of his aims was to reshape the Israeli public's image of Jewish functionaries.

Hausner used both documentation and witnesses to prove Eichmann's guilt. He summoned to the stand more than a hundred witnesses; however, most of them did not know Eichmann and their testimony did not pertain to his actions. In his account of the trial Hausner wrote:

> In order merely to secure a conviction, it was obviously enough to let the archives speak; a fraction of them would have sufficed to get Eichmann sentenced ten times over. But I knew we needed more than a conviction; we needed a living record of a gigantic human and national disaster. . . . In any criminal proceedings the proof of guilt and the imposition of a penalty . . . are not the exclusive objects. Every trial also has a correctional and educational aspect. . . . Much the more so in this exceptional case.[3]

Unlike the kapo trials, where survivors' accounts served as the grounds for conviction, Hausner's use of witnesses was primarily for educational purposes. In his selection of former functionaries to testify, Hausner would choose those who could help him "correct" the impression left by the kapo trials that Jewish functionaries had had a role in the annihilation of the Jews.

In his questioning Hausner attempted to reframe the negative view of Jewish functionaries. He asked a witness, "In Auschwitz, there were also kapos of a different category—Jews. Were there also some who treated the prisoners well?" To another person testifying on the stand he asked, "There were *Blockälteste* of various kinds in Auschwitz, I understand. There were good ones and evil ones?" Regarding the Jewish police, he queried one survivor: "Dr. Peretz, you mentioned the Jewish police. I understand that in Kovno the Jewish police were also not hated by the populace?"[4]

Witness after witness affirmed the prosecutor's attempt to cast functionaries in a positive view. "Most of them were good," one woman declared. "There were people who fulfilled what was described as functions at Auschwitz, Jews and non-Jews, who showed a human approach," an Auschwitz survivor stated. Another testified, "There were good *Blockälteste,* but there were also bad ones. The good *Blockälteste* could help, and many did, even at personal risk to themselves. They endangered their position and themselves by helping prisoners. They had many opportunities to help and, indeed, many took advantage of that and helped." In this telling, the functionaries had joined the rebels opposing the Nazis.[5]

One of the witnesses, fifty-one-year-old Raya Kagan, who had served as a file clerk in administrative offices at Auschwitz, did not initially give Hausner the answer he expected. Upon hearing Hausner ask, "Were there also fair and honest women amongst the *Blockälteste?*" Kagan interrupted, "Yes. There were kapos like that, but that was exceptional." Hausner was unhappy with that response. "Yes, but there were women who were fair, both in the role of kapos and the role of *Blockälteste?*" he insisted. Yes, the witness conceded, "also in the role of kapos."[6]

Two months into the trial, Hausner called to the stand Vera Alexander, one of those to whom he had been referring in his opening speech when he said, "It is extraordinary that even in the midst of this inferno there were many Jews who succeeded in preserving the divine image and were not broken." Alexander, an artist and art critic, agreed to testify in court only after the attorney general persuaded her by saying that after "so much poison had been poured on *Blockältestes* and kapos, it is very essential that something good will also be heard."[7] Hausner wanted to balance the negative view of functionaries, and within the binary frame that he created of "good" and "evil," he chose to portray them as righteous.

He asked, "You became a *Blockälteste.* In what block was that?"

"At first I was a *Blockälteste* in Block 3 in Camp A," she responded.

"Tell me, Mrs. Alexander, how was it possible to be a *Blockälteste* in Auschwitz and to maintain the stance of being created in God's image and maintain the image of a human being?" Hausner inquired, seeking to establish a positive image of the former functionary and to shift the criterion of worthy behavior from loyalty to the nation to adherence to personal moral and religious values.

"It was not easy," she replied. "One needed a lot of tact and much maneuvering. On the one hand, one had to obey orders and to fulfill them and, on the other hand, to harm the prisoners as little as possible and to assist them," she responded. Her answer reinforced the idea that to achieve good in Auschwitz, one was forced at times to do harm.

Hausner continued to pose questions aimed at highlighting examples of a camp functionary who acted honorably and to avoid questions that could bring up what some might see as questionable behavior and actions.[8] "We have been told that you saved women from being put to death. How did you do that? Tell us of some cases." Alexander described to the court how the Nazis selected women for death. "I tried, not always successfully, to remove them from the ranks. Sometimes I managed to place girls in a commando that was going out from Auschwitz to work. This was not heroism on my part—it was my duty," she declared.

Alexander also described how she stole food, blankets, and clothing to support prisoners. She hid a woman and her infant until the Germans discovered them. A supervisor caught her informing new arrivals about camp dangers. Luckily, he did not execute her, but only whipped her.[9]

Following Alexander's testimony, newspaper reports described "a humane, noble individual from Auschwitz who risked her life to save prisoners from death." The newspaper critic Joseph Harif wrote, "Until now we have heard of the rigid and cruel character of the Jewish 'kapo,' the Jewish block functionary who abused his brethren. . . . Now the prosecutor has sought to teach us and future generations that there were also others. As a living symbol he has laid before us the image of Vera Alexander."[10]

In drawing a sharp distinction between victim and perpetrator, Hausner broke through the accepted view of camp functionaries as brutes. In the same spirit, he also brought into question the negative view that many in Israeli society had of Jewish leaders in Europe during the war. During an interview of Hausner halfway through the trial, journalist Raphael Bashan said to him, "Here, Mr. Attorney General, I arrive at a very sensitive and explosive point. Why did they not rebel? Why did they go like sheep to the slaughter? Did the Jewish leaders point the nation in the right direction?"

Hausner was clearly agitated by the question:

One must understand, one must understand once and for all, that a system of disguise, deception, and temptation was organized with such efficiency that I would not take it upon myself to formulate how this or that Jewish leader should have acted. . . . And it is not true that they did not revolt! They did revolt! In all kinds of ways. What do we know about the spiritual courage demonstrated by Jewish leaders who refused to collaborate with the Nazis and understood very well that their proud, negative answer meant an immediate death sentence for them and their families?[11]

Instead of blaming the leaders, Hausner chose to portray them as part of the rebel movement—a radical transformation of their image from only a few years earlier.

In February 1961, two months before the courtroom doors opened for Eichmann's trial, Hausner traveled to the Ghetto Fighters Kibbutz (Lohamei HaGeta'ot), near Israel's border with Lebanon, to talk with two of the most extolled members of the underground movement, Antek Zuckerman and Zivia Lubetkin. In their small kibbutz apartment, the prosecutor asked the couple for their blessing; more important, he sought to convince them to come to Jerusalem and relate to the court their experiences in the Warsaw ghetto.[12]

Initially, Lubetkin was unenthusiastic. She feared that in cross-examination the defense would force her or her husband to expose details that could tarnish the reputation of the rebel movement. In a government meeting that took place a week later, Hausner explained Lubetkin's reluctance to testify. The Warsaw ghetto uprising had become a myth, "a legend by whose light mothers will educate our sons," he pointed out to the ministers. Eichmann's lawyers would surely expose the fact that "the reality is not all glamorous." It might well come to light that the rebel movement had assassinated the heads of the Jewish police and Jewish functionaries, as well as that "Jews had died due to other Jews' informing. . . . I can fully understand Lubetkin, why she was not eager to testify," Hausner concluded, "but she will testify."[13]

Lubetkin and Zuckerman's testimony began on May 3, 1961, a day on which Israel Radio, after ceasing to broadcast the trial for a few weeks, resumed its live coverage. Both Lubetkin and Zuckerman, standing across from the bulletproof glass booth in which Eichmann sat, recalled the horrors of the ghetto. They also detailed the heroic April 1943 revolt by a few hundred poorly armed Jewish rebels against

Yitzhak (Antek) Zukerman, a rebel leader, testifies at the Eichmann trial.

dozens of well-armed Nazis. Lubetkin spoke of the movement's goal "to organize the youth, as I have said, in order to promote within themselves, despite the degradation and depression, a feeling of Jewish self-respect."[14]

When Lubetkin completed her account, the presiding judge, Moshe Landau, asked the defense attorney, Robert Servatius, if he wanted to question her. "I have no questions for the witness," he replied from behind the defense table.[15] Nor did Servatius have any questions for Antek Zuckerman. Possibly with the aim of not alienating the public, the defense attorney chose not to expose the inter-Jewish tensions that had existed during the Holocaust. In fact, twelve survivors had offered to testify for the defense by exposing Jews who they believed had acted in an immoral manner. Servatius turned them down.[16]

At this point Hausner's worry that the defense would spotlight stories of Jewish treachery seemed to be behind him. Then one voice spoke from the bench. It was Judge Benjamin Halevi, who in 1955 had ruled that Rudolf Kastner had concealed information from Hungarian Jewry about their fate and in so doing had "sold his soul to the devil," that is, to Eichmann. The two other jurists on the panel, Moshe Landau and Yitzhak Raveh, had each overseen one previous kapo trial, but none of those trials had as much prominence as the Kastner case.[17]

Halevi scrutinized Zuckerman's testimony. "You mentioned that you attacked an officer of the Jewish police, if I understand correctly. Who was he?" The judge focused on a brief remark Zuckerman had made in his testimony about an August 1942 attempt to kill the ghetto's head of Jewish police, Josef Shaminski, whom the underground deemed a collaborator.

"Yes. He was a converted Jew, a colonel in the Polish police before the war . . . who before the war had no contact with Jewish life," Zuckerman elaborated.

"Why did you attack him to kill him?" the judge wanted to know.

"We couldn't execute all the traitors. He was a collaborator—even though he did not carry arms." There had been Jewish policemen who thought that they would save their families or their wives by collaborating and revealing places where Jews were hiding or where there were auxiliary units, he continued. "We deemed it correct to take vengeance on them, and we did so. But he was only the first in a longer list."[18]

Adolf Eichmann seated in a bulletproof glass booth at his trial in Jerusalem.

Halevi returned to the topic of Jewish collaborators when Hausner raised the matter of Kastner's actions. From the beginning Hausner had feared that the defense would divert attention from Eichmann by re-kindling the Kastner controversy, which just a few years earlier had rent Israeli society. In a meeting with newspaper editors, he urged them not to raise the sensitive topic in their publications. In the pre-trial gov-ernment meeting on February 26, 1961, he said, "I want to avoid this debate [about Kastner]. I do not wish to defend the Jewish Agency in our array of arguments against the Nazis." He told the government that "it is very easy to sit on the bench . . . in Jerusalem and declare: 'This is how Kastner should have acted when he was in Budapest.' Who knows how each of us would have acted in 1944?"[19]

Hausner knew, however, that it would be impossible to avoid the Kastner affair completely, so he decided to call to the stand Joel Brand and his wife, Hansi, who together with Kastner in 1944 had negotiated with Eichmann and his men about saving one million Hungarian Jews in exchange for 10,000 trucks. Hausner anticipated that if he did not call them to testify, the defense would do so. If Hausner called them first, he could frame the couple's testimony in a way that was beneficial to the prosecution.[20]

In a lengthy cross-examination of Hansi Brand that focused on the Budapest-based Committee for Aid and Rescue's negotiations with Eichmann, Judge Halevi posed an unexpected question: "Did the committee ever discuss the possibility of eliminating him, Eichmann, of killing him?" The implication was that instead of collaborating with Eichmann in misleading Hungarian Jewry, the committee could have halted the deportations by assassinating him.[21]

She replied:

We had various reports from various countries about what happened to partisans and people who undertook anything against the Germans. I do not wish to blow my own trumpet, nor do I wish to blow the committee's trumpet—we bore this in mind, what we could achieve. Let us assume that we go in to see him, we are not checked, and one of us shoots him. What would we achieve by that? I must say that frankly and sincerely: We were a committee for the aid and rescue of our people, and none of us was a *gibor*, a hero.

The witness spoke in fluent German, pronouncing just one word, *gibor* (hero), in Hebrew. By doing so she seemed to dismiss the obsession of many Israelis with heroism. In fact, she explained, had they assassinated Eichmann, it might have resulted in the speeding up of the extermination process or in some other form of retaliation that would have been far worse.[22]

Later, in cross-examining Eichmann, Halevi returned to the issue of collaboration. "The Jewish functionaries were given duties . . . which greatly facilitated emigration," the judge asserted.

"Yes, that is true."

"Yes, and then that could be switched very rapidly and simply to deportation," Halevi continued.

"Yes," answered the man who had overseen Nazi Germany's deportation of Jews to the death camps.

"Then there was the idea of the Jewish Councils, particularly for Poland? . . . And later for Hungary, too?" Halevi stated.

"Yes."

"As instruments of German policy regarding the Jews, these Jewish Councils—shall we say—considerably facilitated the implementation of measures against the Jews?" Halevi asked, driving the point home.

"Yes," Eichmann responded.

"And saved a great deal of manpower and staff."

"Yes . . ."

"These [the Jewish Councils] made it possible, by misleading the victims, to facilitate the work, and also to harness the Jews themselves to work for their own destruction," Halevi concluded, thus revealing his view that a few Jews partook in the destruction of their own nation.[23]

Hannah Arendt's View of Collaborators

One observer shared Halevi's discomfort with the prosecution's evasion of the question of the role Jews had played in their own extermination. Hannah Arendt, a refugee from Nazi Europe who had become an intellectual celebrity in New York and who reported on the trial for the *New Yorker* magazine, shared Halevi's assessment of Kastner as someone who had crossed moral lines.[24] In a set of articles, later published as the book *Eichmann in Jerusalem*, Arendt expressed revulsion at prosecutor Gideon Hausner's choice to focus solely on the perpetrator. Relying on Raul Hilberg's research, Arendt wrote, "To a Jew this role of the Jewish leaders in the destruction of their own people is undoubtedly the darkest chapter of the whole dark story. . . . In Amsterdam as in Warsaw, in Berlin as in Budapest, Jewish officials could be trusted to compile the lists of persons and of their property, to secure money from the deportees to defray the expenses of their deportation and extermination, to keep track of vacated apartments, to supply police forces to help seize Jews and get them on trains, until, as a last gesture, they handed over the assets of the Jewish community in good order for final confiscation."[25]

In Arendt's view, "The Jerusalem trial failed to put before the eyes of the world in its true dimensions . . . the most striking insight into the totality of the moral collapse the Nazis caused in respectable European society—not only in Germany but in almost all countries, not only among the persecutors but also among the victims." Totalitarian regimes, this political scientist argued, brought about the moral disintegration of both perpetrator and victim societies, including Jewish society. The Nazis had caused the victims' leaders to participate in and further their own people's annihilation.[26]

Arendt criticized Israel's attorney general for repeatedly asking witnesses, "Why did you not rebel?" She thought that by asking this question he created a smokescreen to obscure the unpleasant question of why the Jewish Councils had caused Jews to go obediently to the trains. In drawing a stark distinction between "saintly victims" and "diabolical perpetrators," she believed, Hausner omitted those who stood in between perpetrator and victim.[27] In the early phase of ghettoization, when it was still possible to oppose the Germans, the members of the Jewish Councils "cooperated" with the Nazis, and so according to Arendt, Jewish community leaders bore some responsibility for the devastating results of the Holocaust. "This leadership, almost without exception, cooperated in one way or another, for one reason or another, with the Nazis. The whole truth was that if the Jewish people had really been unorganized and leaderless, there would have been chaos and plenty of misery but the total number of victims would hardly have been between four and a half and six million people."[28]

Arendt's argument, which focused on the ghetto's Jewish leadership and made no mention of the functionaries in the concentration camps, provoked a public outcry, mostly among Jewish leaders and organizations in the United States.[29] The Anti-Defamation League called her book "evil," not only in response to her account of the Jews but also because of her reference to Eichmann's actions as demonstrating "the banality of evil."[30] Others pointed to her overarching statements about the actions of the Jewish leadership, which in fact had responded in diverse ways. Some ghetto leaders indeed acquiesced to Nazi demands, but many others opposed them.[31] Critics highlighted the hyperbolic language in her description of the Jewish leaders' actions as the "darkest chapter of the whole dark story," her characterization of them as handing over assets to the Germans in a "last gesture," and her labeling of Rabbi Leo Baeck as a Jewish Führer.[32]

In Israel, one renowned scholar, Gershom Scholem, wrote Arendt a personal letter deploring her style and tone, which he found "heartless, frequently almost sneering and malicious." Scholem went further, asserting that Arendt had distanced herself from the Jewish community. "In the Jewish tradition there is a concept hard to define and yet concrete enough, which we know as *Ahabath Israel:* 'Love of the Jewish People. . . .' In you, dear Hannah, as in so many intellectuals who came from the German Left, I find little trace of this."[33]

Scholem, a Kabbalah scholar, questioned Arendt's harsh judgment of the Judenräte:

> Which of us can say today what decisions the Elders of the Jews—whatever we choose to call them—ought to have arrived at in the circumstances? . . . There were the *Judenrat* for example; some among them were swine, others were saints. . . . There were among them also many people in no way different from ourselves, who were compelled to make terrible decisions in circumstances that we cannot even begin to reproduce or reconstruct. I do not know whether they were right or wrong. Nor do I presume to judge. I was not there.[34]

In the spirit of Hausner's view, Scholem presented two extreme sides, swine and saints, with no one in the middle. He also adopted the view, advanced by Attorney General Cohn at the Kastner trial, that anyone who had not been there was not qualified to make a moral judgment. This approach would come to dominate the public view in Israel and stifle both moral debate and historical analysis of the actions of the victims, including the leaders of the Jewish Councils and Jewish functionaries.

Israelis Question the Treatment of Survivors

Haim Gouri, a highly regarded poet and author who fought in the Israeli War of Independence, attended the Eichmann trial from the opening session on April 11, 1961, until the court issued its verdict on December 15 of that year. Daily he published reflections on the proceedings in a left-leaning newspaper, *La-Merhav*. Those accounts reveal how the trial transformed the view of the Holocaust for Gouri and his generation.

At first Gouri felt deep discomfort with the testimonies he heard. In the days following Israel's thirteenth Independence Day, one of the former heads of the Jewish community in Vienna, Morris Fleischmann, described in court how in Vienna in 1938, on orders of the Nazis, he got on his knees to wash the sidewalk with a cloth and hot water. "I did not want to listen to this broken little man go on and on about his sufferings, his ills and indignities, the way the mob jeered at him and his fellow Jews," wrote Gouri, then thirty-eight years old. "I did not want to see him, and I did not want to hear him. I would have preferred to have gone today to the military parade at the stadium, to see Jews at their strongest and most beautiful. But with an uncanny force, this Morris Fleischmann grabbed hold of us by the scruff of our necks, as if to say, 'Sit still and hear me out.'"[35]

Three weeks into the trial, Gouri was losing his patience with the witnesses. "They were part of the endless, uninterrupted procession that was laying out for us the map of Jewish torment, a map that corresponded precisely to the map of the Third Reich at the height of its power." A young attorney told Gouri, "It's crazy to call such witnesses. Hausner's going to turn us all to stone. He doesn't realize he mustn't do this." Like others born and raised in Israel, these men impatiently awaited the testimony of the rebels. As Gouri wrote, "From time to time, we felt like asking Hausner, 'When are we going to get to the revolt?'"[36]

As the trial progressed, however, Gouri's attitude changed. Five months into the trial he wrote:

If a new leaf has been turned over, it is inside us. We now see things differently.

> We have set aside a Memorial Day for the Holocaust and Heroism and in doing so have drawn a subtle distinction between the two, as if we had juxtaposed them as complementary but different.
>
> The Holocaust was a source of shame to us, like some awful blemish, visible to all. But the heroism we embraced as a shred of pride, giving us the right to hold our heads high . . .
>
> But we must ask forgiveness of the multitudes whom we have judged in our hearts, we who were outside that circle. And we often judged them without asking ourselves what right we had to do so.[37]

In their hearts, he was saying, Israelis had been judging not only functionaries but all survivors. Now they would be forced to look hard at their own attitudes.

The Eichmann trial also meant that Israelis ceased to look upon themselves as divided between those who survived the Holocaust and those who had not been at risk. Rather, a unified sense of victimization spread throughout the diverse Israeli population.

In a gathering of schoolteachers in the southern town of Beersheba, the head of that municipality's education department, Dov Barnea, a survivor, told the educators that to overcome in the Holocaust one had to hunker down and wait: "Each one had to consider and choose the way most appropriate for him [to await salvation]. One of the ways: to serve as a kapo. One mustn't necessarily exclude it! Many of them did good deeds. . . . Which one of us feels entitled to judge them? The *goyim* [non-Jews] who [following the war] tried their collaborators were overjoyed when they had an opportunity to try a Jew. But we must always stand by our compatriots."[38]

But while these changes led many to shift their view of Jewish functionaries, there were nevertheless some, including a number of individuals within the legal system, who continued to demand accountability from those who had served the Nazis.

CHAPTER NINE

ABSOLVING ORDINARY FUNCTIONARIES

IN EARLY 1963, the case of *Attorney General v. Hirsch (Henryk) Barenblat* opened in Tel Aviv District Court. Barenblat, whom a Polish court had in 1948 acquitted of collaboration (discussed in Chapter 1), immigrated to Israel in 1959 and served as the assistant conductor of the Israeli Opera House. This case was one of three that ran either concurrently with the trial of Adolf Eichmann or within a year of his execution on May 31, 1962.[1]

In the opening hearing, Judge Jacob Gavison, who chaired the panel, turned to the defendant and read aloud the first of twelve counts:

> The abovementioned defendant, together with others, on an unknown date in the summer of 1942 . . . helped hand over persecuted people to an enemy administration, by rounding up and arresting dozens of orphaned children from the local orphanage, forcibly dragging them from the building and handing them over to the Gestapo, and helping to transfer them to the train boxcars that transported them to the Nazi death camp.

"Not guilty," Barenblat responded.

Gavison read the second count:

> The abovementioned defendant, in August 1942 . . . while serving as commander of the Jewish police in the town of Bedzin, Poland . . . helped hand over persecuted people to an enemy administration, by assisting the Nazis in assembling the town's Jews in the . . . sports fields . . . so a selection could be conducted and, together with members of the Jewish police, maintaining order during the selection; making sure, together with others, to lead thousands of Jews to concentration areas, to guard them there, so they would not escape, and from there, under guard, to lead approximately 5,000 Jews, including the elderly, women, and children to the death trains.

"Not guilty," Barenblat said.

The lead judge went on to read nine additional counts. With a steady voice, Barenblat repeated "Not guilty" nine more times.

The judge came to the twelfth and final count, an allegation that stood out from all the other charges in this and all the previous trials:

> The abovementioned defendant, in the time of the Nazi rule, in the town of Bedzin, Poland . . . was in 1941 and until early 1942 a member of the Jewish police and, beginning in 1942 . . . was appointed to serve as commander of the Jewish police in Bedzin, a position in an "enemy organization" which he filled until October 1943, in the service of the Jewish Council and the Nazi authorities, one of whose aims was to assist in carrying out actions of an enemy administration against persecuted people.[2]

For the twelfth and final time, the forty-six-year-old Barenblat declared, "Not guilty."[3]

Behind the legalistic language of the twelfth count stood a momentous accusation: that the Jewish Councils and Jewish police served as tools of the Nazi authorities, and that their members were collaborators who aimed to further the Nazis' destructive goals. Proving that the Jewish Councils and Jewish police were "enemy organizations" would mark anyone who had served in them, regardless of his or her intent or actions, as a felon who had collaborated with the Nazi regime.[4]

The last time an Israeli court had deliberated a count based on the third paragraph of the law, entitled "Membership in Enemy Organization," was when Attorney General Gideon Hausner charged Adolf Eichmann with three such counts. The Jerusalem District Court convicted Eichmann on all three counts for his membership in the SS, the SD, and the Gestapo.[5] But in 1963, Hausner, who seems not to have believed in the criminality of the Jewish Councils and Jewish police, was preparing to leave his position as attorney general and was not behind Barenblat's indictment. It was the ambitious, Israeli-born deputy district attorney of Tel Aviv, twenty-nine-year-old David Libai, who prosecuted Barenblat. Libai hoped that, just as Hausner had used the Eichmann trial to litigate against the entire Nazi regime, he would turn the Barenblat trial into a reckoning for the Jewish Councils and Jewish police.[6]

Sixty-year-old witness David Liver took the stand in a trial that for the first time did not pit one camp survivor against another, but in which, instead, rebels accused members of the Jewish police of betraying their communities. To establish the twelfth count, the prosecution called a series of witnesses who, one after the other, equated the Jewish police with the German authorities. Liver, whom members of the Bedzin's underground viewed as their mentor, held in the deepest contempt all who had served in the Jewish police. "For me," he told the court, "it was enough that he [Barenblat] had a police hat on his head to view him in a negative light." The Jewish police "received their orders from the chairman of the Jewish Council, and the chairman of the Jewish Council received his orders from the Gestapo. As a result, they did all that the Germans wanted, and did it in the best possible way." The implication of these words was that the Jewish police were a direct arm of the Germans.[7]

Liver's younger brother Aryeh, who commanded the local underground organization La-krav, concurred with his brother's testimony. "Of course I hated the Jewish Council, and I hate [them] now; there was nothing to like about them," he told the judges. "The job of the Jewish Council was to carry out all the tasks given to them by the Germans." Judge Haim Ehrlich questioned the witness: "What would have happened if all Jews had decided that no one would accept a position in the Jewish Council, or that the Jewish Council would be dismantled?"

"I believe that the Germans would have been unable, on their own, to conduct the annihilation they carried out. It's hard for me to imagine it," Aryeh said, echoing Arendt's assessment that chaos within a leaderless Jewish community would have resulted in fewer casualties. Regardless of the question of whether the Germans could have achieved their goal without Jewish collaboration, he then added a moral argument: "I knew one thing: that we should not do the Germans' work for them."[8]

Had the Jewish Council done any good? defense attorney Aryeh Rosenblum asked, hoping to present a different view of the despised organization.

At first they had assisted the widowed and elderly with food and money, Aryeh Liver answered. The council also managed hospitals.

Even these seemingly positive actions, however, ended up serving the Nazis' annihilation plans. After the Germans ordered the Jewish Council to select deportees to Auschwitz in May and June 1942, clerks turned to the lists of the poor, the elderly, and the sick to choose those to ship out of town. In the underground, Aryeh Liver said, "we knew that any collaboration with the Germans . . . would help in fulfilling their main goal of annihilating the Jews." With these words he expressed the common assumption that all German actions, including the establishment of the Judenräte, were premeditated actions aimed toward carrying out the pre-planned extermination of the Jews, an assumption that later research would dispel.[9]

Judge Ehrlich followed up: "Did the underground have an organized plan in the event [that the council would be dismantled], such as smuggling residents out to the forest, sabotage activities, and so on?"

"There was no organized plan," the witness responded.[10]

"We saw no chance of saving people," Isaac Neuman, another member of the rebel movement, testified. Instead, he explained, the underground chose to prepare for battle, to salvage the nation's honor, a principle that the rebels believed was worth dying for. In Auschwitz, the rebel Haim Waxberg, who had briefly battled the Germans, encountered the head of Bedzin's Jewish Council, Haim Molchadsky. "I arrived here honorably; I was caught after being injured in the leg and head [battling the Germans], while [you] were led here with contempt," he told the man who had deported many of the town's Jews, including Waxberg's three children.[11]

Just after he completed presenting the prosecution's case and before handing the floor over to the defense in mid-July 1963, Libai requested permission to address the court. With permission granted, he announced, "After examining the evidence brought before the court, the prosecution has come to the conclusion that it did not present enough evidence regarding the twelfth count. . . . I ask to clear the defendant of the twelfth count." The first eleven counts of the indictment, he explained, detailed the defendant's criminal actions, and the twelfth count—membership in an enemy organization—added nothing to the previous counts. Rather, "the court is being asked to decide and rule on a painful, fundamental historical dilemma that is still the subject of debate."[12]

The prosecution's request to withdraw the twelfth and final count must have surprised spectators in the courtroom gallery. Exactly four months earlier, on opening day, Libai had told the court that he had "plenty of material" with which to convict the defendant on this count. And indeed, in twelve court sessions, prosecution witnesses repeatedly demonstrated how the Jewish Council and Jewish police had followed Nazi commands and served an enemy organization. Just four weeks earlier, Libai had rejected a defense proposal to withdraw the twelfth count. "The charges stand as they appear in the indictment," Libai had asserted then.[13]

While the prosecution presented its case in public, behind the scenes the newly appointed attorney general, Moshe Ben-Zeev, and the state attorney, Tzvi Bar-Niv, were deliberating whether to remove the twelfth count from the indictment. Convicting Barenblat for membership in an enemy organization could result, as one newspaper pointed out, in "putting thousands of Israeli citizens on trial." Was it wise and morally just, the legal experts asked, to try *all* members of the police and councils? Should not individuals' actions and intentions be considered in deciding whether to indict them? In the end, the ministry's leaders opted not to prosecute all of them as criminals and directed Libai to rescind the charge.[14]

Defense attorney Rosenblum added his voice to the prosecutor's request. The three judges consented and cleared Barenblat of the twelfth count.

* * *

The first witness to take the stand for the defense was Bedzin Jewish policeman #34, Hirsch Barenblat. The defendant, a former music professor, wrote one reporter, "stood by the witness stand with his head held high." At one point during his testimony Libai asked him to cut his answers short, but Barenblat raised his voice and replied, "Excuse me, but I must express all of my thoughts. In this trial I'm the one fighting for my life, not you."[15]

"What did you feel in your heart when you acted as a Jewish Council member in Bedzin, as commander of the Jewish police?" the defense lawyer asked, turning to Barenblat's conscience.

"I felt that the Jewish Council tried to support the Jews, and so too with regard to my own work. If there was anything negative about this work, the most respected Jewish residents of Bedzin would not have sat in the Jewish Council," he said.[16]

The police served the people, he continued. They made sure that no resident stepped by mistake outside the borders of the unwalled ghetto into non-Jewish areas. Crossing the line, even inadvertently, could result in the offender being deported to Auschwitz. In addition, Barenblat testified, the Jewish police ensured the fair distribution of food. And together with the council's housing department, the police resolved housing disputes between residents.[17]

Barenblat went on to list the council's positive actions. Hundreds of refugees from around Poland had arrived in Bedzin and remained in the town without permits, living in constant fear of imminent deportation. But Moniek (Moses) Merin—the extremely controversial head of the Zaglebie regional Jewish Council (in full, the Center of Councils of Elders of the Jewish Community in Eastern Upper Silesia), which oversaw various towns, including Bedzin—"got German consent that these Jews be held in a labor camp in Bedzin," Barenblat said, calling that a "great achievement."[18]

The testimony turned to the time when Barenblat assumed command of the Jewish police. At first he had rejected outright an offer from the head of the local Bedzin Jewish Council, Molchadsky, to head the police force. When Barenblat reported the offer to Herschel Springer, the leader of the Jewish underground, "Springer berated me, [saying I was crazy to turn down] such an opportunity that would have enabled the underground to have a head of police with whom they have connections. He influenced me so much that I went back to Molchadsky and told him that I was willing to take on the job."[19]

Refuting Barenblat's account, Libai pointed out that in fact he had started cooperating with the underground when he learned that the Germans had deported two Jewish Council heads, Molchadsky and Merin, to Auschwitz, long after he had taken command of the police. It was not until mid-1943, after he finally understood that collaborating with the Nazis would not shield him from the fate of all other Jews, that he switched sides from the police to the underground in the hope that this would save him.[20]

"It is not true that I thought that way," the defendant countered. "The truth is that from the beginning of my work [in the Jewish police] I helped the underground."[21]

But all of Barenblat's actions on behalf of the underground took place in 1943, when the fate of the Jews had become clear, and not in 1942, when he had helped the Nazis gather them for deportation, Libai pointed out.

Only "in the middle of 1943 did concrete actions to save Jews begin," the defendant responded. "Up until then there was no real resistance, and [the Jews] went 'as an ox goes to slaughter' [Proverbs 22:7]."

"Unfortunately," one of the judges remarked, "there were also ox leaders."[22]

Barenblat also had to answer for the role he had played in one key event that witnesses repeatedly testified about, the "Great Punkt," which transpired on August 12, 1942. On that day, the council ordered all Bedzin's Jews to assemble on the town's sports field. The reason for the assembly, the heads of the council announced, was so that the Germans could renew the Jews' documentation. As early as 5 A.M., thousands of Jews streamed to the Ha-Koah sports field. All hoped to make a good impression on the Germans.[23]

Once at the sports field, the assembled people lined up in front of three desks, behind which sat Jewish Council workers. With no prior notice, at 10 A.M. armed Gestapo men surrounded the field. Nazi officers took up positions by the desks. They processed the masses, dividing them into three distinct groups—one made up of elderly people and children, another of young men and women, and finally one of middle-aged people. The Nazis tore parent from child, husband from wife. A mother struggled to reunite with her daughter, a husband cried out for his wife, a grandfather huddled over a grandchild. Barenblat's policemen secured the boundaries between the groups, pushing back anyone who attempted to cross the lines. That night, at least 5,000 people—by some estimates as many as 10,000—never returned home. The next morning, the Nazis, accompanied by Jewish policemen, led thousands of Bedzin's Jews to trains destined for Auschwitz.[24]

One of the rebels whose account was brought before the court, Hayka Klinger, described how her friends witnessed Barenblat's men blocking Jews' frantic attempts to cross to safety. In one instance, a Jewish policeman spotted a mother who had crossed the group lines. He caught up with her and tossed her baby carriage in the air. Her infant son fell to the ground and died instantly. "We registered the name of that policeman in our hearts," Klinger wrote in her diary.[25]

Following the Great Punkt, Klinger, whose diary was presented to the court as evidence, had written:

> The hatred of the Jewish police grew. One day, they will make a reckoning with them. . . . [T]he Jewish council's true face in all its "glory" has been exposed. We already knew that they would blindly implement any German order and that they served only as a tool to mislead the Jews; day after day they poison[ed] the Jewish public, deflecting its eyes from its tragic fate, dulling and weakening its power of defiance and revolt. It was essential to open the public's eyes and expose the role of the "community council."[26]

Barenblat, the prosecution held, had commanded his policemen as they blocked Jews from fleeing and crossing group lines. He and his men delivered the Jews to the train boxcars.

Barenblat disputed Libai's charges. He had not harmed anyone on the sports field that day in August 1942. On the contrary, he asserted, he saved many. When night fell, rain began to pour and German guards seeking shelter slipped away. Then Barenblat and his men cut a hole in the fence surrounding the field and directed Jews to escape.[27]

Barenblat also argued that at the time of the Great Punkt he served only as second deputy police commander. The responsibility fell on the shoulders of the commander, Romek Goldmuntz, not on him. Besides, he had not known the Germans planned to murder those deported, he said. He had heard only that they would have a harsh life.[28]

The next day, Barenblat continued testifying about events related to the Great Punkt. Just days before that event, he had traveled thirty kilometers east to the neighboring town of Olkusz, where he observed the deportation of the town's Jews. En route back to Bedzin he took with him a young boy, presenting him as his son, "because there was a danger he might die. . . . When I returned to Bedzin I already knew that [the residents of Olkusz] had been shipped to their deaths. Therefore, when there was an assembly at the Bedzin sports field I already feared that people would be shipped to their deaths."

Libai seized the moment: "After being in Olkusz and seeing what happened to the Jews, and which task had been given to the Jewish policemen, why did you not submit your resignation when you returned to Bedzin and tell Haim Molchadsky that you were unwilling to go on filling this kind of position?"

At that point Barenblat changed his story. Upon returning from Olkusz, he now said, "I did not yet know that the deported were being sent to their deaths. All I knew was that they were being sent to Auschwitz and that it is a concentration camp." Besides, he added on a more personal note, "it was not easy then to resign and become a [simple] policeman. I myself had a family, and I was unfit for difficult labor; and also I saw that in this position [of police officer] I could help many Jews."

"Meaning to help a few and assist in the deportation of thousands?" Libai asked, questioning the defendant's moral choice.

"If it was not possible to save everyone, at least I was able to save a few," Barenblat responded, repeating an argument advanced by the heads of Jewish Councils, including Merin and Molchadsky, who had advocated following German orders.

Libai kept pressing. "At the same time that you saved individuals, you as a policeman, deputy commander, or commander, possibly even in situations where you had no option, assisted the Nazis in assembling thousands of Jews and deporting them to Auschwitz and [you] made their deaths possible."

"No more than [any] other of the Jewish Council members," Barenblat concluded.[29]

After five consecutive days of testimony in which the prosecution and the court grilled him with questions about his choices and decisions, Barenblat stepped down from the witness stand and back into the dock. When the court resumed its hearings after the Jewish New Year, the lead judge ordered all the spectators in the gallery out of the courtroom. For reasons of "state security," the next defense witness would utter his name only behind closed doors. After the war, forty-one-year-old Lt.-Col. Zeev Liron (Londoner), a native of Bedzin, had joined the first combat pilot course of the Israel Air Force and now served as the head of its intelligence.[30]

The audience reentered the court hall, and the thoughtful and contemplative Liron began testifying. He admitted that he had tried to avoid coming to court. Asked to explain, he said, "The defendant was not the main reason for my unwillingness to give a [police] deposition.

Regardless of whether I would have had to testify for the prosecution or the defense, in general I'm against Holocaust-related trials and I am opposed in principle to this trial, because to this very day I cannot understand this complicated subject called 'the Holocaust.'" A court hearing, he seemed to be saying, could result in only one of two verdicts, guilty or innocent—a dichotomy that in no way captured the complexity of life under Nazi rule. In this, his opinion differed from that of many other members of the underground.[31]

Liron himself could not find anything positive to say about the Jewish Council and police: "I can't believe that anyone can express a positive [view] of these organizations." The heads of the council and police were not true leaders of the Jews, but rather "leaders" who served the Germans and obeyed their commands, he explained. But he then added that "in future years a historian may [see it] differently."[32]

Like others, Liron resented the Jewish police and Judenrat, but unlike others, he was able to admit, "Regretfully, I must say that the Jewish Council presented the situation correctly—that in the labor camps one works and one survives—and I say this despite my opposition to the Jewish Council." He himself had heard Merin say that if Jews worked and benefited the Germans, the Nazis would wish to preserve some. "We are in a war," the witness quoted Merin, "[and] the enemy wants to destroy us because we are Jews, some of us earlier and some later. There is only a war of attrition. The question is only how many of us will make it to the end, possibly one hundred thousand, possibly fifty thousand, and possibly thirty thousand." It was as if one's arm was gangrenous, and to save one's life one must amputate the arm, Merin concluded.

Merin's principle was good and acceptable, Liron said, "as long as it did not harm that person himself, his body, or the members of his household." The moment this doctrine touched their own family, the members of the Jewish Council and police opposed deportations.[33]

Liron also recounted one event that demonstrated the problematics of resisting the Nazis: the disproportionate retaliation, with no moral limits, with which they reacted to any measure of Jewish resistance. On August 1, 1943, the Germans caught Liron and put him and Barenblat's wife at the time, Machla, in a freight train that departed Bedzin for Auschwitz, one of the last shipments of Jews from town. A short time into the fifty-kilometer journey, Liron pulled out a concealed handgun. Through the boxcar's narrow window, he shot at an SS man positioned on the train's rooftop. The train stopped. SS guards jumped off and sprayed the locked boxcar with bullets, hitting people within. Many fell wounded, including Machla. "She died before we arrived in Auschwitz," Liron said. Barenblat, who throughout the trial remained largely emotionless, could not hold back his tears.[34]

Another underground member, who testified on behalf of Barenblat despite his own wife's displeasure, also had nothing good to say about the Jewish police as an organization. Kalman Blachash referred to the service of the Jewish police as "idolatry." Asked to assess the defendant, the witness hesitated. "On the one hand, Barenblat was the commander of the Jewish police, and on the other hand, Barenblat was a person with whom I met from time to time. I had a kind of conflict. Now, too, I would not have come to testify, had I not been ordered to come," the witness said. "I can't render any opinion, either positive or negative," he said at last, then fell silent.[35]

The courtroom remained quiet for minutes as the witness struggled for words. "It appears," one journalist wrote, "that a conflict unfolded in the witness's soul between a Jew who had seen with his own eyes the tragedy of local Jews whose fate was decided and a person who had become friendly with the head of the Jewish police."

It was, however, not friendship alone that shaped Blachash's testimony; it was also deep gratitude. Twenty years earlier, Barenblat had warned Blachash that the police were on their way to arrest his younger brother. That information saved his brother's life.

Barenblat broke the silence, shouting out in Polish: "The Moor has done his duty; the Moor may go."

Blachash uttered a few words, then stopped briefly. Then, measuring each word, he said, "I think that someone else in place of Barenblat could have been a much worse police commander. . . . In his role as police commander he did not behave badly."[36]

When the court clerk called out the name of a new witness, Barenblat, who had been following the proceedings attentively, covered his face with his hands. The witness, described in one newspaper as a woman who looked "younger than her real age, and whose face showed the beauty of her youth," also avoided looking at him. Just three years earlier, after twelve years of marriage, Miriam (Kasia) Barenblat had divorced Hirsch Barenblat. Now, just as in his trial in Poland in 1948, she had come to testify in his defense. And now, just as then, the defense hoped she would help acquit him.[37]

During the war, Kasia, who did not look Jewish, had served as a messenger in the underground, smuggling paperwork, money, and people in and out of the ghetto. Before she departed on one of her missions, the heads of the underground told her that if she ran into trouble she should contact Barenblat for help.

In September 1943, Kasia fell into the hands of the Germans. They transferred her to the Sosnowiec Jewish police for deportation to Auschwitz. As she had been advised, she asked her guards to inform Barenblat that she was in custody. The following morning, the Bedzin police commander rolled a bread cart into the Sosnowiec police post. Kasia concealed herself under the bread loaves, and Barenblat pushed the cart out of the police post and rolled it to the Bedzin ghetto. He had saved Kasia's life. Kasia fell in love with her savior and moved in with him. They would marry and have one child.

Barenblat took a risk not only to save her but also to save several other Jews, Kasia testified. At the end of 1943, she and Barenblat lived in a camp with a few dozen laborers whom the Germans had left behind to collect the property of the town's deported Jews. On December 9, Barenblat enticed the camp's German guards to come into his office for a drink. While they were indulging, twenty-eight men and women escaped in small groups. Barenblat and Kasia were the last to leave. They went into hiding in a bunker belonging to the Nowak family, where they stayed for some weeks until their escape to Slovakia.[38]

On the eve of Yom Kippur in 1963, the defense rested its case, and the sides turned to their summations. Libai opened his two-day summation with the question "Who was Mr. Barenblat from Bedzin, what were his actions, and how should we assess them?"[39] In an echo of what Liron and Blachash had said, Libai said, "My view is that no one at that time was completely black or completely white."[40] He went on, "I do not argue that he assisted in the annihilation but only in handing over Jews to an enemy administration. I do not accuse the defendant of wishing to annihilate Jews, or of lending a hand in their annihilation, but only of handing them over."

These words represented a shift in the prosecution's mind-set, matching a similar shift in the public's attitudes toward collaborators that had begun with the Eichmann trial. More and more, functionaries were seen not as an integral part of the murder machine but only as people who had "lent a hand" to it.[41]

"Even those among the Jews who were given various jobs [in the police or council] did not act because of zeal like the Nazis' zeal, but rather because of the same condition [of persecution and duress] under which all the Jews lived," proclaimed Libai, affirming a fundamental difference between the Jewish Councils and police, on one hand, and Nazi organizations, on the other.[42]

Still, Libai continued, Barenblat was responsible for his choices and actions and should pay a price for having handed over Jews. Libai pointed out once more that following his visit to the town of Olkusz, Barenblat had known the fate that awaited Jews selected at the sports field. His duty was to warn them or at least resign his post and refuse to participate in the Great Punkt. The defendant himself had testified that such a resignation was possible.[43] "He assisted the Nazis, and he [bears partial responsibility for] thousands going to their deaths, in a shocking and orderly manner, like sheep to the slaughter," Libai concluded, returning to the point that the leadership of the Jewish communities in Europe shared responsibility for their people's having followed Nazi orders with no resistance.[44]

In his summation, the defense attorney, Rosenblum, told the court that—unlike the defendants in previous kapo trials, who had acted on the basis of illegal commands handed down by the Nazis—Barenblat had acted under the directives of the council, "within the communal framework and its organized life."[45] "Here a Jew is standing trial for his actions within an acknowledged institution [the police] established by the only authorized Jewish body that existed in the town of Bedzin in the time of the Holocaust, the Jewish Council." He reiterated that "under absolutely no circumstances should one decontextualize the defendant's [acts] from the reality of those days but also from the Jewish organization in whose name and on behalf of which he acted as he did."

Convicting Barenblat for his actions would be equivalent to finding the entire Jewish leadership during the Holocaust guilty of collaboration, he asserted.[46]

The Jewish Council of Bedzin, he contended, acted the way many other councils did. "Possibly here or there, there was someone with more control of his morality and heroism, like the head of the Jewish Council in Warsaw who committed suicide. . . . However, the question is, What happened to the Warsaw ghetto because of Czerniakow's behavior? Was anyone saved thanks to it?" Rosenblum asked rhetorically. Barenblat was only human, and one could not expect him to have sacrificed his own life to save others, he argued (although that seems to have been the expectation of some of the Knesset members behind the Nazis and Nazi Collaborators Punishment Law).

Rosenblum was presenting the court with a different perspective on the appropriate life of Jewish communities during the Holocaust, one devoid of national heroism and animating ideology and focused only on preserving organized communal life.[47]

* * *

On February 5, 1964, three and a half months after the conclusion of arguments, the Tel Aviv District Court returned a twenty-four-page verdict. The judges spoke of the Nazis' formation of the Jewish Councils:

> In order to carry out their satanic plan with maximum efficiency, they used methods of deception—spreading lies, using tactics of psychological warfare, and exploiting human weaknesses. [The Germans] forcibly enslaved those Jewish Councils . . . to their will, gradually turning them, through threats, great pressure, extortion, and punishment, on the one hand, and false promises, acts of treachery, and promotion of false hopes, on the other hand, into tools in their hands, making their despicable business easier. They gave them the sort of internal autonomy granted to submissive serfs and turned them into persecutors of their brethren.

Had the twelfth charge remained in the indictment, the three judges hinted, they would have proclaimed Barenblat guilty of membership in an enemy organization. In this statement, they explicitly indicated that in their view the Jewish Council and police were morally deplorable.[48]

The Hirsch Barenblat case as covered in the magazine *Ha-Olem ha-Zeh*. The headline reads: "The Barenblat Trial—The Verdict."

The court dismissed outright the defense's argument that Barenblat had acted under the authority of the council—an argument frequently heard from German defendants after the war, that as soldiers they had to follow their superiors' commands. By his own admission, the judges pointed out, Barenblat could have resigned, and chose not to do so. He had executed his despicable job "for selfish reasons," the judges wrote. "The defendant was not an innocent agent of Molchadsky or of Merin, but rather a sane adult who understood the consequences of his actions, knowing the malicious and wicked purpose of the enemy administration."[49]

Even so, the judges refused to see the defendant as abnormal. They made a point of saying, "We are far from seeing the defendant as a sadistic monster who mistreated Jews because of despicable instincts."[50]

> The defendant appears to us as a person who thought mainly about himself and his family. In the position of commanding the Jewish police he saw, up to a certain point, shelter and protection for himself and his family as well as a job that protected him from harsh physical work and a way to assure himself and members of his family a tolerable standard of living and income in the inferno of those days. . . . Defense witness Hertzberg defined him as "a little man," and indeed he is. And this kind of little person has always existed and will continue to exist among all peoples and in all countries. . . . Indeed, what is astonishing and characteristic of this historical period is that in the atmosphere of [the] extraordinary pressure of those days, moral concepts and values changed and little people, educated and likable people, did not refuse a life-saving anchor even if it meant taking part in the handing over of their fellow Jews to the murderous Nazis. Surely, the defendant did not do this willingly, and one cannot view it otherwise, because among those handed over to an enemy administration were some of his friends and acquaintances. . . . The Israeli legislator who spoke in 1950 in the name of the people did not want to forgive these likable people, normal in normal times, who sinned against the [Jewish] people for selfish reasons in that abnormal time.[51]

Judges Jacob Gavison, Michael Harpazi, and Haim Ehrlich found Barenblat guilty of five offenses. In doing so, they were expressing the judgment that ordinary men, in acting to save their lives, had behaved criminally. The implicit expectation behind the judges' opinion was that in the harsh circumstances of wartime Europe, people should have acted heroically and even sacrificed their lives in order to resist the Nazis' actions. Rejecting the point of view offered by Rosenblum, in which Jewish organized life during the Holocaust was devoid of ideology and heroism, the court sided with the viewpoint of the rebel movement, with its focus on communal heroism.

The five counts on which the court found Barenblat guilty included the handing over of persecuted people, assault, and unlawful compulsory labor. Based on the account of a sole witness, Abraham Fischel, "who gave a vivid description of those sights, as if he still saw them," the court found that Barenblat had dragged fifty or sixty children, eight to thirteen years of age, out of an orphanage's attic and into the hands of the Nazis. "There is no way that we, the judges of Israel, can justify the handing over of defenseless Jewish children to the hands of the wicked Nazis, so as to delay the death of others."[52] They also found him guilty of handing over 5,000 Jews in the Great Punkt.[53] The court sentenced Barenblat to five years' imprisonment.[54]

Outside the courtroom, both the prosecutor and the defense lawyer issued statements to journalists. Such a sentence, Barenblat's lawyer said in a quavering voice, "does not leave him a lot of hope for some kind of a life. In addition, his son will have difficulty in taking pride in a father convicted of such a crime. It is difficult to describe in human words the blow that has descended upon him."

Libai followed, repeating his argument from the summation that he did not view Barenblat as a Nazi. "Surely the monsters were the others, the Nazis," he said, expressing a view barely heard from an Israeli prosecutor prior to the Eichmann trial—and one that Libai himself had not expressed at the opening of the Barenblat trial. "Yet he has been convicted of assisting the Nazi regime on a scale of which no person in Israel has ever before been convicted," as previous convictions had focused on acts of harassment of a few hundred people and not on deportations of many thousands to their deaths.[55]

The day after the verdict, the Mapai party newspaper, *Davar*, published an editorial that expressed ambivalence about the Barenblat trial. "In truth, it may be said that part of the Israeli public treats these trials, in which the Nazis and Nazi Collaborators Punishment Law is invoked, with mixed feelings. After all, to some degree, they too [the defendants] were, in carrying out their crimes victims of the Nazi beast—moral victims who in their weaknesses participated in an unprecedented crime, and a crime against their people." A writer in a different newspaper anticipated that the Barenblat trial would be the last of this type.[56]

Other newspapers, however, praised the verdict and continued to point accusing fingers at collaborators like Barenblat. In a lengthy opinion piece in the anti-establishment newspaper *Ha-Olam Ha-Zeh*, editor Uri Avnery labeled the Barenblat trial "an important trial, to a certain extent more important than the Eichmann trial." The Eichmann trial presented colossal events that human beings could not truly comprehend, whereas the Barenblat trial focused on a tiny subset of events that every person could grasp. "This is its significance, but this is also the danger it involves. It is easy to forget that Barenblat was not alone, that his actions were not the actions of an individual. He was a very small cog in a very large machine."[57]

The larger machine within which Barenblat operated was "the Jewish police, the arm of the Jewish councils, which was a criminal organization," Avnery wrote. Barenblat's trial, he pointed out, confirmed Hannah Arendt's controversial thesis that Eichmann and his handful of assistants could not have executed millions on their own. The cooperation all over Europe of thousands of Jewish accomplices was essential. Had the Jewish leaders refused to cooperate, the result would not have been as horrendous.[58]

The Jewish organizations consisted of normal people, neither sadists nor evil people, Avnery continued. These ordinary men and women joined the Jewish organizations for one of several honorable reasons. "One said, in the Jewish Council I will be able to exert [my] influence. . . . The second said, The annihilation will take place anyway. If so, it is better that the day-to-day handling be in the hands of Jews who can prevent the worst horrors, instead of in the hands of sadistic SS men. A third said, If I do not go, a worse Jew will be found. Therefore, it is better that honest Jews serve in these institutions. A fourth said, I have a family. I must save it. . . ." They all saved some, he wrote. But "most important: without them the annihilation would not have been possible!" A refusal to judge and punish ordinary men and women who collaborated with the Nazis, Avnery seemed to indicate, would be like sweeping the dirt under the rug.[59]

The Supreme Court Clears an Ordinary Man

One day after the district court sentencing, Barenblat's attorney submitted an appeal to the Supreme Court in Jerusalem. Not once had the Supreme Court overturned the conviction of a collaborator, though in several instances it had commuted sentences.[60]

In mid-April 1964, the highest court in the land heard the arguments of both sides, and later that month, the court administrator summoned the two sides back to court. On Friday, May 1, Supreme Court president Yitzhak Olshan announced that the panel had decided to vacate Barenblat's conviction. After serving three months, the former police commander of Bedzin was free to go. That Saturday night, Barenblat sat in a Tel Aviv concert hall and enjoyed pianist Vladimir Ashkenazy's performance with the Israel Philharmonic.[61]

Weeks after announcing its verdict, the court issued its opinions. Haim Cohn, now sitting as a judge, had, more than ten years earlier, advanced the Nazis and Nazi Collaborators Punishment Law in the Knesset, and then as attorney general pursued many of the cases against Jewish collaborators. In this case, however, his lead opinion gave a detailed legal justification for the court's unanimous decision to overturn the district court's ruling.

Regarding the first count in the indictment, which accused Barenblat of rounding up and handing over to the Gestapo dozens of orphaned children, the district court had accepted the testimony of a single witness to the event and convicted Barenblat. In clearing Barenblat, Cohn explained that while for an ordinary charge, a single solid piece of testimony would have sufficed for conviction, that was not sufficient for a horrendous accusation like this. Cohn also questioned the validity of Fischel's testimony. Although he did not doubt its honesty, he surmised that Fischel's "testimony was based on misapprehension, even in good faith; or, that the recollection of the many different horrors that the witness saw with his own eyes or experienced had become blurred and confused in the course of the twenty years that had passed since then."[62] In years to come, Fischel would remain bitter about this dismissal of his testimony, expressing the view that non-survivors would never understand him and his fellow survivors.[63]

In dismissing this charge, Cohn not only returned to the theme of questioning the stability of witnesses and their accounts, which first arose in the Banik trial, but he went further, arguing that with such a grave accusation, one had to weigh the testimony in the context of all the other evidence before the court. None of the two dozen testimonies and none of the survivor memoirs referred to such a harrowing event as handing over helpless children to the Nazis. "It is simply not possible and it is inconceivable that an incident like this could have happened and been committed by one of the Jews, or even by the Jewish police, without the entire community knowing of it and being shocked, and without it being written about in the histories of the times."[64]

Such a statement might be true of an average community in normal times, when stronger members express concern and empathy toward weaker ones. Yet in the abnormal conditions of the Holocaust, it was "normal" practice in Jewish communities to surrender the poor, weak and ill first. Thus, contrary to Cohn's argument, it is *not* inconceivable that the community was not alarmed by the surrendering of the orphaned children. And indeed, in the nearby Sosnowiec community and in other communities, the Jewish police assisted the Nazis in transferring orphaned children into Nazi hands.

Furthermore, in defending himself against the accusation of surrendering the orphaned children, Barenblat had admitted that he was present in mid-1942 when the Nazis seized the children. He claimed that the Germans' arrival meant he had to scratch his early morning attempt to smuggle the children into safe hiding places. However, it seems very unlikely that Barenblat had attempted to save the orphaned children, as in no other instance in this period had he participated in operations that opposed the Nazis. Only later, in mid-1943, when he learned he had no chance of saving himself, did he begin to act against them.

Finally, the testimony of Fischel, then twenty-two, was supported by the recollections of one orphaned child who had been ten years old at the time. Reuven Wekselman, who could not remember how he was saved, testified that "I was caught together with a group of children [in the orphanage] and they [the Jewish police] began to carry us with real force via the stairs. When I got down I saw in front of me the defendant and three policemen."[65] The court, understandably, did not want to rely on an account by someone who had been just ten years old at the time. Yet the combination of similar events taking place in other Jewish communities in the area, Barenblat's own account of being present when the children were taken, and the accounts of two witnesses who testified about the children being pulled out of the orphanage supports a conclusion that the Jewish police, headed by Barenblat, took an active role in this action.[66]

Cohn also disagreed with the district court judges' interpretation of the felony described in the fifth paragraph of the law, regarding "handing over" people. The lower court had concluded that when, during the Great Punkt, Barenblat prevented Jews from crossing from a group destined for deportation to one destined for release, he had delivered up Jews to an enemy administration. "May we say that the prevention of escape from an enemy administration is equivalent to delivery to that administration? I am afraid that in so doing we exceed by far the broadest meaning denoted by the word 'delivery,'" Cohn said, without offering his own distinction between "delivering up" and "preventing escape."[67]

Whereas Cohn's opinion gave the legal justification for clearing Barenblat on the various charges in the indictment, the two remaining justices, Olshan and Landau, dedicated parts of their opinions to addressing a count that was no longer in the indictment: the charge of membership in an enemy organization.

After the war, Olshan wrote, a public debate raged regarding the behavior of the Jewish Council members. Views ranged from seeing the community leadership as "responsible" for the harsh results of the Holocaust to those who "justified" the councils' cold-blooded calculations and their decisions to surrender some with the hope of saving others. All points of view in this debate are legitimate, Olshan held, and the court of history, not the court of law, will determine which is right. It seems he had concluded that issues of collaboration during the Holocaust were too complicated for the court to resolve.

Olshan then harshly criticized the prosecution for its formulation and presentation of the twelfth charge. He acknowledged that the councils and police had "benefited" the German regime, "for otherwise, the Nazis would not have been interested in establishing and maintaining them."[68] Yet "even the most extreme critics have not charged that the Judenrat or the Jewish police aimed to assist the Nazis in the extermination of Jews," Olshan wrote.[69] In leveling against the defendant the accusation not only of having benefited the Nazis in his actions but also of having identified with the Nazis' aim, the prosecution created a "tendentious environment" that distorted witnesses' testimony, he wrote.[70]

Justice Landau, who had headed the panel that judged Eichmann, joined Olshan in issuing a moral statement expressing his disapproval of the charges presented by the prosecution:

> And it is also the bitter truth that "in the atmosphere of [the] extraordinary pressure of those days, moral concepts and values changed." But it would be hypocritical and arrogant on our part—on the part of those who never stood in their place and on the part of those who succeeded in escaping from there, like the prosecution witnesses— to make this truth a cause for criticizing those "little men" who did not rise to the heights of moral supremacy when mercilessly oppressed by a regime whose first aim was to remove the human image from their faces. And we are not permitted to interpret the elements of the special offenses defined in the Nazis and Nazi Collaborators (Punishment) Law, 1950, by some standard of moral conduct only few are capable of attaining. One cannot impute to the legislator an intention to demand a level of conduct that the community cannot sustain, especially as we are dealing with ex post facto laws. Nor should we deceive ourselves in thinking that the oppressive weight of the terrible blow our nation suffered would be lifted were the acts committed there by our persecuted brethren judged according to the standard of pure morality.[71]

The Supreme Court determined that there was no justification for judging normal people who served in the Jewish Councils or police for their choices and actions in an abnormal time. Unlike the minister of justice, Pinchas Rosen, who in early 1950 stated that the Nazis and Nazi Collaborators Punishment Law would allow those from the Jewish Council and Judenrat "to clear those who are innocent," the court now saw those men and women as innocent unless proven otherwise. This would mark the shift into the fourth and final stage of the trials, a point at which the legal authorities viewed functionaries as normal people who could not be expected to have behaved extraordinarily in difficult times, such as Nazi times.[72]

In upholding earlier rulings in the kapo trials, Cohn did, however, point out that some of the functionaries deserved punishment. Felons such as Jacob Honigman and Joseph Paal, he wrote, were "sadistic tyrants" and "monsters." And while in the Barenblat ruling the Supreme Court absolved functionaries who acted out of fear, it would not absolve functionaries who acted out of cruelty. The court had established a new standard by which to try collaborators. While cruelty had been mentioned in previous trials, it had not served as a criterion to determine whether someone should be tried. In an earlier case, deputy Tel Aviv district attorney Dinari had pointed out that "for the court it does not matter if there was sadism or not in determining if the action was criminal."[73] But following Barenblat's verdict the Supreme Court would henceforth require evidence of cruelty if prosecutors wanted to try a Jew for collaboration—a move that had no reference within the law and further minimized the law's applicability.[74]

One Last Conviction of a Cruel Kapo

The clearing of Barenblat did not bring an end to survivors' complaints against Jewish functionaries. Debating what to do with one such complaint, the deputy attorney general, Shmuel Kwart, wrote in the Justice Ministry's internal correspondence that "in light of the result of the Barenblat appeal, I do not believe that an investigation should be begun on a complaint like this that relates to a Jewish policeman's handing over of Jews as part of his job in 1942–1944." Responding to Kwart, Attorney General Moshe Ben-Zeev, who would later issue a directive to all district attorneys stating that "one should not submit a criminal indictment based on the Nazis and Nazi Collaborators Punishment Law, 1950, without prior consent from the attorney general," ordered Kwart to direct the northern district of the police to pursue an investigation of that complaint. He did not see any reason for a wholesale cessation of indictments, and so he would require an investigation before deciding what to do with any particular complaint.[75]

While most of these investigations never led to an indictment, one case did develop into a full-blown trial. On the evening of August 5, 1971, Sonia Punk took a break from watching television in her Rishon Lezion apartment and walked into her kitchen. As she stood by the window looking out, a car pulled up in front of her neighbor's home. Two teenage boys emerged, followed by a red-haired woman, all evidently tourists. "That moment I almost fainted," she said later at the police station. The red-haired woman who stepped out of the car was Lube Gritzmacher (Meskup), who had been Punk's *Lagerältester* in the Landsberg concentration camp in Germany.[76]

Punk not only reported Gritzmacher's arrival to the police but also informed the community of survivors from the Landsberg camp, including her sister, Mary Daniels. Word of the arrival from Germany of "Red-Haired Lube," as she was known by former inmates, spread among the camp's survivors. Two weeks later, the police located Gritzmacher and arrested her. And eight months later, in March 1972, the case of *Attorney General v. Lube Gritzmacher* opened in Tel Aviv District Court.

"Lube Gritzmacher was cruel. She always walked around with a stick in her hand and would hit women and send them out to work despite their being ill," said Ahron Punk, a witness who had observed her actions from the male section of the camp.[77] "She was a bad and cruel woman, and it is hard to find words to describe her behavior toward the Jewish women," testified survivor Berta Schwartz in her police deposition. She would "strike the arms and legs without any consideration for the cries or screams of the woman. She knew how to hurt sensitive parts of the body." All of this took place, a few witnesses stated, when no Germans were around. In morning roll call, "she would pass between the lines of women, striking on the right and on the left, and abusing women with no reason. Her cruelty had no bounds," Schwartz continued. "The women interned in Landsberg camp were in her hands and she could let them live or kill them."[78]

Once Lube Gritzmacher entered the camp laundry room where inmates were washing the Germans' clothes and noticed that Mary Daniels was washing her own clothes with the soap meant for the Germans' laundry. "You shall not use our German soap for your needs," she screamed at Daniels. "I will kill you like a dog." She grabbed a metal rod to hit Daniels, who tried to block the blow. Daniels's left middle finger was broken by the impact.[79]

Some survivors showed interest not only in Red-Haired Lube but also in her husband, Itzik Gritzmacher. In the Tel Aviv courtroom, survivor Aryeh Segalson, who would become a district judge in the same courthouse, testified that Itizk Gritzmacher "was a kapo in the concentration camp. He was the terror and horror of the men's camp. And the defendant was his lover. They conducted orgies."[80]

In 1945, as mentioned in Chapter 1, Itzik Gritzmacher was sitting at the head of a table at a memorial service arranged by the American forces at a Bad Tölz movie theater. Halfway through the ceremony, one survivor called out, "Let us take revenge on the Jewish SS men among us!" and dozens of skeletal survivors charged at him and his fellow kapos. To give him enough time to escape, Itzik Gritzmacher's lover, Lube, tried to block the crowd.[81] A year later, in 1946, Itzik Gritzmacher was spotted in France and taken into custody. He was tried in the town of Rastatt, Germany. The court sentenced him to four years' imprisonment, and Lube, who had given birth to a boy, was left to care for the baby on her own. Upon her husband's release from prison, the family settled in a small village in Beckingen, Saarland, Germany, and opened a coffee shop.[82]

The Israeli court refused to accept Lube Gritzmacher's refutation of the accusations and her contention that the accusations were a "libel" concocted by the women from one Lithuanian city, or that survivors wanted to take revenge on her for her husband's behavior or for her having chosen to reside in Germany, where other accused collaborators like Barenblat also ended up settling. Secretly, representatives of the German embassy in Tel Aviv attempted to assist the defense by collecting archival material to dispute the prosecution witnesses' accounts.[83]

At the culmination of Gritzmacher's trial in September 1972, judges Yitzhak Raveh, Haim Deborin, and Shmuel Kwart convicted her on two counts of assault, including one for breaking Daniels's finger. The panel sentenced her to three months' imprisonment. In their ruling, the judges stated that "when we speak of defendants who were themselves persecuted . . . while we do take this issue into account, we cannot, on the other hand, ignore another consideration, which is that these defendants used their special status in the camp in which they served to treat their brethren and others cruelly." The status of a persecuted person, the court made clear, did not give that victim impunity to act in a "cruel" and "sadistic" manner. With this case, the trials against Jewish functionaries in Israel came to an end.[84]

EPILOGUE

In the summer of 2013 I visited Shulamit Valenstein, who had served for eighteen years as a prosecutor and for twenty years as a judge in Tel Aviv. Over tea and cookies we schmoozed about family and news until I finally turned the conversation to the subject I had come about: her role in the kapo trials. Upon hearing about my interest, this lucid and charming eighty-eight-year-old looked at me in surprise. She had had no role in those trials, she told me, either as a prosecutor or as a judge; in fact, she had never even heard of them.

I pulled from my files a copy of the Julius Siegel indictment and handed it to her. Seeing her signature on the page, she now believed me that she had indeed prosecuted four alleged collaborators, all of whom the courts convicted and sentenced to jail time.[1]

It was not only Valenstein who had obliterated from personal memory her role in the kapo trials. In his autobiography, former Knesset member Yohanan Bader writes briefly about the legislative process leading up to passage of the Nazis and Nazi Collaborators Punishment Law in 1950: "I should confess that when we worked on the bill we believed that it had only symbolic value. However, it eventually served as a basis for the Eichmann trial."[2] Bader appears to have forgotten the law's original rationale, which was to serve as a basis for trying Jewish functionaries. More important, he put out of his mind the entire set of trials that followed this legislation.

In his autobiography, former attorney general and justice Haim Cohn writes that he and Justice Minister Rosen agreed that "in a Jewish state it would not suffice to have a general law pertaining to genocide. There is a need for a special law that authorizes courts in the State of Israel to have Nazi criminals tried and punished." Not only does Cohn neglect to mention the original intent of the law, but he barely refers to the more than thirty trials conducted under his stewardship.[3]

How is it that a prosecutor in the kapo trials completely forgot her role in them? How is it that a legislator and a jurist present a misleading account of the legislation's goal and impact? The answer, I believe, is more complex than memory failure.

For decades, the Israel State Archives have limited access to all documents related to these trials. Only recently, and thanks in part to the efforts of researchers, has it permitted access to the court files. As I write these words, the sixty-year-old police files are undergoing a lengthy process of declassification.

Furthermore, Yad Vashem Martyrs and Heroes Remembrance Authority, the official custodian of Holocaust memory in Israel, does not refer to the kapo trials even once in its 4,200-square-meter permanent exhibition. As of 2019, the Yad Vashem archive did not show on its public computers even one of the documents it holds pertaining to the kapo trials. In short, Israeli institutions have been suppressing the memory of the kapo trials for fear of tainting the image of the victims.

A factor in this suppression of memory is "I was not there, so I cannot judge": the notion that no one who did not live through those times and experiences could morally judge Holocaust survivors for their actions. As we have seen, the Eichmann trial and the controversy over Hannah Arendt's overarching criticism of the Judenräte led some intellectuals, most notably Gershom Scholem, to adopt this approach. With a few exceptions, a taboo developed with regard to discussing instances in which Jews acted harshly during the Holocaust.[4]

This taboo on discussing the questionable behavior of Jewish functionaries in the camps enabled the rise of a strong identification with the victims among Israelis. Identification with victims and their plight went beyond empathy for parents or grandparents and resulted in Israelis as a group viewing themselves as victims. The 1973 Yom Kippur War, in which the armies of Egypt and Syria launched a surprise attack against Israel, caused many to believe the state was on the brink of extinction and that only Israel's victory saved them from a second holocaust. The rise to power of Menachem Begin in 1977, a prime minister who viewed the Holocaust as a key lesson about Jewish isolation in the world, further advanced the centrality of the Holocaust in

Israeli society's identity. The citizens of the most powerful state in the Middle East came to identify themselves as living constantly on the brink.

In the opening ceremony on Holocaust Memorial Day in 1984, Prime Minister Yitzhak Shamir described the Jewish state as an embodiment of survivors:

> The wounds are still open, the severed organs have not yet regenerated. Day in and day out we feel the absence of the six million, our brethren and sisters, who were not fortunate enough to come with us to the homeland. Our brothers and sisters, fathers and mothers, massacred and burnt, accompanied and accompany us in our daily existence in all fields of life and development. They were with us in all our wars, in all our struggles, from the past to this very day. Only in the unseen presence of the six million can one explain the establishment of the state and its continuous existence in face of the world nations and warmongers who spit venom and hatred towards us.[5]

In Shamir's view, the spirit of the dead inspires the nation in its continuous battles, just as survivors have an everyday presence in Israeli life. The Holocaust, he explained in another speech, is an event from which "we have not recovered and there is no chance we ever will." As a nation persecuted for generations, he explained, victimization defines Jews' psyche.[6]

With this shift of perspective, Israelis no longer saw the six million martyrs as those "who went like sheep to the slaughter." As early as 1970, the National History Curriculum adopted a new definition of victims, describing them all as resisters, as people who made "an effort to maintain a human visage and Jewish uniqueness." The Israeli educational establishment could not tolerate the portrayal of Jews as weak, and instead offered an apologetic approach that treated all victims as resisters and heroes. Educators blended into a single group rebels who held rifles and victims who prayed, the former exhibiting physical heroism, the latter spiritual resistance.

One prism through which members of Israel's establishment viewed the Holocaust was that of national victory or defeat. As one senior IDF officer put it, "I do not want to say that we won when we lost there six million, but for sure they [the Germans] did not win." With these words, this officer, who despite being born after the war defined himself as "a survivor of Auschwitz," framed the Holocaust as a battle between Germany and the Jewish state.[7]

This identification of Israelis as continuous victims was a far cry from the attitude at the inception of Zionism, when leaders disparaged Jewish sacrifices. Following the 1903 Kishinev pogrom, the poet Hayim Nahman Bialik wrote "The City of Slaughter," in which he decried the fate of the Jewish people:

> And I am sorry for you, my children, and my heart goes out to you;
> your sacrifices are sacrificed for nothing—and neither you nor I
>   know
> why you died,
> nor who nor what for,
> and there's no point to your deaths as there was no point to your
>   lives.[8]

Bialik, like many other leaders of the era, hoped that Zionism would bring with it an alteration in the course of Jewish history. No longer would the Jews be a people who lived at the mercy of others, a group acted upon; rather, they would take their fate into their own hands and form their own history.[9]

Israelis' perception of themselves as victims also represented a partial return to their Jewish ancestral roots. According to this view, the Holocaust was the latest event in the continuous persecution of Jews, as expressed in the Passover night epigraph "In every generation, they [the non-Jews] rise up to destroy us." Many add to this epigraph, "In every generation, we must see ourselves as if we have survived the Holocaust and founded this country." Combining these two sayings empowered the new "commandment" of remembering the Holocaust with both a religious imperative and a national one.[10]

Some opposed this embrace of victimization as the raison d'être of Israeli society. President Chaim Herzog expressed reservations about the message communicated to the younger generation of Israelis:

> One must not kneel beneath this burden of remembrance. We must not cast this heavy shadow over the future of the State of Israel. We must carry this burden as a searing package; to pass it on as a legacy

and to teach the youth generation the chapters of that period of the Holocaust and its lessons. Not to encumber them with the dark cloud which encumbered us, but to allow them, as free men and women, to survey the vista of a bright panorama of hope, and a future of peace.[11]

Others held that memory of the Holocaust not only blocked the youth's vision but in fact harmed them. In 1988, Holocaust survivor and history of science professor Yehudah Elkana decried the perpetuation of the belief that "we are the eternal victim." In his view, continuously teaching the Holocaust had an immediate negative result: "I have become more and more convinced that the deepest political and social factor that motivates much of Israeli society in its relations with the Palestinians is not personal frustration, but rather a profound existential 'Angst' fed by a particular interpretation of the lessons of the Holocaust and the readiness to believe that the whole world is against us." Elkana thought that Israelis' definition of themselves as victims allowed them to hold a self-righteous view. He believed Israelis "need to forget the Holocaust" and must let go of "the domination of the historical 'remember!' over our lives." The past had come not only to dominate Israeli identity but also to shape its political and social present and future. Identifying oneself as a victim justified questionable behaviors, especially when it came to the occupation of Palestinian territory.[12]

But the 1980s calls of Herzog and Elkana went unheeded, and the Holocaust and the view of the Jewish nation as an eternal victim continued to dominate the landscape. What's more, Israelis felt that the Holocaust gave them the right to cross boundaries. Just before noon on September 4, 2003, three Israeli F-15 fighter jets took off from Radom Military Air Base and flew 200 kilometers southwest over the lush green Polish landscape, planning a symbolic flight over the Auschwitz death camp. Polish air controllers notified the pilots that they would be permitted to go no lower than 14,000 feet, high enough that the planes would be difficult to see from the ground. Prior to takeoff, however, a senior commander in the Israeli air force, Major General Eliezer Shkedi, told the lead pilot, Brigadier General Amir Eshel, that "the last time the Poles told us what to do was sixty years ago. Do whatever you need to do." The implication was that the status of victimhood permitted the Israeli Air Force to carry out that flight over Auschwitz however it saw fit.

Eshel and the other two pilots, all descendants of Holocaust survivors, brought their fighter jets down to 1,200 feet, flying just above the camp's red brick gate, train rails, crematorium, and barracks. As the roar of the engines reverberated over Auschwitz, Eshel read out from his cockpit lines that echoed through loudspeakers to the two hundred Israeli officers and soldiers standing below in formation: "We pilots of the Israel Air Force, flying in the skies above the camp of horrors, arose from the ashes of the millions of victims and shoulder their silent cries, salute their courage, and promise to be the shield of the Jewish people and its nation Israel."[13] In a nutshell, these words positioned the pilots of one of the most powerful air forces in the world as an incarnation of Auschwitz's victims, co-opting the hopes and bravery of the millions of dead in the service of defending the Jewish state. Israeli pilots, considered by many as the pinnacle of Israeli society, declared that their power emanated from the human remains in the death camps.

Such a powerful identification with Holocaust fatalities as heroes and the use of them to define Israel does not allow room to study the stories of how one victim harassed or harmed another. The common adoration of victims as heroes disturbed Primo Levi. In Levi's view, using the term "hero" was "illusionary," "misleading," and "untrue," a rhetoric that did not allow the exposure of the moral gray zone as it relates to the Holocaust.[14] In a society that portrays all victims as heroes, the kapo trials and the moral dilemmas they spawned remain to this day outside the public memory of the Holocaust. Unlike the public controversy about the Judenräte that resulted from Arendt's statements, the kapo trials and the people at the center of them are hidden from public sight.

The absence of a debate around the role of Jewish functionaries in camps enabled the development of a streak of sentimental victimhood. A 1980s high school textbook wrote of the Nazis' attempts to sow discord among camp inmates, "According to many survivors' accounts, the Nazis did not succeed in that plot. Human solidarity, friendship, political views, religious faith, the silent prayer of the heart—all these had to go underground, but they did not cease to operate, to beat in the hearts of the prisoners, and to exist within the camp regime."[15]

Textbooks like this presented dichotomous portrayals of Jews and Germans on opposite ends of a continuum, with an abyss in between. Speaking of the victims and perpetrators, Primo Levi said, "To divide into black and white means not to know human nature. It's a mistake, it is useful only for celebrations."[16] These schoolbooks fail to present the complex position and life of victims and encourage a simplistic, ahistorical view of victimhood. Furthermore, they rob the victims of their humanity, of their weaknesses and virtues.

Levi offered a different perspective:

> The network of human relationships inside the Lagers was not simple: it could not be reduced to two blocs of victims and persecutors. Anyone who today reads (or writes) the history of the Lager reveals the tendency, indeed the need, to separate evil from good, to be able to take sides, to emulate Christ's gesture on Judgment Day: here the righteous, over there the reprobates. . . .
>
> From many signs it would seem the time has come to explore the space which separates (and not only in Nazi Lagers) the victims from the persecutors. . . . Only a schematic rhetoric can claim that that space is empty: it never is, it is studded with obscene or pathetic figures (sometimes they possess both qualities simultaneously) whom it is indispensable to know if we want to know the human species, if we want to know how to defend our souls when a similar test should once more loom before us, or even if we only want to understand what takes place in a big industrial factory.[17]

As the cases of Jewish functionaries demonstrate, the camps contained not only victims and perpetrators but also those who lived in the gray zone. Considering these figures has the potential to complicate our understanding of our existence. While we cannot judge them, we must deliberate on their dilemmas in order to deepen our own humanity.

NOTES

ABBREVIATIONS

Archiv MZV	Czech Ministry of Foreign Affairs Archive, Prague
BGA	Ben-Gurion Archives, Ben-Gurion University of the Negev
CZA	Central Zionist Archives, Jerusalem
ISA	Israel State Archives, Jerusalem
MFA	Israel Ministry of Foreign Affairs
RG	Record Group
UNRRA	United Nations Relief and Rehabilitation Administration
YVA	Yad Vashem Archives, Jerusalem
ZIH	Jewish Historical Institute, Warsaw, Poland

INTRODUCTION

1. Verdict, *Attorney General v. Yehezkel Jungster, Piske Din*, vol. 5 (1951–1952), criminal case 9 / 51, 165. All translations in the book are by the author unless otherwise indicated.

2. Verdict, *Attorney General v. Yehezkel Jungster, Piske Din*, vol. 5 (1951–1952), criminal case 9 / 51, 157.

3. The Nazis and Nazi Collaborators Punishment Law, 5710-1950, passed Aug. 1, 1950, provided the basis for these charges. The text of the law in English is at http://www.mfa.gov.il/mfa/mfa-archive/1950-1959/pages/nazis%20and%20nazi%20collaborators%20-punishment-%20law-%20571.aspx. As I point out in a later endnote, this translation is not always accurate.

4. Cited in Yechiam Weitz, *The Man Who Was Murdered Twice: The Life, Trial and Death of Israel Kastner* (Jerusalem: Yad Vashem, 2011), 219; cited in Shalom Rosenfeld, *Tik Pelili 124/ 53: Mishpat Gruenwald Kastner* (Tel Aviv: Karni, 1955), 280.

5. Indictment, Mar. 10, 1963, *Attorney General v. Hirsch Barenblat*, ISA, RG/32/LAW/15/63, para. 12.

6. Verdict, *Hirsch Barenblat v. Attorney General, Piske Din*, vol. 18 (2) (1964), criminal case 77 / 64, pp. 105–106.

7. Verdict, *Hirsch Barenblat v. Attorney General, Piske Din*, vol. 18 (2) (1964), criminal case 77 / 64, pp. 90–91.

8. *Attorney General v. Lube Gritzmacher (Meskup)*, ISA, RG/32/LAW/116/71.

9. Testimony of Avraham Fischel, July 4, 1963, *Attorney General v. Hirsch Barenblat*, ISA, RG / 32 / LAW / 15 / 63, pp. 79–80.

10. Testimony of Malka Goldstein, Nov. 27, 1951, *Attorney General v. Elsa Trenk*, ISA, RG / 32 / LAW / 2 / 52, p. 35.

11. Primo Levi, "The Gray Zone," in *The Drowned and the Saved*, trans. Raymond Rosenthal (New York: Vintage, 1989), 44–45, 49, 59. In coining the term

"choiceless choices," Lawrence Langer seems to take a stronger view than Levi about victims' inability to act in a moral manner in what he defined as a nonmoral world. See Langer's *Versions of Survival* (Albany: State University of New York Press, 1982), 72–75.

12. Adam Brown, *Judging "Privileged" Jews: Holocaust Ethics, Representation, and the "Grey Zone"* (New York: Berghahn, 2013), 15–16. In "The Gray Zone," Levi is writing of the Sonderkommando (units consisting of prisoners forced to work in the gas chambers and crematoriums). See Levi, "Gray Zone," 59–60. See also René Wolf, "Judgement in the Grey Zone: The Third Auschwitz *(Kapo)* Trial in Frankfurt 1968," *Journal of Genocide Research* 9, no. 4 (2007): 617–635; Susan Pentlin, "Holocaust Victims of Privilege," in *Problems Unique to the Holocaust*, ed. Harry James Cargas (Lexington: University Press of Kentucky, 1999), 26, 39; Sander H. Lee, "Primo Levi's Gray Zone: Implications for Post-Holocaust Ethics," *Holocaust and Genocide Studies* 30, no. 2 (2016): 277–278, 280.

13. Levi, "Gray Zone," 40, 43, 46, 47; Brown, *Judging "Privileged" Jews*, 48.

14. Giuseppe Grassano, "A Conversation with Primo Levi (1979)," in Primo Levi, *The Voice of Memory: Interviews, 1961–1987*, ed. Marco Belpoliti and Robert Gordon (New York: New Press, 2001), 132. Although in this interview Levi is referring to German political prisoners as an example of those who need to be judged, his statement is general, and there is no reason to believe that he excludes Jewish functionaries from this requirement of judgment. In "The Gray Zone," he explicitly says of an act of pity by a specific SS man that "it is enough . . . to place him too, although at its extreme boundary, within the gray band" ("Gray Zone," 58). See also Brown, *Judging "Privileged" Jews*, 58.

15. The Nazis and Nazi Collaborators Punishment Law; see https://mfa.gov.il /mfa/mfa-archive/1950-1959/pages/nazis%20and%20nazi%20collaborators%20-punishment-%20law-%20571.aspx (last accessed Apr. 23, 2019).

16. Knesset member Mordechai Nurock, *Divrei ha-Knesset*, Nov. 29, 1949, 187; *Maariv*, June 22, 1949.

17. This preference for social over criminal judgment draws from the view of Lawrence Douglas, who argues that atrocity trials should be viewed as didactic trials. See Douglas, "Crimes of Atrocity, the Problem of Punishment and the Situ of Law," in *Propaganda, War Crimes Trials and International Law: From Speaker's Corner to War Crimes*, ed. Predrag Dojčinović (New York: Routledge, 2012), 281–283.

I. FROM REVENGE TO RETRIBUTION IN POST-NAZI EUROPE

1. *Herut*, Aug. 30, 1955; Dov Shilanski, *Hashekhah le-or ha-yom: ma'avako shel tsair Tsiyoni be-Lita uva-mahanot* (Jerusalem: Yad Vashem, 2006), 480–482; Aryeh Segalson, *Be-Lev ha-ofel: Kilyonah shel Kovnah ha-Yehudit—Mabat mi-bifnim* (Jerusalem: Yad Vashem 2003), 502–504.

2. Tuvia Friling, *A Jewish Kapo in Auschwitz: History, Memory and the Politics of Survival*, trans. Haim Watzman (Boston: Brandeis University Press, 2014), 69.

3. Executive Committee of the Labor Union, Sept. 5, 1945, BGA, pp. 28–29. One witness spoke of having seen two policemen being lynched after liberation

in the Sudetenland. See testimony of Yerachmiel Barkai, May 25, 1953, *Attorney General v. Tsvi Shapshevsky*, ISA, RG/32/LAW/486/52, p. 12.

4. Police deposition of Abraham Fried, May 21, 1950, in *Attorney General v. Abraham Fried*, ISA, RG/32/LAW/8/51.

5. See Laura Jockusch and Gabriel N. Finder, "Introduction: Revenge, Retribution and Reconciliation in the Postwar Jewish World," in *Jewish Honor Courts: Revenge, Retribution and Reconciliation in Europe and Israel after the Holocaust*, ed. Laura Jockusch and Gabriel N. Finder (Detroit: Wayne State University Press, 2015), 11–12.

6. Testimony of Mendel Kleider, *Attorney General v. Jacob Honigman*, Nov. 8, 1950, ISA, RG/31/LAW/3/51, pp. 9–11. See also July 11, 1951, testimony of Mendel Kleider, who testified about the listing of the "sadistic kapos," including Rosenzweig, and conducting a "trial" of these kapos; ibid., p. 89.

7. Calel Perechodnik, *Am I a Murderer? Testament of a Jewish Ghetto Policeman* (Boulder, CO: Westview, 1996), 46, 26. For another story of a policeman who felt regret and asked a rebel leader to kill him, see Yitzhak (Antek) Zuckerman, *A Surplus of Memory: Chronicle of the Warsaw Ghetto Uprising* (Berkeley: University of California Press, 1993), 637.

8. Stanislaw Adler, *In the Warsaw Ghetto: The Memoirs of Stanislaw Adler* (Jerusalem: Yad Vashem, 1982), 212. See also Susan L. Pentlin, "Holocaust Victims of Privilege," in *Problems Unique to the Holocaust*, ed. Harry James Cargas (Lexington: University Press of Kentucky, 1999), 27.

9. Zuckerman, *A Surplus of Memory*, 636–637.

10. Jewish Agency Management Meeting, Feb. 24, 1946, BGA. For another account of this event, see the account of Ruth Eliav, File 165, Dec. 4, 1978, pp. 57–58, BGA.

11. David Ben-Gurion, "Zav Tel Hai," *Ba-Marakhah* 3 (1948): 119–121.

12. Hanokh Patishi, *Mahteret be-madim: ha-"Haganah" veha-hayalim ha-Erets-Yiśre'elim be-tsava ha-Briti 1939–1946* (Tel Aviv: Misrad ha-bitahon-hotsa'ah le-or, Universitat Hefah, 2006). For details about a different revenge operation headed by Abba Kovner, see Dina Porat, *Me-ever le-Gashmi: parashat Hayav shel Aba Kovner* (Tel Aviv: Am Oved, 2000), 227–247.

13. For the most detailed account of the event, see testimony of Abu (Avinoam) Horwitz, Dec. 14, 1955, Haganah Archives, 98.4, p. 19.

14. Testimony of Yochanan Zeid, Dec. 14, 1955, Haganah Archives, 98.4, p. 20.

15. Interview with Mordecai Surkis, Feb. 1, 1978, Yad Tabenkin Archives, Ramat Efal, 36.1, file 8, p. 6. Years later, Meir Davidson questioned the legitimacy of these actions: "We did not know legal procedures, rules of evidence, and rules of testimony. I think we crossed lines" (Mar. 14, 1967, Haganah Archives, 102.2, p. 44). Yisrael Libratovsky took an apologetic view and at one point even denied his actions. See Dec. 14, 1955, Haganah Archives, 98.4, pp. 19–20; 1966, 93.7, p. 25.

16. One of the two Jewish Brigade soldiers who observed this "trial" and wrote a letter home about it was Uri Sharfman. See Uri Sharfman, *Im nahagim Ivriyim be-milhemet ha-'olam ha-sheniyah* (Kefar Tavor: Gal-On, 2006), 84.

17. Davidson, *Vilah Pezanah* (Tel Aviv: Ma'arakhot, 1969), 89.

18. Laura Jockusch, "Rehabilitating the Past? Jewish Honor-Courts in Allied Occupied Germany," in *Jewish Honor Courts: Revenge, Retribution and Reconciliation in Europe and Israel after the Holocaust,* ed. Laura Jockusch and Gabriel N. Finder (Detroit: Wayne State University Press, 2015), 68.

19. Abraham S. Hyman, *The Undefeated* (Jerusalem: Gefen, 1993), 163–164.

20. For more on the difference between revenge and retribution, see Jockusch and Finder, "Introduction," 22–23 n. 4; Jockusch, "Rehabilitating the Past?," 69–70.

21. Abraham Hyman, Jan. 27, 1947, p. 15, Rabbi Philip Bernstein Collection, Rare Books, Special Collections and Preservation, University of Rochester, Rochester, NY; Hyman, *Undefeated,* 163–164. For another assessment about the quality of judgment in these courts in general, see the view of Mrs. E. Robertson, who writes on March 24, 1947: "Its proceedings were conducted with great dignity and impartiality and it enjoyed the full confidence of the Camp Director and of the displaced persons." UNRRA, United Nations Archives and Records Management Section, Displaced Persons—General—Camp Courts, S-0437-0018-09.

22. Cited in Jockusch, "Rehabilitating the Past?," 61–62.

23. Jockusch, "Rehabilitating the Past?," 68–72.

24. Jockusch, "Rehabilitating the Past?," 69–72; Margarete Myers-Feinstein, *Holocaust Survivors in Post-War Germany, 1945–1947* (Cambridge, UK: Cambridge University Press, 2010), 243–244; Angelika Königseder and Juliane Wetzel, *Waiting for Hope: Jewish Displaced Persons in Post–World War II Germany,* trans. John A. Broadwin (Evanston, IL: Northwestern University Press, 2001), 136; Hyman, *Undefeated,* 161; Rivka Brot, "Ben kehilah lemedinah: mishpathem shel meshatfe-peulah im ha-Natsim," Ph.D. diss., Tel Aviv University, 2015, 113–114.

    For references to imprisonment resulting from DP camp honor courts, see, for example, UNRRA, United Nations Archives and Records Management Section, S-0425-0019-10 Legal Matters—Military Government Courts and S-0437-0018-09, Displaced Persons—General—Camp Courts. Cases of imprisonment were rare, as they exceeded the authority given to the honor courts by the military government, which (as I detail later) came to question even the mere existence of the honor courts themselves. For an example of holding a suspect in detention, either for fear that he would attempt to influence witnesses' testimonies or for fear of his safety, see the case of Julius Siegel, July 10, 1946, court transcript, CZA, S5 / 10.099, p. 1; David Engel, "Why Punish Collaborators?," in *Jewish Honor Courts: Revenge, Retribution and Reconciliation in Europe and Israel after the Holocaust,* ed. Laura Jockusch and Gabriel N. Finder (Detroit: Wayne State University Press, 2015), 29–48.

25. Mrs. E. Robertson, Director of Area Team 1062, to Mr. R. W. Collins, Mar. 24, 1947, UNRRA, S-0437-0018-09, Displaced Persons—General—Camp Courts.

26. Team Letter no. 152, A. T. Berney-Ficklin, District Director of UNRRA District Office Stuttgart, Oct. 29, 1945, UNRRA, S-0425-0019-10, Legal Matters—Military Government Courts. In one instance, a Munich honor court transferred the case of a Jewish police member from Warsaw to an

American military court; however, the outcome remains unknown. Jock-usch, "Rehabilitating the Past?," 73.

27. The exact number of trials remains unclear. Jockusch cites the head of the American Jewish Distribution Committee in the American Zone, Leon Schwartz, who speaks of 397 cases. Jockusch, however, found a paper trail of many fewer cases and estimates the number to be between 100 and 150. Jockusch, "Rehabilitating the Past?," 56, 80 n. 34. In Berlin sixty-five such trials took place; ibid., 55.

28. Gabriel N. Finder and Alexander V. Prusin, "Jewish Collaborators on Trial in Poland," in *Polin: Studies in Polish Jewry*, ed. Gabriel N. Finder, Natalia Aleksiun, Antony Polonsky, and Jan Schwarz (Oxford, UK: Littman Library of Jewish Civilization, 2008), 20:128–129; David Engel, "Who Is a Collaborator? The Trials of Michal Weichert," in *The Jews in Poland*, ed. Slawomir Kapralski (Krakow: Jagiellonian University, 1999), 2:359.

29. Finder and Prusin, "Jewish Collaborators," 135–136; Engel, "Who Is a Collaborator?," 339–370.

30. Engel, "Who Is a Collaborator?," 358–359.

31. Engel, "Who Is a Collaborator?," 339–340.

32. Cited in Finder and Prusin, "Jewish Collaborators," 137.

33. Gabriel N. Finder, "The Trial of Shesl Rotholc and the Politics of Retribution in the Aftermath of the Holocaust," *Gal-ed—On the History and Culture of Polish Jewry* 20 (2006): 72–73; Ewa Kozminska-Frejlak, "'I'm Going to the Oven Because I Wouldn't Give Myself to Him': The Role of Gender in the Polish Jewish Civic Court," in *Jewish Honor Courts: Revenge, Retribution and Reconciliation in Europe and Israel after the Holocaust*, ed. Laura Jockusch and Gabriel N. Finder (Detroit: Wayne State University Press, 2015), 254, 264, 277 n. 139.

34. Engel, "Who Is a Collaborator?," 367–370.

35. Engel, "Who Is a Collaborator?," 367–370.

36. For a document related to Henryk (Hirsch) Barenblat's stay in Czechoslovakia, see the Czech National Archives, Policejni reditelstvi Praha, file B 411/8 and file B 144/9.

37. Verdict of District Court of Sosnowiec, *Attorney General v. Henryk Barenblat*, ISA, RG 32/LAW/15/63 N/9.

38. Testimony of Henryk Barenblat, Jan. 29, 1948, ZIH, file of Henryk Barenblat, 313/5.

39. Testimony of Symcha Zlotowski and of Nathan Piorun, Jan. 29, 1948, ZIH, file of Henryk Barenbalt, 313/5.

40. Testimony of Isaac Fylenda, Jan. 29, 1948, ZIH, file of Henryk Barenblat, 313/5.

41. Testimony of David Klajman and Rozka Felczer, Jan. 29, 1948, ZIH, file of Henryk Barenblat, 313/5.

42. Testimony of Maria (Kasia) Szancer, Jan. 29, 1948, ZIH, file of Henryk Barenblat 313/5.

43. Verdict of District Court of Sosnowiec, no date available, *Attorney General v. Henryk Barenblat*, ISA, RG/32/LAW/15/63 N/9.

44. Shane Darcy, *Collective Responsibility and Accountability under International Law* (Ardsley, NY: Transnational, 2007), 257, 271–278.

45. Verdict of District Court of Sosnowiec, no date available, *Attorney General v. Henryk Barenblat*, ISA, RG / 32 / LAW/15/63 N / 9.

46. Indictment of Henryk Barenblat, May 16, 1949, ZIH, file of Henryk Barenblat, 313 / 5; Engel, "Who Is a Collaborator?," 368–370.

47. Cited in Avihu Ronen, "Ha-Punkt ha-gadol: 12.8.1942 ha-gerush ha-hamoni shel Yehudi Zaglembyeh," *Masuah* 9 (April 1989): 118–120. For more on Bedzin and especially on the German occupation of the town, see Mary Fulbrook, *A Small Town near Auschwitz: Ordinary Nazis and the Holocaust* (Oxford: Oxford University Press, 2012).

48. Haykah Klinger, *Mi-yoman ba-geto* (Merhavyah, Israel: Sifriyat ha-po'alim, 1959), 77.

49. Prosecution indictment, May 16, 1949, ZIH, file of Henryk Barenblat, 313 / 5.

50. Prosecution indictment, May 16, 1949, ZIH, file of Henryk Barenblat, 313 / 5; Jockusch, "Rehabilitating the Past?," 60.

51. The citations here are taken from the indictment because the case did not move on to the honor court. Prosecution indictment, May 16, 1949, ZIH, file of Henryk Barenblat, 313 / 55.

52. Cited in Avihu Ronen, *Nidona le-hayim: yomana ve-hayeha shel Haikeh Klinger* (Tel Aviv: Yediot Aharonot, 2011), 223.

53. Testimony of Henry Diament, Mar. 11, 1948, ZIH, file of Henryk Barenblat, 313 / 5.

54. See Finder and Prusin, "Jewish Collaborators," 137, 148; Engel, "Who Is a Collaborator?," 368–369.

55. ZIH, file of Julius Siegel, 313 / 1, p. 13. On this trial, see Rivka Brot, "Julius Siegel: Kapo in Four (Legal) Acts," *Dapim Journal: Studies on the Holocaust* 25 (2011): 65–127.

56. Cited in Brot, "Julius Siegel," 78 n. 33.

57. Indictment of Julius Siegel, no date available, CZA, S5 / 10.099.

58. Testimony of Julius Siegel, June 29, 1946, CZA, S5 / 10.099.

59. Barish Wacksberg, July 7, 1946, CZA, S5 / 10.099.

60. Testimony of Moritz Herschteil, June 29, 1946, CZA, S5 / 10.099. On Lindner, see Fulbrook, *Small Town*, 242; and Stephan Lehnstedt, "Correction and Incentive: Jewish Ghetto Labor in East Upper Silesia," *Holocaust and Genocide Studies* 24, no. 3 (2010): 408.

61. Testimony of Abraham Timberg, YVA, O3 / 8211.

62. Testimony of Moritz Herschteil, June 29, 1946, CZA, S5 / 10.099.

63. *Ba-Derech*, June 11, 1946, and July 26, 1946.

64. World Zionist Congress honor court transcript, July 18, 1946, CZA, S5 / 10.099.

65. Testimony of Julius Siegel, July 18, 1946, CZA, S5 / 10.099.

66. Testimony of Julius Siegel, July 19, 1946, CZA, S5 / 10.099.

67. Verdict in the case of Julius Siegel, July 19, 1946, CZA, S5 / 10.099.

68. Aryeh Stern to Justice Ministry, Sept. 27, 1948, ISA, RG / 32 / LAW/475/52.

69. Aryeh Stern to Justice Ministry, Sept. 27, 1948, ISA, RG / 32 / LAW/475/52.

2. TENSIONS AMONG SURVIVORS IN MANDATORY PALESTINE

1. *Haaretz*, Dec. 7, 1945; *Ha-Mashkif*, Dec. 7, 1945. See also Haganah Archive, 8-59, for a report of the scuffle on the bus and the statement that Golda Meyerson (Meir) was investigating the case.

2. *Haaretz*, Jan. 6, 1946; *Ha-Mashkif*, Jan. 6, 1946.

3. *Ha-Mashkif*, Jan. 8, 1946; *Iton Meyuhad*, 9 Shevat 5706 [Jan. 11, 1946].

4. Cited in Itamar Levin, "Ha-edim ma'ashimim ve-dorshim: sekirah rishonit al Yehudim she-nehshadu be-Yisrael be-shituf peulah im ha-Natsim," *Cathedra* 162 (2017): 104.

5. *Haaretz*, Dec. 26, 1945.

6. For other encounters, see, for example, *Iton Meyuhad*, 24 Adar 5705 [Mar. 9, 1945]; *Mishmar*, June 11, 1946; *Haaretz*, July 15, 1946.

7. *Mishmar*, Nov. 17, 1944.

8. *Mishmar*, Nov. 17, 1944.

9. *Haaretz*, Dec. 7, 1945.

10. *Ha-Mashkif*, Jan. 6, 1946, Dec. 7 and 13, 1945.

11. *Yediot Aharonot*, June 14, 1948.

12. *Iton Meyuhad*, 1 Sivan 5706 [May 31, 1946].

13. *Ha-Tzofeh*, Jan. 9, 1946.

14. *Iton Meyuhad*, 9 Shevat 5706 [Jan. 11, 1946].

15. *Mishmar*, June 11 and Sept. 2, 1946; *Ha-Boker*, *Davar*, and *Haaretz*, Sept. 1, 1946. For another case in which a victim was tried for assaulting an alleged collaborator, see *Ha-Boker*, Nov. 14, 1949.

16. *Mishmar*, Mar. 8, 1944.

17. For another example of Klinger's presentation, see Avihu Ronen, *Nidona le-hayim: yomana ve-hayeha shel Haikeh Klinger* (Tel Aviv: Yediot Aharonot, 2011), 412.

18. Executive Committee of the Histadrut, Mar. 15, 1944, Moreshet Archive, C.53.1.24, p. 11. For the response of the leadership to this criticism, see Ronen, *Nidona le-hayim*, 415–418.

19. Some went even further than Klinger and viewed the lack of any significant actions by Palestine Jewry as a treachery of the Jewish cause. See Tom Segev, *The Seventh Million* (New York: Hill and Wang, 1993), 180–183.

    Isaiah Trunk, in *Judenrat: The Jewish Councils in Eastern Europe under Nazi Occupation* (New York: Macmillan, 1972), 32–34, explains the disproportionate numbers by noting that the most religious members of communities, who typically wore traditional garb, could not appear in front of the Germans in such clothing. Another barrier to membership in the councils that limited participation by traditional Jews was their lack of knowledge of the German language. Finally, Trunk points out that the views held by the political party of the Bund, which promoted autonomous Jewish life in Europe, also hindered their ability to take part in the councils. One ultra-Orthodox newspaper points out the absence of Haredi Jews in the Judenrats and takes credit for it. See *Ha-Mivtzar*, Elul 5718 (Aug. 1958).

20. Zivia Lubetkin, *Aharonim 'al ha-homah: devarim ba-ve'idah ha-5 shel ha-Kibuts ha-Me'uhad be-Yagur 8 be-Yuni 1946* (Ein Harod, Israel: Hakibbutz

Hameuchad, 1946), 4–5. See also Belah Guterman, *Tsivyah ha-ahat: sipur hayah shel Tsivyah Lubetkin* (Jerusalem: Hotsa'at ha-Kibuts ha-mewuhad and Yad Vashem, 2011), 291–297; and Roni Stauber, *Ha-Lekah la-dor: Sho'ah u-gevurah ba-mahashavah ha-tsiburit ba-arets bi-shenot ha-hamishim* (Jerusalem: Yad Izhak Ben-Zvi, 2000), 26–27.

21. Lubetkin, *Aharonim 'al ha-homah*, 15–16.

22. *Davar*, June 10, 1946.

23. *Sefer ha-Shomer ha-Tsair* (Merhavyah: ha-Shomer ha-tsa'ir, 1956), 1:589; Stauber, *Ha-Lekah la-dor*, 28–33. See also Dina Porat, *Hanhagah be-milkud: ha-Yishuv nokhah ha-Sho'ah, 1942–1945* (Tel Aviv: Am Oved, 1986), 437.

24. Lubetkin, *Aharonim 'al ha-homah*, 48.

25. Yoav Gelber, *Shorshe ha-havatselet: ha-modi'in ba-Yishuv, 1918–1947* (Tel Aviv: Ministry of Defense, 1992), 460–463; Report on the Actions of the Haifa Office for Investigation of the Situation of the Jews in the Nazi Diaspora (1943–1945), Sept. 10, 1945, CZA S25 / 7823; see also CZA, S25 / 8883.

26. Meeting with M.S. (possibly Moshe Shertok-Sharett), May 23, 1945, CZA, S25 / 7825; Report on the Actions of the Haifa Office for Investigation of the Situation of the Jews in the Nazi Diaspora (1943–1945), Sept. 10, 1945, CZA, S25 / 7823; letter to Mr. Tabori, June 13, 1945, CZA, S25 / 7831. Henryk Barenblat's name appears on another list; see "Jewish Collaborators with German Authorities in Poland," Jan. 8, 1945, CZA, S25 / 7828.

27. Note from Nov. 27, 1944, CZA, S25 / 7828 (no sender or recipient listed).

28. Note from Nov. 27, 1944, CZA, S25 / 7828 (no sender or recipient listed).

29. Letter from the Haifa Bureau of Investigations to the Political Department, the Jewish Agency, Jerusalem, Dec. 27, 1944, CZA, S25 / 7823.

30. Meeting of Executive Committee of the Histadrut, Sept. 5, 1945, BGA, p. 29; Hanna Yablonka, *Ahim zarim: nitsole ha-Sho'ah bi-Medinat Yiśra'el, 1948–1952* (Jerusalem: Yad Yitshak Ben-Tsevi, 1994), 57.

31. Transcript of meeting, Jewish Agency Board of Directors, Dec. 27, 1942, BGA, pp. 3–4. See also Porat, *Hanhagah be-Milkud*, 438.

32. Directors of the Jewish National Council meeting, Oct. 15, 1945, CZA, J1 / 7262.

33. Meeting of Executive Committee of the Histadrut, Sept. 5, 1945, BGA, p. 29.

34. Jewish National Council meeting, Oct. 1, 1945, CZA, J1 / 7262, p. 28.

35. Executive Committee of the Histadrut, Sept. 5, 1945, BGA, p. 29; see also Jewish National Council meeting, Oct. 1, 1945, CZA, J1 / 7262, p. 2. See Gideon Rafael in letter from the Haifa Bureau of Investigations to the Political Department, Jewish Agency, Jerusalem, Dec. 27, 1944, CZA, S25 / 7823.

36. Office of the Situation of Exile Jewry meeting, Haifa, May 23 or 29, 1945, CZA S25 / 7825, p. 45.

37. In pre-mandatory Palestine, the Jewish population had only a court for civil cases, not one for criminal justice. Transcript of meeting, Jewish Agency Board of Directors, January 13, 1946, CZA, S51 / 168, p. 26 (11452). On this trial see Rivka Brot, "Julius Siegel: Kapo in Four (Legal) Acts," *Dapim Journal: Studies on the Holocaust* 25 (2011): 65–127.

38. On the castigation in schools, see testimony of Tsipora Beisky, May 3, 1959, *Attorney General v. Hannoh Beisky*, ISA, RG / 32 / LAW/137/59, p. 6. For a

moral discussion on the theoretical question of whether to ban a child of a kapo, see the children's magazine *Ha-Tsofeh le-Yeladim* 27 (5713 [1953]): 440 and 32 (5713 [1953]): 502–503.

39. Letter from Kibbutz Ein ha-Mifratz to secretariat of ha-Kibbutz ha-Artzi, Feb. 5, 1945, Moreshet Archive, D.1.6186.

40. Haifa Bureau of Investigations, Report 286 on the Jewish militia in Kolomyya, Feb. 12, 1945, CZA, S26/296. See the same report in CZA, S25/7828.

41. Menashe Hutschnecker to Mr. Shefer, RSJA, June 12, 1945, CZA, S26/296.

42. Emphasis in the original. Association of Former Residents of Kolomyya to Jewish Agency, Apr. 13, 1945, CZA, S26/296.

43. Y. Kirsh, Association of Former Residents of Kolomyya, to Menashe Hutschnecker, n.d., CZA, S26/296; Menashe Hutschnecker to Mr. Shefer, RSJA, n.d., CZA, S26/296.

44. Haifa Bureau of Investigations, Report 286 on the Jewish militia in Kolomyya, Feb. 12, 1945, CZA, S26/296. See same report in CZA, S25/7828.

45. Haifa Bureau of Investigations, Report 286 on the Jewish militia in Kolomyya, Feb. 12, 1945, CZA, S26/296. See same report in CZA, S25/7828.

46. Menashe Hutschnecker to Mr. Shefer, RSJA, June 12, 1945, CZA, S26/296.

47. Menashe Hutschnecker to Mr. Shefer, RCJA, June 12, 1945, CZA, S26/296.

48. Menashe Hutschnecker to Mr. Shefer, RCJA, June 12, 1945, CZA, S26/296.

49. Shefer to Menashe Hutschnecker, July 2, 1945, CZA, S26/296; transcripts of witness testimonies pertaining to the case of Hutschnecker, July 22, 1945, and August 13, 1945, CZA, S26/296.

50. Hartglas to Menashe Hutschnecker, Sept. 24, 1945, CZA, S26/296.

51. Yitzhak Gruenbaum, *Bi-yeme hurban ve-Sho'ah* (Jerusalem: Hotsa'at Haverim, 1946), 192.

52. Gruenbaum, *Bi-yeme hurban ve-Sho'ah*, 192; see also Stauber, *Ha-Lekah la-dor*, 17–18; Dina Porat, "Asah ha-kol le-amet et michtavch: Yithazk Gruenbaum peiluto ve-hitbatuyotav be-tekufat ha-Shoah," in *Sho'ah mimerhak tavo: ishim ba-Yishuv ha-Erets-Yiśre'eli ve-yahasam la-Natsizm vela-Sho'ah, 1933–1945* (Jerusalem: YadIzhak Ben-Zvi, 2009), 462–463.

53. In London, writes Antek Zuckerman, the representation of Polish Jewry split into two parts. Members of one group suspected that some representatives in the other group, who were members of the Ichud party, were former members of the Jewish Councils and they refused to appear with them in one delegation; *Yetsi'at Polin: 'al "ha-Berihah" ve-'al Shikum ha-Tenu'ah ha-Halutsit* (Tel Aviv: ha-Kibuts ha-me'uhad, 1988), 45. In the Zionist Conference that took place in Basel in 1946, Zionist leaders conducted an unofficial hearing on Rudolf Kastner. Sometime later an investigation committee also examined allegations against Moshe Krausz, who was also involved in the rescue attempts of Hungarian Jewry. See Yechiam Weitz, *The Man Who Was Murdered Twice: The Life, Trial and Death of Israel Kastner* (Jerusalem: Yad Vashem, 2011), 49–52.

54. Tuvia Friling, *A Jewish Kapo in Auschwitz: History, Memory and the Politics of Survival*, trans. Haim Watzman (Boston: Brandeis University Press, 2014), 156.

55. See the final report of the Polish Communist Party examination committee in Friling, *A Jewish Kapo*, 131–132. Friling's book presents a detailed and comprehensive account of the case of Eliezer Gruenbaum. See also Galia Glasner-Heled and Dan Bar-On, "Displaced: The Memoir of Eliezer Gruenbaum, Kapo at Birkenau—Translation and Commentary," *Shofar: An Interdisciplinary Journal of Jewish Studies* 27, no. 2 (2009): 1–23.

56. Friling, *A Jewish Kapo*, 138.

57. Friling, *A Jewish Kapo*, 88, 138–139. Eliezer lost his hair as a teenager.

58. Friling, *A Jewish Kapo*, 139.

59. Executive Committee of the Labor Union, Sept. 5, 1945, BGA, p. 29.

60. Directors of Jewish National Council, meeting, Oct. 15, 1945, CZA, J1 / 7262, p. 28.

61. Friling, *A Jewish Kapo*, 173.

62. A. Rubin to Yitzhak Gruenbaum, May 21, 1946, and attached letter, CZA, A127 / 1156; Friling, *A Jewish Kapo*, 172–173.

63. Tuvia Friling, *Mi atah Le'on Berz'eh? Sipuro shel kapo be-Oshvits: Historya, politika ye-zikaron* (Tel Aviv: Resling, 2009), 316.

64. Roman Frister, *Deyokan atsmi im tsaleket* (Tel Aviv: Devir, 1993), 302.

65. See the IDF memorial for Haim Aharoni (Molchadsky): http://www.izkor.gov .il/HalalKorot.aspx?id=23625 (last accessed Apr. 22, 2019). Author interview with Menachem Liewer, June 19, 2012.

66. Personal correspondence of author with the Tel Aviv municipal offices of Hevrah Kadisha, Jan. 12, 2014. In the cemetery registry book, an indecipherable mark that is either an exclamation mark or a question mark appears by the word *malshin*. On my visit to the cemetery in January 2014, the staff could not point to the exact location of Simcha Baumblat's burial site.

67. *Mishmar, Haaretz,* and the *Palestine Post,* Apr. 6, 1947; *Haaretz,* Apr. 16, 1947; *Haaretz* and *Hatzofeh,* Jan. 8, 1948; *Davar,* Jan. 9, 1948.

68. Medical examiner burial license (personal communication of author with the Tel Aviv municipal offices of Hevrah Kadisha, Jan. 12, 2014).

69. *Haaretz,* Jan. 8, 1948.

70. *Haaretz,* Jan. 8, 1948.

71. Levin, "Ha-edim ma'ashimim ve-dorshim," 96–97; Rena Weiss, police deposition, July 28, 1949, *Attorney General v. Raya Hanes,* ISA, RG / 32 / LAW/140/51; Blumah Klein, police deposition, July 28, 1949, ISA, RG / 79 / IP/3713/5. See also a letter to the editor that refers to Jewish kapos as "Nazis," *Ha-Dor,* Sept. 29, 1950.

72. Organizational Committee to Board Member of Jewish Agency, Apr. 22, 1949 CZA S5 / 10.099; letter from organizational department to Dr. P. Merez, Dec. 7, 1948, CZA, S5 / 10.086. For another case involving Rudolf Kastner heard by the World Zionist Congress honor court, see Weitz, *The Man Who Was Murdered Twice,* 49–52.

73. Yitzhak Levi to Honor Court, World Zionist Congress, May 13, 1949, CZA, S5 / 10.086.

74. Honor Court, World Zionist Congress, May 5, 1949, CZA, S5 / 10.086.

75. Honor Court, World Zionist Congress, May 20, 1949, CZA, S5 / 10.086.

76. Honor Court, World Zionist Congress, May 20, 1949, CZA, S5 / 10.086.
77. Letter from Shmuel Eliashiv to the World Zionist Congress, Dec. 14, 1949, CZA, S5 / 10.999.

3. THE NAZIS AND NAZI COLLABORATORS PUNISHMENT LAW

1. Testimony of Yerachmiel Yanovsky, Mar. 18, 1951, *Attorney General v. Joseph Paal*, Magistrates Court Judicial Inquiry, District Court file, ISA, RG / 31 / LAW/48/51.
2. Testimony of Yerachmiel Yanovsky, Mar. 18, 1951, *Attorney General v. Joseph Paal*, Magistrates Court Judicial Inquiry, District Court file, ISA, RG / 31 / LAW/48/51, p. 7.
3. *Ha-Boker*, Feb. 28, 1949. In no instance did the State of Israel extradite anyone accused of committing crimes during World War II. One request for extradition of a Holocaust survivor who lived in Israel, Jacob Kozeleuk, was filed by the Czechoslovakian consulate in Israel. A brief reference to this request is in ISA, MFA/130/1884/7 (no date, no names). An amateur historian, Amir Haskel, has written a book about Kozeleuk attempting to clear his name. See Amir Haskel, *Soher mi-blok 11* (Yavneh: Hotsa'at Shorashim, 2013). At one point Israeli authorities did consider requesting information about "Jewish collaborators" from the Belgian authorities but ended up not doing so. Israeli Diplomatic Mission in Belgium to Foreign Ministry Legal Advisor, Apr. 18, 1951, ISA, MFA/130/1884/7.
4. Mordechai Nurock, *Divrei ha-Knesset*, Nov. 29, 1949, 187.
5. *Al ha-Mishmar, Haaretz*, and *Ha-Boker*, Sept. 6, 1949.
6. *Maariv*, Aug. 17, 1949.
7. *Ha-Boker, Ha-Tzofeh*, and the *Palestine Post*, Oct. 10, 1948.
8. *Davar*, Oct. 19, 1948.
9. *Ha-Boker*, June 7, 1949. For other examples, see *Davar, Haaretz*, and the *Palestine Post*, Mar. 27, 1949; *Davar*, Jan. 29, 1950.
10. *Maariv*, June 22, 1949; Hanna Yablonka, "Ha-Hok le-asiyat din ba-Natsim u-be-ozrehim: hebet nosaf li-she'elat ha-Yisre'elim ha-nitsolim ve-ha-Shoah," *Cathedra* 82 (Dec. 1996): 139; Laura Jockusch, "Rehabilitating the Past? Jewish Honor-Courts in Allied Occupied Germany," in *Jewish Honor Courts: Revenge, Retribution and Reconciliation in Europe and Israel after the Holocaust*, ed. Laura Jockusch and Gabriel N. Finder (Detroit: Wayne State University Press, 2015), 53.
11. *Davar*, Mar. 17, 1949.
12. Joseph Gorski to Head of Criminal Investigation Unit, July 6, 1949, ISA, RG / 74 / IP/2162/45. For the role of Israel Police in the investigation of Jewish functionaries' actions in the Holocaust, see Uri Kossovsky, "'U-be-Ozreihem': tafkidah shel Mishteret Yisra'el be-Hakiraht Hashudim be-Shituf Pe'ulah im ha-Natsim," *Police and History* 1 (2019): 184–217.
13. Ram Salomon to Police Inspector, Oct. 18, 1949, ISA, RG / 74 / IP/2162/45.
14. *Új Kelet*, Dec. 17, 1949. For a seminar paper written about the Banik trial, see Lachan Sarid, "Mishpato shel Andrej Banik: ha-mishpat ha-rishom lefi ha-hok le-asiyat din ba-Natsim u-be-ozrehim," Hebrew University Faculty of Law, 2012.

15. Testimony of Tsvi Roth, May 31, 1951, *Attorney General v. Banik*, ISA, RG/33/LAW/121/51; Banik diary, Czechoslovak Embassy in Tel Aviv, Box 8, Archiv MZV.

16. Banik diary, Czechoslovak Embassy in Tel Aviv, Box 8, Archiv MZV.

17. For more on the formation of the Hlinka Guard, see Yeshayahu Jelinek, "Storm Troopers in Slovakia: The Rodobrana and the Hlinka Guard," *Journal of Contemporary History* 6, no. 3 (1971): 97–119.

18. Testimony of Yitzhak Freiman, Dec. 20, 1949, *Attorney General v. Banik*, ISA, RG/33/LAW/121/51.

19. All quotes from the police investigation of Banik, Dec. 20, 21, and 27, 1949, Jan. 1 and 3, 1950, *Attorney General v. Banik*, ISA, RG/33/LAW /121/51.

20. Police investigation of Banik, Dec. 20, 21, and 27, 1949, Jan. 1 and 3, 1950, *Attorney General v. Banik*, ISA, RG/33/LAW/121/51.

21. *Ha-Boker, Herut*, 1950; *Haaretz*, Nov. 24, 1950; *Yediot Aharonot*, Dec. 15, 1950; *Maariv*, Apr. 5, 1951. For another case of a non-Jew suspected of collaboration arrested on Allenby Street in Tel Aviv, see *Ha-Boker, Ha-Tzofeh*, and the *Palestine Post*, Oct. 10, 1948.

22. *Ha-Mashkif*, Jan. 17, 1946; *Maariv* and *Al-Hamishmar*, Mar. 5, 1948; *Maariv*, May 4, 1951.

23. Expulsion order, ISA, MFA/130/1884/6.

24. N. Stavi, Assistant Inspector General, Investigation Branch, Israel Police Force Headquarters, to Consulate General, Czechoslovak Republic, Jerusalem, Mar. 7, 1950, Czechoslovak Embassy in Tel Aviv, Box 8, Archiv MZV; *Ha-Boker*, Sept. 27, 1950; Israel Attorney General to Czechoslovak Consul General, Dec. 24, 1950; Foreign Ministry Legal Advisor to Attorney General, Apr. 19, 1951, ISA, MFA/130/1884/7.

25. The Nazis and Nazi Collaborators Punishment Law (1950) has been discussed in several works. See Yehudit Dori Deston, "Mishpat Demyanyuk: sofah shel asiyat din ba-Natsim u-ve-ozrehim be-Medinat Yisre'el," Ph.D. diss., Hebrew University of Jerusalem, 2017, 39–48; Itamar Levin, *Kapo be-Alenbi: ha-amadat Yehudim la-din be-Yiśra'el be-ashmat siyu'a la-Natsim* (Jerusalem: Yad Izhak Ben-Zvi & Moreshet, 2015), 23–40; Rivka Brot, "Ben Kehilah le-medinah: mishpathem shel meshatfe-peulah im ha-Natsim," Ph.D. diss., Tel Aviv University, 2015, 152–181; Hemda Gur-Arie, "Hakarat ha-ne'elam: Ha-Shoah ba-mishpat ha-Yisre'eli," Ph.D. diss., Tel Aviv University, 2007, 173–178; Orna Ben-Naftali and Yogev Tuval, "Punishing International Crimes Committed by the Persecuted: The Kapo Trials in Israel (1950s–1960s)," *Journal of International Criminal Justice* 4 (2006): 130–149; Yablonka, "Ha-Hok le-asiyat din ba-Natsim u-be-ozrehim," 139–146; Yechiam Weitz, "ha-Hok le-asiyat din ba-Natsim ve-ozrehim ve-yahahsah shel ha-hevrah ha-Yisre'elit be-shenot ha-hamishim la-Shoah ve-nitsoleha," *Cathedra* 82 (Dec. 1996): 153–154.

26. On the Crime of Genocide (Prevention and Punishment) Law (1950), see http://preventgenocide.org/il/law1950.htm. On the UN Convention on the Prevention and Punishment of the Crime of Genocide, see http://www.hrweb .org/legal/genocide.html. See also Dori Deston, "Mishpat Demyanyuk," 40.

27. Knesset Constitution, Law, and Justice Committee, Aug. 10, 1949, Knesset Archives, pp. 11–13. Eri Jabotinsky called for the establishment of a special court, but more for political reasons than for judicial ones; *Divrei ha-Knesset*, Mar. 27, 1950, 1153.

28. *Divrei ha-Knesset*, Mar. 27, 1950, 1147–1148. For a similar view, see the remarks of Hannan Rubin, Knesset Constitution, Law, and Justice Committee, Aug. 10, 1949, Knesset Archives, p. 6. See also Nir Kedar, *Mamlakhtiyu: ha-tefisah ha-ezrahit shel David Ben-Guryon* (Jerusalem: Yad Izhak Ben-Zvi, 2009).

29. While there is no explicit reference to this view in the Knesset, prosecutors attempted to get the harshest possible punishments for defendants, including the death penalty, indicating that they did not consider social punishment an option.

30. *Divrei ha-Knesset*, Mar. 27, 1950, 1147, 1148, 1161; Knesset Constitution, Law, and Justice Committee, Aug. 10, 1949, Knesset Archives, pp. 2–4. While the formal name in English is the Nazis and Nazi Collaborators Punishment Law, the title of the legislation is more accurately translated from Hebrew as the Nazis and Nazis' Assistants (or Helpers) Punishment Law. In earlier versions of the bill, the title only spoke about "war criminals," with no distinction between Nazis and Nazi collaborators. *Divrei ha-Knesset*, Nov. 29, 1949, 187.

31. Knesset Constitution, Law, and Justice Committee, Aug. 10, 1949, Knesset Archives, p. 6. The Knesset Constitution, Law, and Justice Committee discussed the possibility of extradition of a Nazis criminal in its deliberations related to the Crime of Genocide (Prevention and Punishment) Law, 1950, Dec. 28, 1949; *Divrei ha-Knesset*, Mar. 27, 1950, 1153. See also Rotem Giladi, "Not Our Salvation: Israel, the Genocide Convention, and the World Court 1950–1951," *Diplomacy and Statecraft* 26 (2015): 473–492.

32. *Divrei ha-Knesset*, June 29, 1949, 868. See also *Divrei ha-Knesset*, Mar. 27, 1950, 1148.

33. On the question of whether the law was formulated with the thought that Nazis might stand trial in Israel and the implications of such a view, see Dori Deston, "Mishpat Demyanyuk," 222–226.

34. *Divrei ha-Knesset*, Mar. 27, 1950, 1154. Gil's view can also be found in an op-ed he published in *Ha-Boker*, Apr. 13, 1950, and in *Hatza'ot hok* 36 (Feb. 28, 1950). See also "Principles of International Law Recognized in the Charter of the Nuremberg Tribunal and in the Judgment of the Tribunal," *Yearbook of the International Law Commission*, 1950, vol. 2, para. 97.

35. Crimes against the Jewish people were already mentioned in passing in the ruling of the Polish State Court in the case of Barenblat (see Chapter 1); earlier, honor courts in DP camps in Germany recognized this offense. See Laura Jockusch, "In Search of Retribution: Nazi Collaborators Trials in Jewish Courts in Postwar Germany," in *Revenge, Retribution, Reconciliation: Justice and Emotion between Conflict and Mediation*, ed. Laura Jockusch, Andreas Kraft, and Kim Wünschmann (Jerusalem: Hebrew University Magnes Press, 2016), 138.

36. Knesset Constitution, Law, and Justice Committee, May 23, 1950, ISA, RG/60/K/25/17, pp. 1–3, 8–9; June 12, 1950, ISA, RG/60/K/25/17, pp. 3–4.

37. Yohanan Bader, *Ha-Knesset va-ani* (Jerusalem: Idanim, 1979), 40–41.

38. Knesset Constitution, Law, and Justice Committee, July 12, 1950, Knesset Archives, pp. 6–7.

39. Roni Stauber, *Ha-Lekah la-dor: Sho'ah u-gevurah ba-mahashavah ha-tsiburit ba-Arets bi-shenot ha-hamishim* (Jerusalem: Yad Izhak Ben-Zvi, 2000), 71–72.

40. Knesset Constitution, Law, and Justice Committee, July 12, 1950, Knesset Archives, p. 7.

41. Knesset Constitution, Law, and Justice Committee, July 12, 1950, Knesset Archives, p. 15.

42. Cited in Stauber, *Ha-Lekah la-dor*, 67–69.

43. Stauber, *Ha-Lekah la-dor*, 71.

44. Nazis and Nazi Collaborators Punishment Law (1950), para. 10.

45. *Divrei ha-Knesset*, Aug. 1, 1950, 2394.

46. *Divrei ha-Knesset*, Aug. 1, 1950, 2395–2396.

47. *Divrei ha-Knesset*, Mar. 27, 1950, 1148.

4. PRELIMINARY COURT EXAMINATIONS

1. Police deposition of Rivka Ugnik (Nugelman), Nov. 19, 1950, *Attorney General v. Dr. Pinchas Pashititzky*, ISA, RG/32/LAW/6/51.

2. Testimony of Josef Singer in District Court, Nov. 29, 1951, *Attorney General v. Elsa Trenk*, ISA, RG/32/LAW/2/52, p. 56. The number 350 is an estimate given by one of the officers on the investigation team, Josef Singer, in testimony in November 1951. Another officer on the team, Tsvi Nusblatt, estimated that in the entire period of the kapo trials they conducted 400 investigations. See Sharon Geva, *El ha-ahhot halo yeduah: giborat ha-Shoah ba-hevrah ha-Yiśre'elit* (Tel Aviv: Migdarim, 2010), 250. The exact number remains unknown.

3. Police deposition of Yerachmiel Barkai, Feb. 1, 1951, *Attorney General v. Tsvi Shapshevsky*, ISA, RG/32/LAW/486/52.

4. Police deposition of Tehila Amster, Sept. 25, 1950, police investigation file of Miriam Goldberg, ISA, RG/79/IP/3713/3. See also *Yediot Aharonot*, June 14, 1948.

5. Nathan Brun, *Mishpat, yetsarim u-politikah: shoftim u-mishpetanim be-sof ha-mandat uve-reshit ha-Medinah* (Tel Aviv: Steimatzky, 2014), 229; for more on the dismissal of the policemen, see ibid., 193–240.

6. *Haaretz*, Jan. 4, 1951.

7. *Haaretz*, Oct. 2, 1950. For one such case of a doctor who fled Israel for Canada, see Erik Ehrlich, ISA, RG/IP/L/2200. See also the movie *Kapo* (Daniel Siton, director, 1999), in which a woman testifies that as a result of the passage of the Nazis and Nazi Collaborators Punishment Law, she decided to leave Israel.

8. Shlomo Sofer, Israel Police Headquarters, to Criminal Division, Tel Aviv District, Sept. 10, 1950, ISA, RG/IP/L/2200. For another case in which the Shin Bet is updated about the status of a suspect, see Criminal Division, Is-

rael Police Headquarters, to the Shin Bet, Case of Moshe Shiff, Mar. 23, 1954, ISA, RG/IP/L/2200. See also Itamar Levin, "Ha-edim ma'ashimim ve-dorshim: sekirah rishonit al Yehudim she-nehshadu be-Yisrael be-shituf peulah im ha-Natsim," *Cathedra* 162 (2017): 97 n. 6, on ten files of investigations by the Shin Bet that are still under a gag order.

9. Testimony of Police Sgt. Tsvi Nusblatt, Nov. 30, 1951, *Attorney General v. Yehezkel Jungster*, ISA, RG/32/LAW/9/51, pp. 22–24; arrest warrant for Yehezkel Jungster, Feb. 18, 1951, police investigation file, ISA, RG/IP/L/2200.

10. Police complaint of Abraham Hendler, Mar. 8, 1951, *Attorney General v. Mordechai Friedman*, ISA, RG/32/LAW/7/51.

11. Summary of police investigation, Jan. 2, 1951, police investigation file of Mordechai Goldstein, ISA, RG/IP/L/2200; letter from Horowitz to the officer in charge, Mar. 19, 1950, in police investigation file of Mordechai Goldstein, ISA, RG/IP/L/2200.

12. Police deposition of Leib Hass, Mar. 1, 1951, *Attorney General v. Shimon Zuckerberg*, ISA RG/33/LAW/168/52; police deposition of Esther Hass, Mar. 5, 1951, in *Attorney General v. Shimon Zuckerberg*, ISA RG/33/LAW/168/52.

13. Police deposition of Yerachmiel Barkai, Feb. 1, 1951, *Attorney General v. Tsvi Shapshevsky*, ISA, RG/32/LAW/486/52; police deposition of Genia Kempinski, Feb. 15, 1951, in *Attorney General v. Tsvi Shapshevsky*, ISA, RG/32/LAW/486/52; police deposition of Josef Rosenbaum, May 15, 1951, *Attorney General v. Tsvi Shapshevsky*, ISA, RG/32/LAW/486/52.

14. Michael Avatichi to Head of Investigation Department, Dec. 4, 1950, police investigation file of Miriam Goldberg, RG/79/IP/3713/3.

15. Police deposition of Hillel Itzkovitch, Oct. 29, 1950, and Apr. 14, 1951, *Attorney General v. Abraham Fried*, ISA, RG/32/LAW/8/51.

16. Police deposition of Abraham Fried, May 21, 1950, in *Attorney General v. Abraham Fried*, ISA, RG/32/LAW/8/51.

17. Police deposition of Elimelech Rosenwald, Jan. 29, 1952, *Attorney General v. Elimelech Rosenwald*, ISA, RG/32/LAW/990/53.

18. Police deposition of Miriam Goldberg, Dec. 4, 1950, *Attorney General v. Miriam Goldberg*, ISA, RG/32/LAW/14/51.

19. Police deposition of Mordechai Goldstein, Jan. 27, 1950, *Attorney General v. Mordechai Goldstein*, ISA, RG/32/LAW/93/51.

20. Police deposition of Elsa Trenk, Aug. 18, 1950, *Attorney General v. Elsa Trenk*, ISA, RG/32/LAW/2/52.

21. Police deposition of Yehezkel Jungster, Feb. 14, 1951, *Attorney General v. Yehezkel Jungster*, ISA, RG/32/LAW/9/51.

22. Police deposition of Elsa Trenk, Aug. 18, 1950; the other official warning was issued on Sept. 7, 1950, in *Attorney General v. Elsa Trenk*, ISA, RG/32/LAW/2/52. On the view of the survivor community, see Rivka Brot, "Ben kehilah le-medinah: mishpathem shel meshatfe-peulah im ha-Natsim," Tel Aviv University, Ph.D. thesis, 2015, pp. 183–195.

23. These fifteen indictments all made their way to the district court level. As pointed out later in this chapter, in the first year after passage of the legislation the magistrates court heard thirty cases, and it seems likely that in some instances that court blocked the cases from proceeding to the district court

level. However, I was unable to locate in the archives any cases in which the magistrates court blocked a case from reaching the district court level.

24. *Maariv*, Aug. 24, 1950; *Ha-Dor*, Aug. 16, 1950; *Kol Ha-Am*, Aug. 17, 1950; *Jerusalem Post*, Aug. 25, 1950. The only discussion of the Banik trial is in a seminar paper by Lahan Sarid, "Mishpato shel Andrej Banik: ha-mishpat ha-rishom lefi ha-hok le-asiyat din ba-Natsim u-be-ozrehim," Hebrew University of Jerusalem, Law Faculty, 2012.

25. Counts 8–10, Indictment of Andrej Banik, Sept. 7, 1950, case 3827/50, Jerusalem Magistrates Court, Czechoslovak Embassy in Tel Aviv, Box No. 8, Archiv MZV.

26. *Davar*, Aug. 14, 1950; *Kol Ha-Am*, Aug. 17, 1950.

27. *Ha-Dor*, Aug. 16, 1950.

28. *Ha-Dor*, Aug. 16, 1950; *Kol Ha-Am*, Aug. 17, 1950; Sarid, "Mishpato shel Andrej Banik."

29. Miriam Ben-Porat, *Mi-Ba'ad la-gelimah* (Jerusalem: Keter, 2010), 73–74; Attorney General Haim Cohn to Czechoslovak Consul General, Apr. 19, 1951, ISA, MFA/130/1884/7. Ben-Porat also worked on other cases; see Levin, "Ha-edim ma'ashimim ve-dorshim," 116.

30. *Ha-Boker*, Sept. 27, 1950.

31. *Yediot Aharonot*, Oct. 4, 1950.

32. Indictment of Andrej Banik, Sept. 7, 1950, case 3827/50, Jerusalem Magistrates Court, Czechoslovak Embassy in Tel Aviv, Box No. 8, Archiv MZV.

33. *Attorney General v. Andrej Banik*, Sept. 7, 1950, case 3827/50, Jerusalem Magistrates Court, Czechoslovak Embassy in Tel Aviv, Box No. 8, Archiv MZV.

34. Patricia M. Wald, "Dealing with Witnesses in War Crime Trials: Lessons from the Yugoslav Tribunal," *Yale Human Rights and Development Journal* 5, no. 1 (2002): 217–218; Telford Taylor, *The Anatomy of the Nuremberg Trials* (New York: Knopf, 1992), 148; Marie Bénédicte Dembour and Emily Haslam, "Silencing Hearing? Victim-Witnesses at War Crimes Trials," *European Journal of International Law* 151 (2004): 167.

35. *Attorney General v. Andrej Banik*, Sept. 7, 1950, case 3827/50, Jerusalem Magistrates Court, Czechoslovak Embassy in Tel Aviv, Box No. 8, Archiv MZV; Nazis and Nazi Collaborators Punishment Law, para. 15. Another defense attorney in Banik's case was Alfred David Levhar, but since Doron is the one who appeared in front of the court, I mention only him.

36. *Haaretz*, Nov. 17 and Nov. 22, 1950; *Ha-Boker*, Nov. 17 and Nov. 21, 1950; *Jerusalem Post*, Nov. 23, 1950; State Attorney to the Legal Advisor of the Foreign Ministry, Nov. 23, 1950, ISA, MFA/130/1884/6.

37. Letter from Consul Necas to Attorney General Haim (Herman) Cohn, Nov. 22, 1950, Czechoslovak Embassy in Tel Aviv, Box No. 8, Archiv MZV.

38. Copy of a letter from the National Committee of Hummene to Joseph Dobrovodsky, Oct. 23, 1950, ISA, MFA/130/1884/6.

39. See, for example, a cable sent from the Prague-based Israeli diplomatic mission to the Foreign Ministry's legal advisor in Jerusalem on May 18, 1951. When the local authorities in Czechoslovakia learned of these affidavits, they

sent a lengthy letter to Israel's attorney general arguing that the witnesses' testimony pertained to a different person, Antow Banik, who had already been sentenced to twelve years of imprisonment in Czechoslovakia. Consulate General of the Czechoslovak Republic to Haim (Herman) Cohn, Attorney General, Apr. 17, 1951, ISA/130/1884/7.

40. State Attorney to the Legal Advisor of the Foreign Ministry, Nov. 23, 1950, ISA, MFA/130/1884/6; Ben-Porat, *Mi-Ba'ad la-Gelimah*, 73–74. About the view that the trials of Banik, Hanes, and Trenk, all former citizens of Czechoslovakia, constituted a diplomatic provocation, see MFA/130/1884/7 (no dates, no names referenced). In Israel the Foreign Ministry's legal advisor questioned why the Czechoslovak authorities made such efforts to assist Banik. He wrote that it may have been a result of their concern for their country's "prestige" as well as a result of the tendency "in this country, as in other countries in Eastern Europe, to occlude the crimes against Jews in these countries during the world war." See Foreign Ministry Legal Advisor to Israel Attorney General, May 15, 1951, MFA/130/1884/7.

41. *Haaretz*, Dec. 20, 1950.

42. J. Doron to the Czechoslovak Consul, Jerusalem, Jan. 26, 1951, Archiv MZV, Czechoslovak Embassy in Tel Aviv, Box No. 8. For Hebrew version, see Dec. 19, 1951, ISA, RG/33/LAW/121/51.

43. *Ha-Boker*, Jan. 10, 1951; *Herut*, Jan. 10, 1951.

44. *Jerusalem Post*, Sept. 17, 1950; *Ha-Boker*, Sept. 28, 1950. See also, for example, a headline regarding the opening of the trial of Jacob Honigman in *Ha-Boker*, Oct. 26, 1950: "Began the Investigation of the Accused of Murdering Jews in the Camps."

45. It has proven impossible to locate all cases that went before the magistrates court, as it seems that cases that were cleared may have been disposed of by the archives. I therefore rely for these numbers on the *Jerusalem Post* of July 1, 1951. For an analysis of the trial of Elsa Trenk, see Rivka Brot, "Ha-Ezor ha-afor shel shituf peulah be-vet-ha-mishpat," *Teoria Ubikoret* 40 (Summer 2012): 157–187.

46. Mark Dvorzhetski, *Ha-Dor*, Nov. 3, 1950. For more on the image of women as collaborators, see Geva, *El ha-ahhot halo yeduah*, 251–269; Brot, "Ben kehilah le-medinah," 297–298.

47. *Davar*, Mar. 11, 1951.

48. *Maariv*, May 4, 1951.

49. Testimony of Idit Leizerovich, Tel Aviv Magistrates Court, Oct. 8, 1950, *Attorney General v. Raya Hanes*, ISA, RG/32/LAW/140/51, pp. 8–9; see also testimony of Shoshana Fogel, Tel Aviv Magistrates Court, Oct. 26, 1950, *Attorney General v. Raya Hanes*, ISA, RG/32/LAW/140/51, pp. 28–29.

50. Fourth and first counts, indictment of Raya Hanes, *Attorney General v. Raya Hanes*, ISA, RG/32/LAW/140/51.

51. First count, indictment of Elsa Trenk, *Attorney General v. Elsa Trenk*, ISA, RG/32/LAW/2/52.

52. Testimony of Shoshana Bloch, Tel Aviv Magistrates Court, Sept. 27, 1950, in *Attorney General v. Elsa Trenk*, ISA, RG/32/LAW/2/52, pp. 13–14; see also

Frida Schwartz, Tel Aviv Magistrates Court, Sept. 27, 1950, *Attorney General v. Elsa Trenk*, ISA, RG/32/LAW/2/52, pp. 15–16.

53. Testimony of Berta Wosner, Tel Aviv Magistrates Court, Sept. 27, 1950, *Attorney General v. Elsa Trenk*, ISA, RG/32/LAW/2/52, pp. 18–19; see also testimony of Dvora Ashkenazi and Frida Schwartz, Tel Aviv Magistrates Court, Sept. 27, 1950, *Attorney General v. Elsa Trenk*, ISA, RG/32/LAW/2/52, pp. 12, 15.

54. Decision of Judge Shamir, Tel Aviv Magistrates Court, *Attorney General v. Elsa Trenk*, Oct. 16, 1950, ISA, RG/32/LAW/2/52, pp. 35–36.

55. Decision of Judge Waldman, Tel Aviv Magistrates Court, Nov. 7, 1950, *Attorney General v. Raya Hanes*, ISA, RG/32/LAW/140/51, pp. 1–4. In one instance, Judge Joseph Maguri ruled that two counts of crimes against humanity leveled against Miriam Goldberg be replaced with two counts of crimes against the Jewish people, a charge never otherwise brought in the case of a Jewish defendant. In his verdict the judge offered no explanation for his ruling, and it is difficult to understand why he made this change, which pits the defendant against her own ethnic group. Indeed, in the district court indictment, the prosecution chose to charge the defendant with crimes against humanity. Verdict, Apr. 20, 1951, *Attorney General v. Miriam Goldberg*, ISA, RG/74/G/6879/20, p. 11; also see district court indictment, Nov. 29, 1951, ibid.

56. These cases include the cases against Pinchas Pashititzky, Yehezkel Jungster, Mordechai Goldstein, Moshe Puczyc, Abraham Fried, and Mordechai Friedman.

57. Testimony of Pinchas Pashititzky, Dec. 26, 1951, *Attorney General v. Dr. Pashititzky*, ISA, RG/32/LAW/6/51, pp. 40–42.

58. Police investigation of Pinchas Pashititzky, Dec. 5, 1950, *Attorney General v. Dr. Pashititzky*, ISA, RG/32/LAW/6/51; police summary report, Pinchas Pashititzky, Dec. 8, 1950, ISA, RG/IP/L/2200, pp. 1, 5.

59. Police investigation of Pinchas Pashititzky, Dec. 5, 1950, *Attorney General v. Dr. Pashititzky*, ISA, RG/32/LAW/6/51.

60. Decision of Judge Waldman, Tel Aviv Magistrates Court, Nov. 7, 1950, *Attorney General v. Raya Hanes*, RG/32/LAW/140/51, pp. 1–4; decision of Judge Shamir, Tel Aviv Magistrates Court, Oct. 16, 1950, *Attorney General v. Elsa Trenk*, ISA, RG/32/LAW/2/52, pp. 35–36; indictment of Pinchas Pashititzky, Jan. 3, 1951, *Attorney General v. Dr. Pashititzky*, ISA, RG/32/6/51.

61. Testimony of Shalom Lindenbaum, Jan. 15, 1951, *Attorney General v. Dr. Pashititzky*, ISA, RG/32/6/51, p. 6.

62. Testimony of Esther Tugedman, Feb. 1, 1951, *Attorney General v. Dr. Pashititzky*, ISA, RG/32/6/51, p. 12.

63. Testimony of Meir Waxberg, Mar. 4, 1951, *Attorney General v. Dr. Pashititzky*, ISA, RG/32/6/51, p. 17; testimony of Miriam Tagari, Jan. 28, 1961, *Attorney General v. Dr. Pashititzky*, ISA, RG/32/6/51, p. 8.

64. Testimony of Miriam Boymann, Jan. 28, 1951, *Attorney General v. Dr. Pashititzky*, ISA, RG/32/6/51, pp. 6–7.

65. Testimony of Shalom Lindenbaum, Jan. 15, 1951, *Attorney General v. Dr. Pashititzky*, ISA, RG/32/6/51, p. 5; *Ha-Boker*, Feb. 2, 1951.

66. Testimony of Haim Sandrowitz, Feb. 21, 1952, *Attorney General v. Joshua Sternberg*, ISA, RG/32/276/51, pp. 6, 12–13; testimony of Moshe Rosenthal, Feb. 26, 1952, *Attorney General v. Joshua Sternberg*, ISA, RG/32/276/51, p. 23.

67. Statement of Pinchas Pashititzky, Mar. 4, 1951, *Attorney General v. Dr. Pashititzky*, ISA, RG/32/6/51, pp. 18–19.

68. Decision of Judge Waldman, Tel Aviv Magistrates Court, Mar. 28, 1951, *Attorney General v. Dr. Pashititzky*, ISA, RG/32/6/51, p. 20.

5. WEIGHING THE ACTIONS OF JEWISH COLLABORATORS

1. Under pressure from the Czechoslovak consulate, Israel's legal authorities moved Banik's trial from Jerusalem to Haifa. See J. Doron to Czechoslovak Consul, Jerusalem, Jan. 26, 1951, in Czechoslovak Embassy in Tel Aviv, Box No. 8, Archiv MZV.

2. Cohn, opening statement, May 14, 1951, Haifa District Court, *Attorney General v. Banik*, ISA, RG/33/LAW/121/51, p. 8.

3. Cohn, opening statement, May 14, 1951, Haifa District Court, *Attorney General v. Banik*, ISA, RG/33/LAW/121/51, p. 2.

4. Cohn, opening statement, May 14, 1951, Haifa District Court, *Attorney General v. Banik*, ISA, RG/33/LAW/121/51, p. 5.

5. Shalom Rosenfeld, *Tik Pelili 124: mishpat Grinwald-Kastner* (Tel Aviv: Karni, 1955), 290.

6. Testimony of Yitzhak Freiman, May 14, 1951, Haifa District Court, *Attorney General v. Banik*, ISA, RG/33/LAW/121/51, pp. 35–36.

7. Police deposition of Freiman, Dec. 20, 1949, Haifa District Court, *Attorney General v. Banik*, ISA, RG/33/LAW/121/51; testimony of Freiman, Jerusalem Magistrates Court, Dec. 19, 1950, in *Attorney General v. Banik*, ISA, RG/33/LAW/121/51, pp. 47–48; testimony of Freiman, May 14, 1951, in Haifa District Court, *Attorney General v. Banik*, ISA, RG/33/LAW/121/51, pp. 35–36; *Davar*, May 16, 1951.

8. Testimony of Freiman, May 16, 1951, Haifa District Court, *Attorney General v. Banik*, ISA, RG/33/LAW/121/51, p. 49.

9. Affidavit of Ibola Bokorova, Jan. 11, 1951, *Attorney General v. Banik*, ISA, RG/33/LAW/121/51.

10. Testimony of Freiman, May 16, 1951, Haifa District Court, *Attorney General v. Banik*, ISA, RG/33/LAW/121/51, pp. 49–50.

11. *Haaretz*, May 17, 1951; testimony of Freiman, May 16, 1951, Haifa District Court, *Attorney General v. Banik*, ISA, RG/33/LAW/121/51, p. 50.

12. Letter from the Bratislava Attorneys Association, Jan. 30, 1951, court evidence N/5, *Attorney General v. Banik*, ISA, RG/33/LAW/121/51. What remains a slim possibility is that in the case of both the three-year-old boy and the attorney Grossman, the affidavits produced in Czechoslovakia were false. This would require special examination and would resolve neither the internal contradictions in Freiman's testimony nor other problems with his testimony, as discussed later in this chapter.

13. Testimony of Freiman, May 15, 1951, Haifa District Court, *Attorney General v. Banik*, ISA, RG/33/LAW/121/51, pp. 39–40.

14. Arnon to Doron, May 11, 1951, *Attorney General v. Banik*, ISA, RG/33/LAW/121/51, evidence N/1.

15. Testimony of Freiman, May 15, 1951, Haifa District Court, *Attorney General v. Banik*, ISA, RG/33/LAW/121/51, pp. 41–42.

16. Testimony of Freiman, May 15, 1951, *Attorney General v. Banik*, ISA, RG/33/LAW/121/51, pp. 46–47.

17. Letter from Israel Police Headquarters to Doron, May 11, 1951, Haifa District Court, *Attorney General v. Banik*, ISA, RG/33/LAW/121/51, court evidence N/13.

18. Testimony of Nathan Rabinowitz, May 31, 1951, Haifa District Court, *Attorney General v. Banik*, ISA, RG/33/LAW/121/51, p. 216.

19. Prosecution's summation, June 1, 1951, Haifa District Court, *Attorney General v. Banik*, ISA, RG/33/LAW/121/51, p. 227.

20. Verdict, Haifa District Court, *Attorney General v. Banik*, ISA, RG/33/LAW/121/51, p. 6. For another example of doubts expressed by the court of witnesses in the kapo trials, see Judge Yitzhak Raveh, verdict, Mar. 3, 1956, Tel Aviv District Court, *Attorney General v. Elimelech Rosenwald*, ISA, RG/32/LAW/990/53, p. 1.

21. *Haaretz*, May 17, 1951.

22. *Haaretz*, May 31, 1951; testimony of Andrej Banki, May 29, 1951, Haifa District Court, *Attorney General v. Banik*, ISA, RG/33/LAW/121/51, p. 198.

23. Defense trial summary, June 5, 1951, Haifa District Court, *Attorney General v. Banik*, ISA, RG/33/LAW/121/51, pp. 1–2; *Haaretz*, June 6, 1951.

24. Edgar Jones and Simon Wessely, "Psychological Trauma: A Historical Perspective," *Psychiatry* 5, no. 7 (2006): 217; Ira Gäbler and Andreas Maercker, "Revenge after Trauma: Theoretical Outline," in *Embitterment: Societal, Psychological, and Clinical Perspectives*, ed. Michael Linden and Andreas Maercker (New York: Springer, 2011), 42–45.

25. Testimony of Tova-Judith Greenberger, May 17, 1951, Haifa District Court, *Attorney General v. Banik*, ISA, RG/33/LAW/121/51, pp. 62–63.

26. Testimony of Tova-Judith Greenberger, May 17, 1951, Haifa District Court, *Attorney General v. Banik*, ISA, RG/33/LAW/121/51, pp. 66–67.

27. Testimony of Asher Lastovcy, May 18, 1951, Haifa District Court, *Attorney General v. Banik*, ISA, RG/33/LAW/121/51, pp. 75–76.

28. Testimony of Asher Lastovcy, May 18, 1951, Haifa District Court, *Attorney General v. Banik*, ISA, RG/33/LAW/121/51, pp. 77. See also complaint of Asher Lastovcy, Dec. 11, 1949, *Attorney General v. Banik*, ISA, RG/33/LAW/121/51, pp. 1–2.

29. Testimony of Banik, May 24, 1951, Haifa District Court, *Attorney General v. Banik*, ISA, RG/33/LAW/121/51, p. 152.

30. Verdict, Haifa District Court, *Attorney General v. Banik*, ISA, RG/33/LAW/121/51, p. 23.

31. Verdict, Haifa District Court, *Attorney General v. Banik*, ISA, RG/33/LAW/121/51, p. 16.

32. Verdict, Haifa District Court, *Attorney General v. Banik*, ISA, RG/33/LAW/121/51, p. 17; indictment of Banik, Apr. 17, 1951, Haifa District Court, *Attorney General v. Banik*, ISA, RG/33/LAW/121/51, para. 6.

33. Testimony of Alexander Marko, May 22, 1951, Haifa District Court, *Attorney General v. Banik*, ISA, RG/33/LAW/121/51, p. 108.

34. Defense summation, June 5, 1951, Haifa District Court, *Attorney General v. Banik*, ISA, RG/33/LAW/121/51, p. 1.

35. *Ha-Dor*, Aug. 16, 1950; *Kol ha-Am*, Aug. 17, 1950.

36. Testimony of Banik, May 24, 1951, Haifa District Court, *Attorney General v. Banik*, ISA, RG/33/LAW/121/51, p. 150.

37. Police investigation, Jan. 3, 1950, Haifa District Court, *Attorney General v. Banik*, ISA, RG/33/LAW/121/51, evidence T/11.

38. Letter from Necas to Doron, Jan. 3, 1951, Czechoslovak Embassy in Tel Aviv, Box No. 8, Archiv MZV.

39. *Jerusalem Post*, *Davar*, and *Haaretz*, June 11, 1951.

40. Verdict, Sept. 2, 1951, *Attorney General v. Paal*, ISA, RG/31/LAW/48/51, pp. 145–150; verdict, *Paal v. Attorney General*, *Piske Din*, vol. 6 (1952), criminal case 119/51, 501.

41. Sentence, Jan. 23, 1952, *Attorney General v. Mordechai Friedman*, ISA, RG/32/LAW/7/51, pp. 82–83.

42. Sentence, Feb. 8, 1952 *Attorney General v. Miriam Goldberg*, ISA, RG/32/LAW/14/51, p. 9.

43. *Davar*, Nov. 26, 1951; indictment of Elsa Trenk, Nov. 12, 1951, Tel Aviv District Court, *Attorney General v. Elsa Trenk*, ISA, RG/32/LAW/2/52.

44. Prosecution summations, Dec. 7, 1951, *Attorney General v. Trenk*, ISA, RG/32/LAW/2/52, p. 136.

45. Testimony of Vera Schwartz, Nov. 25, 1951, Tel Aviv District Court, *Attorney General v. Trenk*, ISA, RG/32/LAW/2/52, p. 9.

46. Testimony of Deborah Ashkenazi, Nov. 26, 1951, Tel Aviv District Court, *Attorney General v. Trenk*, ISA, RG/32/LAW/2/52, p. 18.

47. Testimony of Hava Gottlieb, Nov. 27, 1951, Tel Aviv District Court, *Attorney General v. Trenk*, ISA, RG/32/LAW/2/52, p. 25.

48. Yehoshua Robert Büchler, "First in the Vale of Affliction: Slovakian Jewish Women in Auschwitz, 1942," *Holocaust and Genocide Studies* 10, no. 3 (1996): 299–325.

49. Hermann Langbein, *Der Auschwitz Prozess: Eine Dokumentation* (Vienna: Europa, 1965), 54. Also see Büchler, "First in the Vale of Affliction," 313.

50. Cited in Büchler, "First in the Vale of Affliction," 310.

51. Testimony of Trenk, Dec. 3–4, 1951, Tel Aviv District Court, *Attorney General v. Trenk*, ISA, RG/32/LAW/2/52, pp. 94–98; *Ha-Boker*, Dec. 5, 1951.

52. Testimony of Trenk, Dec. 4, 1951, Tel Aviv District Court, *Attorney General v. Trenk*, ISA, RG/32/LAW/2/52, p. 108.

53. Testimony of Eirene Markowitz, Dec. 4, 1951, Tel Aviv District Court, *Attorney General v. Trenk*, ISA, RG/32/LAW/2/52, pp. 124–125.

54. See, for example, the discussion in Chapter 6 of the witness Tsvi Schlimmer in the case of Yehezkel Jungster.

55. Nazis and Nazi Collaborators Punishment Law (1950), para. 1.

56. Verdict, Dec. 14, 1951, Tel Aviv District Court, *Attorney General v. Trenk*, ISA, RG/32/LAW/2/52, pp. 8–11; verdict, *Attorney General v. Trenk, Piske Din*, vol. 5 (1951–1952), criminal case 2/52, 147–149. For the requirement that actions constituting a war crime must be carried out against a mass of people and not against individuals, see also verdict, *Attorney General v. Honigman*, Jan. 27, 1952, ISA, RG/31/LAW/3/51, p. 8. In this verdict the judges also specify that the actions must in some sense be systematic and planned ahead of time.

57. Verdict, *Attorney General v. Honigman*, Jan. 27, 1952, ISA, RG/31/LAW/3/51, pp. 9, 28; verdict, *Attorney General v. Jungster, Piske Din*, vol. 5 (1951–1952), criminal case 9/51, 163.

58. Verdict, *Attorney General v. Trenk, Piske Din*, vol. 5 (1951–1952), criminal case 2/52, 151–152. For more on the gap between the language of the verdict and the sentencing, see Rivka Brot, "Ben kehilah le-medinah: mishpathem shel meshatfe-peulah im ha-Natsim," Tel Aviv University, Ph.D. thesis, 2015, pp. 303–305.

59. Verdict, Dec. 14, 1951, Tel Aviv District Court, *Attorney General v. Trenk*, ISA, RG/32/LAW/2/52, pp. 10–11; verdict, *Attorney General v. Trenk, Piske Din*, vol. 5 (1951–1952), criminal case 2/52, 151–152; *Jerusalem Post* and *Haaretz*, Dec. 16, 1951. Trenk's case had the highest number of convictions, excluding cases involving a plea bargain, such as *Attorney General v. Hannoh Beisky*, ISA, RG/32/LAW/137/59 and *Attorney General v. Haim Zilberberg*, ISA, RG/33/LAW/200/60.

60. Police journal, Raya Hanes police investigation file, Tel Aviv District Court, *Attorney General v. Hanes*, ISA, RG/79/L/3713/5; *Davar*, Jan. 30, 1951; *Haaretz*, Jan. 30, 1951; *Jerusalem Post*, Jan. 30, 1951; *Ha-Dor*, Feb. 26, 1951.

61. *Jerusalem Post*, Jan. 30, 1951; *Haaretz*, Jan. 30, 1951. This alteration of the indictment may also have been a consequence of the Jungster verdict, issued early that month, as described in Chapter 6.

62. Testimony of Miriam Tesler, Jan. 15, 1952, Tel Aviv District Court, *Attorney General v. Hanes*, ISA, RG/32/LAW/140/51, p. 3.

63. Testimony of Miriam Meirovitch, Jan. 15, 1952, Tel Aviv District Court, *Attorney General v. Hanes*, ISA, RG/32/LAW/140/51, p. 2.

64. Testimony of Sarah Gross, Jan. 16, 1952, Tel Aviv District Court, *Attorney General v. Hanes*, ISA, RG/32/LAW/140/51, p. 12.

65. Testimony of Sarah Gross, Jan. 16, 1952, Tel Aviv District Court, *Attorney General v. Hanes*, ISA, RG/32/LAW/140/51, p. 12; see also testimony of Hanna Yofeva, Jan. 16, 1952, Tel Aviv District Court, *Attorney General v. Hanes*, ISA, RG/32/LAW/140/51, p. 10.

66. Testimony of Issachar Blau, Jan. 17, 1952, Tel Aviv District Court, *Attorney General v. Hanes*, ISA, RG/32/LAW/140/51, p. 42.

67. Testimony of Sarah Gross, Jan. 16, 1952, Tel Aviv District Court, *Attorney General v. Hanes*, ISA, RG/32/LAW/140/51, p. 11.

68. Testimony of Hanes, Jan. 16, 1952, Tel Aviv District Court, *Attorney General v. Hanes*, ISA, RG/32/LAW/140/51, pp. 6–8; testimony of Shoshana Heikin, Jan. 17, 1952, Tel Aviv District Court, *Attorney General v. Hanes*,

ISA, RG/32/LAW/140/51, p. 15; police investigation of Hanes, July 21, 1949, *Attorney General v. Hanes*, ISA, RG/32/LAW/140/51, p. 1; testimony of Elisheva Singer, Jan. 16, 1952, Tel Aviv District Court, *Attorney General v. Hanes*, ISA, RG/32/LAW/140/51, p. 13; verdict, Judge Zeltner, Jan. 18, 1952, *Attorney General v. Hanes*, ISA, RG/32/LAW/140/51, p. 1.

69. Verdict, Judge Zeltner, Jan. 18, 1952, *Attorney General v. Hanes*, ISA, RG/32/LAW/140/51, p. 2.

70. Testimony of Carola Soroka, Jan. 16, 1952, *Attorney General v. Hanes*, ISA, RG/32/LAW/140/51, p. 2.

71. *Herut*, Jan. 16, 1952; verdict, Judge Zeltner, Jan. 18, 1952, *Attorney General v. Hanes*, ISA, RG/32/LAW/140/51, pp. 3–4.

72. Verdict, Judge Zeltner, Jan. 18, 1952, *Attorney General v. Hanes*, ISA, RG/32/LAW/140/51, p. 4.

73. Verdict, Judge Zeltner, Jan. 18, 1952, *Attorney General v. Hanes*, ISA, RG/32/LAW/140/51, p. 4.

74. Verdict, Judge Zeltner, Jan. 18, 1952, *Attorney General v. Raya Hanes*, ISA, RG/32/LAW/140/51, p. 5.

75. *Ha-Boker*, Sept. 18, 1950, Nov. 30, 1951, Dec. 2, 1951.

76. *Ha-Dor*, Nov. 3, 1950.

77. *Ha-Dor*, Sept. 29, 1950.

78. *Ha-Dor*, Nov. 3, 1950.

79. Ruth Bondy, *Shevarim shelemim* (Tel Aviv: Gevanim, 1997), 44.

80. Letter from Abraham Fried to Haim Matalon, Dec. 23, 1951, *Attorney General v. Fried*, ISA, RG/32/LAW/8/51.

81. Letter from Joseph Paal to the president of the Jerusalem District Court, 24 Adar 5711 [Mar. 2, 1951], *Attorney General v. Paal*, ISA, RG/31/LAW/48/51. When his case advanced to the district court level, Paal was represented by a leading Jerusalem attorney, Eliyahu Meridor. It remains unclear who paid the attorney.

6. DID JEWISH KAPOS COMMIT CRIMES AGAINST HUMANITY?

1. Testimony of Pashititzky, Dec. 26, 1951, *Attorney General v. Dr. Pashititzky*, ISA, RG/32/6/51, p. 134; defense summation, Dec. 30, 1951, Tel Aviv District Court, *Attorney General v. Dr. Pashititzky*, ISA, RG/31/LAW/6/51, p. 169.

2. While the judge in the preliminary examination permitted the prosecution to present the district court with two counts of crimes against humanity, the prosecution chose, possibly for lack of evidence, to omit these counts.

3. Testimony of Rivka Nugelman, Dec. 17, 1951, *Attorney General v. Dr. Pashititzky*, ISA, RG/31/LAW/6/51, p. 26.

4. Testimony of Pashititzky, Dec. 26, 1951, *Attorney General v. Dr. Pashititzky*, ISA, RG/32/LAW/6/51, p. 135.

5. Cited in Levin, *Kapo be-Alenbi*, 426.

6. Testimony of Pinchas Berkowitz, Dec. 18, 1951, Tel Aviv District Court, *Attorney General v. Dr. Pashititzky*, ISA, RG/31/LAW/6/51, pp. 43–44.

7. Testimony of Joseph Lindenbaum, Dec. 18, 1951, Tel Aviv District Court, *Attorney General v. Dr. Pashititzky*, ISA, RG/31/LAW/6/51, pp. 30–31.

8. Testimony of Pashititzky, Dec. 26, 1951, *Attorney General v. Dr. Pashititzky*, ISA, RG / 32 / LAW/6/51, p. 145.

9. Summary of prosecution, Dinari, Dec. 31, 1951, Tel Aviv District Court, *Attorney General v. Dr. Pashititzky*, ISA, RG/31/LAW/6/51, p. 182.

10. Summation of prosecution, Dinari, Dec. 31, 1951, Tel Aviv District Court, *Attorney General v. Dr. Pashititzky*, ISA, RG/31/LAW/6/51, pp. 181–182.

11. Summation of defense, Hagler, Dec. 31, 1951, Tel Aviv District Court, *Attorney General v. Dr. Pashititzky*, ISA, RG/31/LAW/6/51, pp. 172–173.

12. Verdict, Jan. 8, 1951, Tel Aviv District Court, *Attorney General v. Dr. Pashititzky*, ISA, RG/31/LAW/6/51, pp. 3–4; *Herut*, Jan. 9, 1952. It should be pointed out that in other cases the courts acquitted educated people—for example, Moshe Puczyc, who had studied economics and political science at Warsaw University and during the Nazi rule served as deputy commander the Ostrowiec Jewish police. Yet it is difficult to come to any conclusion on this issue due to the small sample of trials. *Attorney General v. Puczyc*, Tel Aviv District Court, ISA, RG/31/LAW/10/51; *Ha-Boker*, Feb. 1, 1952.

13. *Herut*, Jan. 12, 1951.

14. Testimony of Hertzkopf Gleitman, July 23 and July 29, 1951, *Attorney General v. Honigman*, Tel Aviv District Court, ISA, RG/31/LAW/3/51, pp. 140, 147; see also *Ha-Boker*, Jan. 12, 1951; *Davar*, Dec. 1, 1950, and *Kol Ha-Am*, Jan. 19, 1951.

15. Testimony of Rivka Ugnik in Tel Aviv District Court, Dec. 16, 1951, *Attorney General v. Dr. Pashititzky*, ISA, RG/32/LAW/6/51, p. 7. Regarding the actions of Jews as worse than those of Germans, see also *Jerusalem Post*, July 1, 1951, which includes the statement that "many of them [the Jewish kapos] were notorious for their cruelties, which often exceeded that of the Germans."

16. Testimony of Abba Moshenberg, Dec. 3, 1951, *Attorney General v. Jungster*, ISA, RG/31/LAW/9/51, p. 38.

17. Testimony of Meir Ziskovich, Jan. 11, 1951, Tel Aviv Magistrates Court, within the Tel Aviv District Court file, *Attorney General v. Honigman*, Tel Aviv District Court, ISA, RG/31/LAW/3/51, p. 58; see also *Ha-Boker*, Jan. 12, 1951.

18. Testimony of Yehudah Holtzman, Dec. 6, 1951, *Attorney General v. Jungster*, Tel Aviv District Court, ISA, RG/31/LAW/3/51, p. 62.

19. Testimony of David Levkovitch, Nov. 28, 1951, Tel Aviv District Court, *Attorney General v. Jungster*, ISA, RG/31/LAW/9/51, p. 7.

20. Testimony of Jacob Schweizer, Dec. 4, 1951, Tel Aviv District Court, *Attorney General v. Jungster*, ISA, RG/31/LAW/9/51, p. 55.

21. Testimony of Mendel Kleider, July 11, 1951, Tel Aviv District Court, *Attorney General v. Hoingman*, ISA, RG/31/LAW/9/51, p. 86.

22. Testimony of Abba Moshenberg, Dec. 3, 1951, Tel Aviv District Court, *Attorney General v. Jungster*, ISA, RG/31/LAW/9/51, p. 40.

23. *Haaretz*, July 30, 1951; Testimony of Abraham Lehrer, July 29, 1951, Tel Aviv District Court, *Attorney General v. Honigman*, ISA, RG/31/LAW/3/51, pp. 145–146.

24. *Herut, Davar*, Dec. 1, 1950; testimony of Mendel Kleider, Nov. 30, 1950, Tel Aviv Magistrates Court, *Attorney General v. Honigman*, ISA, RG/31 /LAW/3/51, p. 18.

25. *Haaretz*, Nov. 20, 1951; Testimony of Meir Ziskovich, Nov. 19, 1951, Tel Aviv Magistrates Court, *Attorney General v. Honigman*, ISA, RG/31/LAW/3/51, pp. 166–167.

26. In the case of Honigman, the details of the event unfolded both in the preliminary examination in the magistrates court and in the district court, whereas in the case of Jungster the magistrates court judge heard the accounts in the preliminary examination but did not permit their inclusion in the district court indictment. Still, the case did come up in the testimonies given in the district court hearing, but the court did not weigh in on them.

27. One who remembered them healthy was Yehudah Holtzman, Apr. 19, 1951, preliminary examination, Tel Aviv Magistrates Court transcript in Tel Aviv District Court, *Attorney General v. Jungster*, ISA, RG/31/LAW/9/51, p. 13. He also reported that no guard oversaw them.

28. Testimony of Yitzhak Masrodnik, Dec. 5, 1951, *Attorney General v. Jungster*, ISA, RG/31/LAW/9/51, p. 59. Testimony of Yehudah Hambelberg, Feb. 1, 1951, preliminary examination, Tel Aviv Magistrates Court within Tel Aviv District Court file, *Attorney General v. Honigman*, ISA, RG/31/LAW/3/51, p. 86; testimony of Jacob Neufeld, July 15, 1951, *Attorney General v. Honigman*, ISA, RG/31/LAW/3/51, p. 104.

29. Testimony of Abba Moshenberg, July 9, 1951, *Attorney General v. Honigman*, ISA, RG/31/LAW/3/51, pp. 65–67.

30. Testimony of Yehudah Holtzman, Dec. 2, 1950, preliminary examination, Tel Aviv Magistrates Court, *Attorney General v. Honigman*, ISA, RG/31 /LAW/3/51, pp. 44–45.

31. Testimony of Meir Ziskovich, Dec. 2, 1951, *Attorney General v. Jungster*, ISA, RG/31/LAW/9/51, p. 31; testimony of Abba Moshenberg, July 4, 1951, Tel Aviv District Court, *Attorney General v. Honigman*, District Court, ISA, RG/31/LAW/3/51, p. 50.

32. Testimony of Abba Moshenberg, July 9, 1951, Tel Aviv District Court, *Attorney General v. Honigman*, ISA, RG/31/LAW/3/51, p. 67.

33. Meir Ziskovich stated that no German was present at the killing of the Jews; Jan. 11, 1951, preliminary examination, Tel Aviv Magistrates Court, *Attorney General v. Honigman*, ISA, RG/31/LAW/3/51, p. 60. Abba Moshenberg testified that the German commander Kiska was present; July 9, 1951, Tel Aviv District Court, *Attorney General v. Honigman*, ISA, RG/31/LAW/3/51, p. 65. Yehudah Holtzman testified that following the beating the German shot the inmates; Feb. 1, 1951, preliminary examination, *Attorney General v. Honigman*, ISA, RG/31/LAW/3/51, p. 86. One of those who heard shots was Yehudah Holtzman; Dec. 6, 1951, Tel Aviv District Court, *Attorney General v. Jungster*, ISA, RG/31/LAW/9/51, p. 64. Jacob Schweitzer asserted definitively that there were no shots and that the inmates died from the beating by the Jewish kapos; Jan. 4, 1951, Tel Aviv Magistrates Court, *Attorney General v. Honigman*, ISA, RG/31/LAW/3/51, p. 57.

34. Testimony of Jacob Schweitzer, Dec. 5, 1951, *Attorney General v. Jungster*, ISA, RG/31/LAW/9/51, p. 53.

35. Testimony of Jacob Neufeld, Dec. 14, 1950, preliminary examination, Tel Aviv Magistrate Court, *Attorney General v. Honigman*, ISA, RG/31 /LAW/3/51, p. 36.

36. Abba Moshenberg, Jan. 18, 1951, preliminary examination, Tel Aviv Magistrates Court, *Attorney General v. Honigman*, ISA, RG/31/LAW/3/51, p. 68.

37. Testimony of Jacob Schweitzer, Dec. 5, 1951, Tel Aviv District Court, *Attorney General v. Jungster*, ISA, RG/31/LAW/9/51, p. 53.

38. Testimony of Yehudah Holtzman, Dec. 6, 1951, Tel Aviv District Court, *Attorney General v. Jungster*, ISA, RG/31/LAW/9/51, p. 68. See also Holtzman, Apr. 19, 1951, preliminary examination, Tel Aviv Magistrates Court, *Attorney General v. Jungster*, ISA, RG/31/LAW/9/51, p. 13.

39. Testimony of Honigman, Dec. 9, 1951, Tel Aviv District Court, *Attorney General v. Honigman*, District Court, ISA, RG/31/LAW/3/51, p. 224.

40. Testimony of Jungster, Dec. 10, 1951, Tel Aviv District Court, *Attorney General v. Jungster*, ISA, RG/31/LAW/9/51, p. 81.

41. Testimony of Jungster, Dec. 10, 1951, Tel Aviv District Court, *Attorney General v. Jungster*, ISA, RG/31/LAW/9/51, p. 77.

42. The two vehemently rejected the title of "kapo." In the end, both the court and, in the case of Honigman, even the defense attorney used the term "kapo" as a generic term to describe that post in camp; testimony of Jungster, Dec. 10, 1951, *Attorney General v. Jungster*, ISA, RG/31/LAW/9/51, p. 82; *Herut*, Dec. 1, 1950.

43. *Herut*, Dec. 1, 1950; testimony of Honigman, Dec. 11, 1951, Tel Aviv District Court, *Attorney General v. Honigman*, ISA, RG/31/LAW/3/51, p. 234.

44. Testimony of Jungster, Dec. 10, 1951, Tel Aviv District Court, *Attorney General v. Jungster*, ISA, RG/31/LAW/9/51, p. 74.

45. Testimony of Jungster, Dec. 9, 1951, Tel Aviv District Court, *Attorney General v. Jungster*, ISA, RG/31/LAW/9/51, pp. 77–78; testimony of Honigman, Nov. 28, 1951, Tel Aviv District Court, *Attorney General v. Honigman*, ISA, RG/31/LAW/3/51, p. 221.

46. Testimony of Jungster, Dec. 10, 1951, Tel Aviv District Court, *Attorney General v. Jungster*, ISA, RG/31/LAW/9/51, p. 83.

47. Testimony of Honigman, Dec. 9, 1951, Tel Aviv District Court, *Attorney General v. Honigman*, ISA, RG/31/LAW/3/51, p. 225.

48. Testimony of Tsvi Schlimmer, Dec. 11, 1951, Tel Aviv District Court, *Attorney General v. Jungster*, ISA, RG/31/LAW/9/51, pp. 85–87.

49. For the claims of Jungster that he was forced to take his position as kapo, see testimony of Jungster, Dec. 9, 1951, Tel Aviv District Court, *Attorney General v. Jungster*, ISA, RG/31/LAW/9/51, pp. 72–73; Honigman also claimed he had tried to avoid the position, see testimony of Honigman, Nov. 28, 1951, Tel Aviv District Court, *Attorney General v. Honigman*, District Court, ISA, RG/31/LAW/3/51, p. 210.

50. Testimony of Tsvi Schlimmer, Dec. 11, 1951, Tel Aviv District Court, *Attorney General v. Jungster*, ISA, RG/31/LAW/9/51, p. 87.

51. Testimony of Tsvi Schlimmer, Dec. 11, 1951, Tel Aviv District Court, *Attorney General v. Jungster*, ISA, RG/31/LAW/9/51, p. 87.

52. Testimony of Meir Ziskovich, Jan. 11, 1951, Tel Aviv District Court, *Attorney General v. Jungster*, ISA, RG/31/LAW/9/51, p. 29.

53. Testimony of Tsvi Schlimmer, Dec. 11, 1951, Tel Aviv District Court, *Attorney General v. Jungster*, ISA, RG/31/LAW/9/51, p. 87.

54. Testimony of Tsvi Schlimmer, Dec. 11, 1951, Tel Aviv District Court, *Attorney General v. Jungster*, ISA, RG/31/LAW/9/51, p. 90.

55. Some among Israel's intellectual elite shared Hake's concern that trying Jews in Israel for collaboration would point at Jews as responsible for their own catastrophe and allow non-Jews to claim innocence. In a 1951 gathering of intellectuals, a debate developed over the appropriate handling of alleged collaborators. Some participants argued that if Jews did not try their own criminals, how could one expect other nations to pursue justice with their criminals? Others opposed this view: conducting trials in Israel against "Jews who participated in the murder of their people will achieve the opposite effect in the non-Jewish countries. If the Jews committed such crimes, why do you complain about the Nazis?," the non-Jews would argue. *Maariv*, May 4, 1951; see also *Ha-Boker*, Dec. 16, 1951.

56. Honigman defense summation, Dec. 23, 1951, Tel Aviv District Court, *Attorney General v. Honigman*, ISA, RG/31/LAW/3/51, pp. 282–284.

57. Honigman defense summation, Dec. 23, 1951, Tel Aviv District Court, *Attorney General v. Honigman*, ISA, RG/31/LAW/3/51, p. 307.

58. Verdict, Mar. 24, 1954, *Attorney General v. Meir Shmuel Zoltan*, ISA, RG/32/LAW/398/53, pp. 3–4.

59. Honigman defense summation, Dec. 25, 1951, Tel Aviv District Court, *Attorney General v. Honigman*, ISA, RG/31/LAW/3/51, p. 307. For a discussion of the possible goals of war crimes trials, see Lawrence Douglas, "Crimes of Atrocity, the Problem of Punishment and the Situ of Law," in *Propaganda, War Crimes Trials and International Law: From Speaker's Corner to War Crimes*, ed. Predrag Dojčinović (New York: Routledge, 2012), 278–281. See also Yehudit Dori Deston, "Mishpat Demyanyuk: sofah shel asiyat din ba-Natsim u-ve-ozrehim be-Medinat Yisre'el," Ph.D. diss., Hebrew University of Jerusalem, 2017, 15–39.

60. Verdict, *Attorney General v. Honigman*, ISA, RG/31/LAW/3/51, pp. 28–30; verdict, *Attorney General v. Jungster*, *Piske Din*, vol. 5 (1951–1952), criminal case 9/51, 161.

61. Verdict, *Attorney General v. Honigman*, ISA, RG/31/LAW/3/51, p. 12.

62. Verdict, *Attorney General v. Honigman*, ISA, RG/31/LAW/3/51, p. 31.

63. Verdict, *Attorney General v. Jungster*, *Piske Din*, vol. 5 (1951–1952), criminal case, 9/51, 157–158, 166.

64. Verdict, *Attorney General v. Jungster*, *Piske Din*, vol. 5 (1951–1952), criminal case, 9/51, 153, 164. For an opposed view, see the verdict in *Attorney General v. Trenk*, *Piske Din*, vol. 5 (1951–1952), criminal case, 2/52, 142.

65. Verdict, *Attorney General v. Honigman*, ISA, RG/31/LAW/3/51, pp. 8–9, 34; *Herut*, Mar. 24, 1953.

66. Verdict, *Attorney General v. Jungster, Piske Din*, vol. 5 (1951–1952), criminal case, 9/51, 164–165.

67. Verdict, *Attorney General v. Jungster, Piske Din* (1951–1952), criminal case, vol. 5, 9/51, 165.

68. Verdict, *Attorney General v. Jungster, Piske Din*, vol. 5 (1951–1952), criminal case, 9/51, 174–175. The judges in Honigman's case wrote that crimes against humanity consist of a "partnership . . . with the Nazi leadership in their satanic plan to annihilate peoples in general and the Jewish people in particular" (verdict, *Attorney General v. Honigman*, ISA, RG/31/LAW/3/51, p. 9).

69. *Maariv*, May 4, 1951; Knesset Constitution, Law, and Justice Committee, July 12, 1950, Knesset Archives, pp. 6–7. On the punishment required by para. 1 of the Nazis and Nazi Collaborators Punishment Law (1950), see Dori Deston, "Mishpat Demyanyuk," 221–230; Cohn, opening speech, May 14, 1951, Haifa District Court, *Attorney General v. Banik*, ISA, RG/33/LAW/121/51, p. 6.

70. Nazis and Nazi Collaborators Punishment Law 1953, para. 11.

71. Verdict, *Attorney General v. Jungster, Piske Din*, vol. 5 (1951–1952), criminal case, 9/51, 174–175. This view was not shared by some of those who helped draft the law, such as attorney general Haim Cohn, who argued in the opening trial of Banik that the law did not require the death penalty (Chapter 5). In the Eichmann trial, Justice Landau expressed a view similar to Lam's, that para. 1 of the law did not require a death penalty; Deborah E. Lipstadt, *The Eichmann Trial* (New York: Nextbook, 2011), 145.

7. THE FIRST DOUBTS ABOUT THE KAPO TRIALS

1. Hjalmar Horace Greeley Schacht, *Confessions of "The Old Wizard"* (Boston: Houghton Mifflin, 1956), 456; *Maariv*, Nov. 26, 1951. For more on the Schacht affair, see ISA, RG/Police/L/2240/5. A detailed account of the affair is available in Yechiam Weitz, "Nosea over be-sdeh-ha-teufah Lod: parashat 'Schacht be-Lod' u-mashmautah," *Israel: Studies in Zionism and the State of Israel—History, Society, Culture* 9 (2006): 87–107.

2. Weitz, "Nosea over be-sdeh-ha-teufah Lod," 88–91.

3. Weitz, "Nosea over be-sdeh-ha-teufah Lod," 91–92; *Maariv*, Nov. 26, 1951.

4. *Divrei ha-Knesset*, Nov. 26, 1951, 447.

5. *Divrei ha-Knesset*, Nov. 28, 1951, 492.

6. *Herut*, Nov. 28, 1951.

7. *Yediot Aharonot*, Nov. 27, 1951.

8. *Herut*, Jan. 8, 1952.

9. Tom Segev, *The Seventh Million* (New York: Hill and Wang, 1993), 211–222.

10. *Divrei ha-Knesset*, Jan. 9, 1952, 944.

11. *Haaretz*, Apr. 22, 1951; letter from Jacob Henigman to the attorney general, October 24, 1951, Attorney General File, *Attorney General v. Miriam Goldberg*, ISA, RG/74/G/6879/20, pp. 1–2. In January 1952, the court found Miriam Goldberg guilty and sentenced her to ten months' imprisonment, with credit for time already served (verdict, Feb. 8, 1952, Tel Aviv District Court, *Attorney General v. Goldberg*, ISA, RG/32/LAW/14/51, p. 9).

12. District Court Indictment, Nov. 29, 1951, *Attorney General v. Miriam Goldberg*, ISA, RG/32/LAW/14/51; letter from Jacob Henigman to the attorney general, October 24, 1951, and Jan. 20, 1952, Attorney General File, *Attorney General v. Miriam Goldberg*, ISA, RG/74/G/6879/20. Following the Jungster verdict, the attorney general's office replaced a September 1951 indictment of a policeman from the Ostrowiec ghetto, Mordecai Goldstein, that included one count of war crimes and one of crimes against humanity with an indictment that omitted these counts but added other counts of assault. Compare the indictment of September 18, 1951, with that of March 11, 1952, *Attorney General v. Mordecai Goldstein*, ISA, RG/32/LAW/93/52. For more about this trial, see Rivka Brot, "The Gray Zone of Collaboration and the Israeli Courtroom," in *Jewish Honor Courts: Revenge, Retribution, and Reconciliation in Europe and Israel after the Holocaust*, ed. Laura Jockusch and Gabriel N. Finder (Detroit: Wayne State University Press, 2015), 342–352.

   In another case, that of Nathan Brot, following the inquiry process the Tel Aviv Magistrates Court approved the submission to the Tel Aviv District Court of an indictment with two counts of crimes against humanity. The attorney general's office, however, removed those two counts when it submitted the case to the Tel Aviv District Court in July 1952. Compare the judge's decision in the preliminary process of October 23, 1951, with the district court indictment of July 27, 1952. Attorney General File, *Nathan Brot*, ISA, RG/74/G/6879/13.

13. One exception in which the attorney general's office charged the defendant with four counts of crimes against humanity was the 1959 case of Abraham Tikochinsky, who was acquitted. It remains unclear why in this case the state chose to file such charges. See *Attorney General v. Abraham Tikochinsky*, ISA, RG/32/LAW/31/59.

   In two other cases, of Alter Fogel and Hanokh Baiski, the indictments included such counts as crimes against humanity; however, because in both cases a plea bargain (an uncommon practice at the time) was reached, the initial presentation of those charges seems to have been part of a negotiating tactic. See *Attorney General v. Alter Fogel*, ISA, RG/32/LAW/159/56 and *Attorney General v. Hanokh Baiski*, ISA, RG/32/LAW/59/137.

14. Attorney General File, Elimelech Rosenwald, ISA, RG/74/G/6860/6.

15. Verdict, Mar. 4, 1956, Sentence, May 11, 1956, *Attorney General v. Elimelech Rosenwald*, ISA, RG/32/LAW/990/53; Attorney General File, Elimelech Rosenwald, ISA, RG/74/G/6860/6.

16. The court promised to publish its opinion on the case at a later date, but it seems that the justices never did so. See *Yehezkel Jungster v. Attorney General*, Apr. 4, 1952, ISA, RG/30/LAW/7/52.

17. *Herut* and *Yediot Aharonot*, July 18, 1952; letter from Tel Mond Central Prison to Investigation Department, Israel Police, June 21, 1952, Attorney General File, *Jungster*, ISA, RG/74/G/6879/17.

18. *Yediot Aharonot*, Apr. 8, 1952.

19. Honor court verdict in the case of Julius Siegel, July 19, 1946, CZA, S5/10.099.

20. For an account of the previous legal proceedings against Siegel, see Chapters 1 and 3. Also see Rivka Brot, "Julius Siegel: Kapo in Four (Legal) Acts," *Dapim Journal: Studies on the Holocaust* 25 (2011): 65–127.

21. Testimony of Julius Siegel, June 11, 1953, in *Attorney General v. Siegel*, ISA, RG/32/LAW/475/52, p. 54.

22. Testimony of Julius Siegel, June 26, 1946, CZA, S5/10.099, p. 2.

23. Testimony of Julius Siegel, June 11, 1953, in *Attorney General v. Siegel*, ISA, RG/32/LAW/475/52, p. 55.

24. Honor court, Cremona, Italy, testimony of Julius Siegel, June 29, 1946, CZA, S5/10.099, p. 1.

25. Testimony of Julius Siegel, June 11, 1953, ISA, RG/32/LAW/475/52, p. 65.

26. Testimony of Julius Siegel, June 11, 1953, ISA, RG/32/LAW/475/52, p. 68.

27. Honor court, Milan, Italy, testimony of Julius Siegel, July 18, 1946, CZA, S5/10.099, p. 3.

28. Honor court, Milan, Italy, testimony of Julius Siegel, July 18, 1946, CZA, S5/10.099, p. 3.

29. Testimony of Julius Siegel, Tel Aviv District Court, June 11, 1953, *Attorney General v. Siegel*, ISA, RG/32/LAW/475/52, p. 64.

30. See testimonies of Zvi Fogel, Preliminary Process, Mar. 3, 1953, *Attorney General v. Siegel*, ISA, RG/32/LAW/475/52, 17, and of Abraham Fischel, Tel Aviv District Court, May 7, 1953, *Attorney General v. Siegel*, ISA, RG/32/LAW/475/52, p. 25.

31. Testimony of Tsvi Fogel, Tel Aviv District Court, Mar. 13, 1953, *Attorney General v. Siegel*, ISA, RG/32/LAW/475/52, p. 16.

32. Testimony of Yitzhak Presman, *Attorney General v. Siegel*, March 13, 1953, ISA, RG/32/LAW/475/52, p. 10.

33. Verdict, *Attorney General v. Siegel*, July 16, 1953, ISA, RG/32/LAW/475/52, p. 1.

34. Verdict, *Attorney General v. Siegel*, July 16, 1953, ISA, RG/32/LAW/475/52, p. 1.

35. Verdict in the case of Julius Siegel, July 19, 1946, CZA, S5/10.099.

36. Verdict and Sentence, *Attorney General v. Siegel*, July 16, 1953, ISA, RG/32/LAW/475/52. Unlike the procedure in the honor court in Italy, the prosecution of Siegel in Tel Aviv District Court was based on the criminal code and required a much stricter standard of evidence for conviction than the moral code used by the court in Italy. Although the different judicial frameworks permitted different rules of evidence, it still seems that the gap between the procedures was not limited to these rules; it resulted also from the diminishing of accusations and testimony as time passed and from the judge's favorable assessment of the defendant.

37. *Ha-Dor*, Sept. 29, 1950; *Maariv*, May 4, 1951.

38. Nathan Shaham, *Heshbon hadash* (Tel Aviv: Or-Am, 1989), 46. Another famous Israeli writer, Yigal Mossinsohn, published a play that was never performed about a kapo who immigrates to Israel and establishes a new life there: *Adam beli shem* (Tel Aviv: Friedman, 1953). For more on these plays, see Ben-Ami Feingold, *ha-Sho'ah ba-deramah ha-Ivrit: sugyot, tsurot, megamot* (Tel Aviv: Hakibbutz Hameuchad, 2012), 44–59.

39. Shaham, *Heshbon hadash*, 87.

40. Shaham, *Heshbon hadash*, 106.

41. *Al ha-Mishmar*, July 9, 1954; *Davar*, May 7, 1954. For other, mostly negative, critiques of the play see *Herut*, Apr. 30, 1954, and Sept. 27, 1954; *Ha-Tzofeh*, May 14, 1954; *Maariv*, May 26, 1954; *Yediot Aharonot*, Apr. 26, 1954.

42. Shalom Rosenfeld, *Tik Pelili 124: mishpat Grinwald-Kastner* (Tel Aviv: Karni, 1955), 326.

43. *Letters to Friends* no. 17, cited in Rosenfeld, *Tik Pelili*, 16–20.

44. Yechiam Weitz, *The Man Who Was Murdered Twice: The Life, Trial and Death of Israel Kastner* (Jerusalem: Yad Vashem, 2011), 22–26.

45. Weitz, *The Man Who Was Murdered Twice*, 85; Rosenfeld, *Tik Pelili*, 261.

46. Rosenfeld, *Tik Pelili*, 261–262; Weitz, *The Man Who Was Murdered Twice*, 85.

47. *Letters to Friends* no. 17, cited in Rosenfeld, *Tik Pelili*, 16–20. Gruenwald began his attack on Kastner in *Letters to Friends* no. 15.

48. Weitz, *The Man Who Was Murdered Twice*, 89.

49. *Yediot Aharonot*, Mar. 17, 1963; Weitz, *The Man Who Was Murdered Twice*, 90–92. Weitz contends that it is unlikely that Cohn threatened Kastner by saying that if he refused to go along with the lawsuit against Gruenwald, Cohn would be obliged to prosecute Kastner under the Nazis and Nazi Collaborators Punishment Law. However, given the prevalence of such trials in the early 1950s it seems to me completely plausible that Cohn threatened Kastner with such a trial. See Weitz, *The Man Who Was Murdered Twice*, 92, n. 48.

50. Weitz, *The Man Who Was Murdered Twice*, 133.

51. Weitz, *The Man Who Was Murdered Twice*, 118, 122, 232.

52. Rosenfeld, *Tik Pelili*, 322; Weitz, "ha-Hok le-asiyat din ba-Natsim ve-ozrehim: ve-yahasah shel ha-hevrah ha-Yisre'elit be-shenot ha-hamishim la-Shoah ve-nitsoleha," *Cathedra* 82 (Dec. 1996): 163; Leora Bilsky, *Transformative Justice: Israeli Identity on Trial* (Ann Arbor: University of Michigan Press, 2004), 22–25.

53. Tamir summary, Sept. 21, 1954, *Attorney General v. Malkiel Gruenwald*, ISA, RG / LAW/31/124/53, p. 10; Rosenfeld, *Tik Pelili*, 313.

54. Rosenfeld, *Tik Pelili*, 315.

55. Weitz, *The Man Who Was Murdered Twice*, 47, 199, 201; Rosenfeld, *Tik Pelili*, 276.

56. Rosenfeld, *Tik Pelili*, 278, 280. See also Bilsky, *Transformative Justice*, 24–25.

57. In his autobiography, Haim Cohn presents the legislation of the Nazis and Nazi Collaborators Punishment Law as more of a symbolic practice against Nazis than one aimed at Jewish collaborators. Haim Cohn, *Mavo ishi: otobiyografiya* (Or Yehuda: Devir, 2005), 332–336. See also the Epilogue to this book.

58. Cohn, opening statement, May 14, 1951, Haifa District Court, *Attorney General v. Banik*, ISA, RG / 33 / LAW/121/51, p. 5.

59. Rosenfeld, *Tik Pelili*, 290.

60. Weitz, *The Man Who Was Murdered Twice*, 202–203.

61. Rosenfeld, *Tik Pelili*, 311, 371, 400–401. Tamir even offered the prosecution specific paragraphs that could serve as the basis for the indictment; see Rosenfeld, *Tik Pelili*, 372, 401.

62. Rosenfeld, *Tik Pelili*, 423.

63. Cited in Weitz, *The Man Who Was Murdered Twice*, 219.

64. Cited in Weitz, *The Man Who Was Murdered Twice*, 295.

65. *Kol ha-Am*, June 23, 1955 (emphasis in the original); *Herut*, June 28, 1955. In the Knesset, a member of the Communist Party, Esther Vilenska, made an almost identical call; *Divrei ha-Knesset*, June 28, 1955, 2109.

66. Nathan Alterman, *Ha-Tur ha-shevii* (Tel Aviv: Hakibbutz Hameuchad, 1972), 422–423; Weitz, *The Man Who Was Murdered Twice*, 265–266; Dan Laor, *Al shtei ha-Drakhim: dapim min ha-pinqas* (Tel Aviv: Ha-kibutz ha-meuhad, 1989), 114–155; Roni Stauber, *Ha-Lekah la-dor: Sho'ah u-gevurah ba-mahashavah ha-tsiburit ba-arets bi-shenot ha-hamishim* (Jerusalem: Yad Izhak Ben-Zvi, 2000), 123; Gali Drucker Bar-Am, "Revenge and Reconciliation: Early Israeli Literature and the Dilemma of Jewish Collaborators with the Nazis," *Jewish Honor Courts: Revenge, Retribution, and Reconciliation in Europe and Israel after the Holocaust*, ed. Laura Jockusch and Gabriel N. Finder (Detroit: Wayne State University Press, 2015), 282–289; Bilsky, *Transformative Justice*, 69–74.

67. Nathan Alterman, *Al shete ha-derakhim: dapim min ha-pinkas*, ed. Dan La'or (Tel Aviv: Hakibbutz Hameuchad, 1989), 19–22.

68. Alterman, *Ha-Tur ha-shevii*, 416–417. As pointed out by Leora Bilsky and Hemda Gur-Arie, unlike the legal system, which sees things in a binary mode—guilty or innocent—the cultural mode has the ability to view events in dispute in a more complex manner. For more on Alterman's blurring of the lines between rebels and collaborators, see Leora Bilsky and Hemda Gur-Arie, "'Bi-Zekhut ha-mevukhah'—ha-Yudnrat Bi-mevokh ha-mishpat ha-zikaron veha-politikah," *Mishpat u-Mimshal* 12 (2009): 63, 68–70; Bilsky, *Transformative Justice*, 71–74.

69. *Maariv*, Aug. 26, 1955.

70. *La-Merhav*, July 1, 1955.

71. Alterman, *Al shete ha-derakhim*, 19–22; Alterman, *Ha-Tur ha-shevii*, 416–417. See, for example, an analysis of the views of cultural critics such as Meir Ben Gur and David Kenaani in Bilsky, *Transformative Justice*, 78–79; Laor, *Al shtei ha-Drakhim*, 135–140.

72. Segev, *The Seventh Million*, 308.

73. Segev, *The Seventh Million*, 308.

74. Verdict of Supreme Court, Criminal Appeal, *Attorney General v. Malkiel Gruenwald*, *Piske Din*, vol. 12 (1958), criminal case 232/55, 2057–2058.

75. Verdict of Supreme Court, Criminal Appeal, *Attorney General v. Malkiel Gruenwald*, *Piske Din* vol. 12 (1958), criminal case 232/55, 2021–2317.

76. Verdict of Supreme Court, Criminal Appeal, *Attorney General v. Malkiel Gruenwald*, *Piske Din* vol. 12(1958), criminal case 232/55, 2073–2076.

77. Verdict of Supreme Court, Criminal Appeal, *Attorney General v. Malkiel Gruenwald*, *Piske Din* vol. 12 (1958), criminal case 232/55, 2075.

78. Verdict of Supreme Court, Criminal Appeal, *Attorney General v. Malkiel Gruenwald, Piske Din*, vol. 12 (1958), criminal case 232/55, 2302. For more on Agranat's ruling, see Bilsky, *Transformative Justice*, 61–66.

79. Cohn, *Mavo Ishi*, 327.

80. The numbers I mention here are based on the files I was able to locate in the ISA. Due to the difficulty of locating all the kapo trial files, which I mentioned in the introduction, these numbers are mere estimates. The five cases I reference here are *Attorney General v. Alter Fogel*, ISA, RG/32/LAW/377/58 (an indictment in this case submitted in 1956 was canceled for unknown reasons); *Attorney General v. Aryeh Praport*, ISA, RG/32/LAW/377/58; *Attorney General v. Yisrael Zilberberg*, ISA, RG/32/LAW/492/58; *Attorney General v. Hannoch Beiski*, ISA, RG/32/LAW/137/59; *Attorney General v. Abraham Tikochinsky*, ISA, RG/32/LAW/31/59.

81. Haifa Bureau of Investigation, Report 276, Jan. 10, 1945, CZA, S25/7828.

82. Haifa Bureau of Investigation, Report 276, Jan. 10, 1945, CZA, S25/7828; *Davar*, Sept. 27, 1959; *Maariv*, Dec. 16, 1959.

83. Cited in *Maariv*, Dec. 16, 1959.

84. *Kol ha-Am*, Dec. 17, 1959.

85. Cited in *Maariv*, Dec. 16, 1959.

86. Testimony of Moshe Yavlonsky, Tel Aviv Magistrates Court, Nov. 4, 1957, in *Attorney General v. Aryeh Praport*, ISA, RG/32/LAW/377/58, pp. 9–10; police deposition of Moshe Yavlonsky, October 24 and 30, 1957, and police deposition of Tziral Yavlonsky, October 28, 1957, in *Attorney General v. Praport*, ISA, RG/32/LAW/377/58.

87. Testimony of Moshe Yavlonsky, Tel Aviv Magistrates Court, Nov. 4, 1957, in *Attorney General v. Praport*, ISA, RG/32/LAW/377/58, 9–10; police deposition of Moshe Yavlonsky, October 24 and 30, 1957, and police deposition of Tziral Yavlonsky, October 28, 1957, in *Attorney General v. Praport*, ISA, RG/32/LAW/377/58.

88. Tziral Yavlonsky, Nov. 4, 1957, Tel Aviv Magistrates Court, in *Attorney General v. Praport*, ISA, RG/32/LAW/377/58, pp. 13–14.

89. Testimony of Moshe and Tziral Yavlonsky, Tel Aviv Magistrates Court, Nov. 4, 1957, ISA, RG/32/LAW/377/58, 9, 14. See the preliminary process indictment for an indication that the trial was held behind closed doors. Also, for the judge's decision in the district court, see *Attorney General v. Praport*, July 30, 1958, ISA, RG/32/LAW/377/58, p. 2.

90. Police deposition of Mendel Bogonsky, October 21, 1957, in *Attorney General v. Praport*, ISA, RG/32/LAW/377/58.

91. Testimony of Moshe Yavlonsky, Nov. 4, 1957, in *Attorney General v. Praport*, ISA, RG/32/LAW/377/58, 10; testimony of Tziral Yavlonsky, Apr. 13, 1959, in *Attorney General v. Praport*, ISA, RG/32/LAW/377/58, p. 36; testimony of Tziral Yavlonsky, Apr. 13, 1959, in *Attorney General v. Praport*, ISA, RG/32/LAW/377/58, pp. 40–42; testimony of Moshe Yavlonsky, Apr. 13, 1959, in *Attorney General v. Praport*, ISA, RG/32/LAW/377/58, p. 36.

92. Testimony of Tziral Yavlonsky, Tel Aviv District Court, October 25, 1960, *Attorney General v. Moshe and Tziral Yavlonsky*, ISA, RG/32/LAW/53/60,

pp. 4–5; testimony of Michael Avatichi, Tel Aviv District Court, Apr. 13, 1959, *Attorney General v. Praport*, ISA, RG / 32 / LAW/377/58, p. 31.

93. Verdict, Tel Aviv District Court, May 22, 1959, *Attorney General v. Praport*, ISA, RG / 32 / LAW/377/58, p. 5.

94. Prosecution summary, May 11, 1959, *Attorney General v. Praport*, ISA, RG / 32 / LAW/377/58, pp. 59–60.

95. Cited in Weitz, "ha-Hok le-asiyat din ba-Natsim ve-ozrehim," 158.

96. Testimony of Antek Zuckerman, Tel Aviv Magistrates Court, October 25, 1960, *Attorney General v. Moshe and Tziral Yavlonsky*, ISA, RG / 32 / LAW/53/60, p. 3.

97. Testimony of Antek Zuckerman, Tel Aviv Magistrates Court, October 25, 1960, *Attorney General v. Yavlonsky*, ISA, RG / 32 / LAW/53/60, p. 3; verdict, Tel Aviv Magistrates Court, Jan. 26, 1961, *Attorney General v. Yavlonsky*, ISA, RG / 32 / LAW/53/60, p. 2.

8. JUDGING A NAZI AND REFRAMING COLLABORATION

1. Hausner, opening statement, *The Trial of Adolf Eichmann: Record of Proceedings in the District Court of Jerusalem* (Jerusalem: Trust for the Publication of the Proceedings of the Eichmann Trial, in Cooperation with the Israel State Archives and Yad Vashem, the Holocaust Martyrs' and Heroes' Remembrance Authority, 1992), 62.

2. Hausner, opening statement, *The Trial of Adolf Eichmann*, 71.

3. Gideon Hausner, *Justice in Jerusalem* (New York: Harper & Row, 1966), 291–292. See also Hanna Yablonka, *Medinat Yisrael Neged Adolf Eichmann* (Tel Aviv: Sifre Hemed, 2001), 63; Deborah E. Lipstadt, *The Eichmann Trial* (New York: Nextbook, 2011), 77, 141.

4. Testimony of Yisrael Gutman, *The Trial of Adolf Eichmann*, 1156; testimony of Esther Goldstein, *The Trial of Adolf Eichmann*, 1283; testimony of Aharon Peretz, *The Trial of Adolf Eichmann*, 480. See also testimony of Gedalia Ben-Zvi, *The Trial of Adolf Eichmann*, 1298; testimony of Eliezer Karstadt, *The Trial of Adolf Eichmann*, 492.

5. Testimony of Esther Goldstein, *The Trial of Adolf Eichmann*, 1283; testimony of Yisrael Gutman, *The Trial of Adolf Eichmann*, 1156; testimony of Gedalia Ben-Zvi, *The Trial of Adolf Eichmann*, 1298.

6. Testimony of Raya Kagan, *The Trial of Adolf Eichmann*, 1273. Because the official transcript is not fully accurate, I have transcribed parts of this interaction from the video of the testimony. See https://www.youtube.com/watch?v=robxsPItoMo minutes 3:20–3:47 (last accessed Sept. 20, 2016).

7. Hausner, opening statement, *The Trial of Adolf Eichmann*, 71; *Maariv*, June 11, 1961.

8. On Alexander and her testimony, see also Rivka Brot, "Ha-Ezor ha-afor shel shituf peulah," *Teoria Ubikoret* 40 (summer 2012): 178–181; Sharon Geva, *El ha-ahot halo yedu'ah: giborat ha-Shoah ba-hevrah ha-Yiśre'elit* (Tel Aviv: ha-Kibuts ha-me'uhad, 2010), 262–270.

9. Testimony of Vera Alexander, *The Trial of Adolf Eichmann*, 1287.

10. *Maariv*, June 11, 1961.

11. *Maariv*, Sept. 10, 1961.

12. Hausner, *Justice in Jerusalem*, 294–295. Initially there was hesitation among some in the police investigation team about whether to call Zuckerman and Lubetkin as witnesses, but Hausner insisted. See Bella Gutterman, *Tsivyah ha-ahat: sipur hayeha shel Tsivyah Lubetkin* (Tel Aviv: Hotsa'at ha-Kibuts ha-me'uhad, 2011), 389.

13. Hausner, Government Protocol Meeting, Feb. 26, 1961, ISA, http://www.archives.gov.il/archives/#/Archive/0b0717068031be30/File/0b071706 80348359/Item/090717068034884c (last accessed April 23, 2019), pp. 26–27.

14. Testimony of Zivia Lubetkin, *The Trial of Adolf Eichmann*, 402.

15. Testimony of Zivia Lubetkin, *The Trial of Adolf Eichmann*, 409.

16. Geva, *El ha-ahot*, 251–252. Testimony of Antek Zuckerman, *The Trial of Adolf Eichmann*, 419.

17. When he served in 1952 as a district court judge in Haifa, Landau was the judge in the trial of Shimon Zuckerberg, whom he acquitted. See *Attorney General v. Shimon Zuckerberg*, ISA, RG / 33 / LAW/168/52. In 1953, Judge Raveh of the Tel Aviv District Court convicted Elimelech Rosenwald and gave him a one month's suspended sentence. See *Attorney General v. Elimelech Rosenwald*, ISA, RG / 32 / LAW/990/53. Ten years later, he would also sit on the trial of Lube Gritzmacher, which I discuss in Chapter 9.

18. Testimony of Antek Zuckerman, *The Trial of Adolf Eichmann*, 419–420.

19. Hausner, Government Protocol Meeting, Feb. 26, 1961, ISA, http://www.archives.gov.il/archives/#/Archive/0b0717068031be30/File/0b07170 680348359/Item/090717068034884c (last accessed April 23, 2019), pp. 14, 27. See also Leora Bilsky, *Transformative Justice: Israeli Identity on Trial* (Ann Arbor: University of Michigan Press, 2004), 89–91.

20. Hausner, Government Protocol Meeting, Feb. 26, 1961, ISA, http://www.archives.gov.il/archives/#/Archive/0b0717068031be30/File/0b0717068034839 /Item/090717068034884c (last accessed April 23, 2019), 28.

21. Testimony of Hansi Brand, *The Trial of Adolf Eichmann*, 1059. On this issue see also Lipstadt, *The Eichmann Trial*, 97.

22. Testimony of Hansi Brand, *The Trial of Adolf Eichmann*, 1059–1060. See also on this issue Lipstadt, *The Eichmann Trial*, 97.

23. Testimony of Adolf Eichmann, *The Trial of Adolf Eichmann*, 1817–1818. See also Lipstadt, *The Eichmann Trial*, 133–134.

24. Idith Zertal, *ha-Umah veha-mavet: historyah, zikaron, politikah* (Or Yehuda: Devir, 2002), 369; Bilsky, *Transformative Justice*, 93.

25. Hannah Arendt, *Eichmann in Jerusalem* (New York: The Viking Press, 1963 / 1973), 117–118.

26. Arendt, *Eichmann in Jerusalem*, 125–126. See also Leora Bilsky and Hemda Gur-Arie, "'Bi-Zekhut ha-mevukhah'—ha-Yudnrat Bi-mevokh ha-Mishpat ha-zikaron veha-politikah," *Mishpat u-Mimshal* 12, 74–75; Leora Bilsky, *Transformative Justice*, 151–155.

27. Novick, *The Holocaust in American Life* (Boston: Houghton Mifflin, 1999), 141–142.

28. Arendt, *Eichmann in Jerusalem*, 125.

29. Richard I. Cohn, "A Generation's Response to *Eichmann in Jerusalem*," in *Hannah Arendt in Jerusalem*, ed. Steven E. Aschheim (Berkeley: University of California Press, 2001), 253–277.

30. Novick, *The Holocaust in American Life*, 134.

31. Lipstadt, *The Eichmann Trial*, 157–158.

32. Elisabeth Young-Bruehl, *Hannah Arendt: For Love of the World* (New Haven: Yale University Press, 1982), 363.

33. Letter from Gershom Scholem to Hannah Arendt, June 23, 1963, quoted in "'Eichmann in Jerusalem': An Exchange of Letters between Gershom Scholem and Hannah Arendt," in Hannah Arendt, *The Jew as Pariah: Jewish Identity and Politics in the Modern Age*, ed. Ron H. Feldman (New York: Grove Press, 1978), 241.

34. Letter from Gershom Scholem to Hannah Arendt, 243.

35. Haim Gouri, *Facing the Glass Booth*, trans Michael Swirsky (Detroit: Wayne State University Press, 2004), 31.

36. Gouri, *Facing the Glass Booth*, 42–43, 52.

37. Gorui, *Facing the Glass Booth*, 274.

38. *Kol Ha-Am*, July 31, 1961.

9. ABSOLVING ORDINARY FUNCTIONARIES

1. Besides the trial of Barenblat, the trial that opened six weeks after Eichmann's execution was of Zvi Ben-Zeev (Herman Grauzam) in July 1962. See *Attorney General v. Zvi Ben-Zeev* (Herman Grauzam), ISA, RG/32/LAW/160/62. This was the defendant's second trial after the court had acquitted him ten years earlier: *Attorney General v. Zvi Ben-Zeev* (Herman Grauzam), ISA, RG/32/LAW/195/52. One trial that ran parallel to Eichmann's was that of Haim Zilberberg, whom the court convicted and sentenced to one year's imprisonment. See ISA, RG/33/LAW/200/60.

2. Indictment, Mar. 10, 1963, *Attorney General v. Hirsch Barenblat*, ISA, RG/32/LAW/15/63, pp. 1–4. In this chapter, I at times do not draw a distinction between the Jewish police and the Jewish Councils because the terms were used interchangeably in the trial.

3. Indictment, Mar. 10, 1963, *Attorney General v. Hirsch Barenblat*, ISA, RG/32/LAW/15/63; transcript, Mar. 11, 1963, *Attorney General v. Hirsch Barenblat*, ISA, RG/32/LAW/15/63, p. 1. For a detailed account of the Barenblat trial, see Avihu Ronen, Hadas Agmon, and Asaf Danziger, "Collaborator or Would-Be Rescuer? The Barenblat Trial and the Image of a Jewish Council Member in 1960s Israel," *Yad Vashem Studies* 39, no. 1 (2011): 117–167.

4. In 1948, a Polish court cleared Barenblat on a similar count; see Chapter 1. The Nazis and Nazi Collaborators Punishment Law, 1950, para. 9, permitted trying a person again for a crime for which that individual had already been tried abroad.

5. The court convicted him on three such counts but cleared him, because of the statute of limitations, on the matter of membership prior to May 1940. See *ha-Yo'ets ha-Mishpati la-Memshalah neged Adolf Aikhman: pesak ha-din u-gezar ha-din* (Jerusalem: Merkaz ha-hasbarah be-Misrad Rosh ha-memshalah, 1962), 234–236, 257–260.

6. This count did appear once in an indictment, and the court deliberated over it in its decision, in the case of the non-Jewish Andrej Banik; see Chapter 4. Paragraph 3 was also included in a draft indictment against Hannoch Beiski, but it was omitted in the final indictment. See indictments, Mar. 10 and Apr. 9, 1959, *Attorney General v. Hannoch Beiski*, ISA, RG/32/LAW/137/59. At least one Knesset member expressed during the deliberations of the legislation a similar view to that of Libai, that the law should apply to Jewish organizations. See Aryeh Sheftel (Mapai), *Divrei ha-Knesset*, Mar. 27, 1950, 1150. In the draft of what became the Nazis and Nazi Collaborators Punishment Law, the paragraph that related to hostile organizations was the fifth paragraph, and not the third, as it would end up in the final version of the law.

7. Testimony of David Liver, *Attorney General v. Barenblat*, June 7 and 12, 1963, ISA, RG/32/LAW/15/63, pp. 41, 60–62.

8. Testimony of Aryeh Liver, June 13, 1963, *Attorney General v. Barenblat*, ISA, RG/32/LAW/15/63, p. 73.

9. Testimony of Aryeh Liver, Mar. 11 and June 13, 1963, *Attorney General v. Barenblat*, ISA, RG/32/LAW/15/63, pp. 36, 76–77.

10. Testimony of Aryeh Liver, June 13, 1963, *Attorney General v. Barenblat*, ISA, RG/32/LAW/15/63, p. 73.

11. Testimony of Isaac Neuman, Mar. 11, 1963, *Attorney General v. Barenblat*, ISA, RG/32/LAW/15/63, p. 17; testimony of Haim Waxberg, July 7, 1963, *Attorney General v. Barenblat*, ISA, RG/32/LAW/15/63, p. 116. For more on Molchadsky, see Chapter 2 of this book.

12. David Libai, statement to court, July 11, 1963, ISA, RG/32/LAW/15/63, pp. 152–153.

13. David Libai, opening statement, *Attorney General v. Barenblat*, Mar. 11 and June 12, 1963, ISA, RG/32/LAW/15/63, pp. 1–2, 68; *Herut*, June 14, 1963. In a recent interview with Hadas Agmon and Assaf Danziger, Libai said that the omission of the count from the indictment resulted from public pressure following the March 1963 publication of a *Time* magazine article about the trial (Ronen, Agmon, and Danziger, "Collaborator or Would-Be Rescuer?," 132). This argument does not seem tenable for two reasons. First, the article does not focus on issues related to the twelfth count of the indictment. Second, there were four months between the article's publication and the retraction of the count, a period during which the prosecutor continuously presented evidence to support this charge.

14. *Herut*, June 14, 1963; *Attorney General v. Barenblat*, June 12, 1963, ISA, RG/32/LAW/15/63, p. 68.

15. *Maariv*, Aug. 28 and Oct. 21, 1963.

16. *Maariv*, *Davar*, and *Omer*, Aug. 27, 1963.

17. Testimony of Barenblat, Aug. 25 and 28, 1963, *Attorney General v. Barenblat*, ISA, RG/32/LAW/15/63, pp. 157–158, 218.

18. Testimony of Barenblat, Aug. 25, 1963, *Attorney General v. Barenblat*, ISA, RG/32/LAW/15/63, p. 158.

19. Testimony of Barenblat, Aug. 25, 1963, *Attorney General v. Barenblat*, ISA, RG/32/LAW/15/63, p. 167.

20. *Davar*, Aug. 29, 1963.

21. Testimony of Barenblat, Aug. 28, 1963, *Attorney General v. Barenblat*, ISA, RG / 32 / LAW/15/63, p. 221.

22. Testimony of Barenblat, Aug. 28, 1963, *Attorney General v. Barenblat*, ISA, RG / 32 / LAW/15/63, p. 222.

23. Cited in Avihu Ronen, "Ha-Punkt ha-gadol: 12.8.1942 ha-gerush ha-hamoni shel Yehudi Zaglembyeh," *Masuah* 9 (April 1989): 120.

24. For a detailed account, see Ronen, "Ha-Punkt ha-gadol." Also see Mary Fulbrook, *A Small Town near Auschwitz: Ordinary Nazis and the Holocaust* (Oxford: Oxford University Press, 2012), 236–267.

25. Haykah Klinger, *Mi-yoman ba-geto*, (Merhavyah: Sifriyat ha-po'alim, 1959), 77.

26. Klinger, *Mi-yoman ba-geto*, 81–82.

27. Testimony of Barenblat, Aug. 25, 1963, *Attorney General v. Barenblat*, ISA, RG / 32 / LAW/15/63, p. 162.

28. Testimony of Barenblat, Aug. 25, 1963, *Attorney General v. Barenblat*, ISA, RG / 32 / LAW/15/63, p. 161.

29. Testimony of Barenblat, Aug. 27, 1963, *Attorney General v. Barenblat*, ISA, RG / 32 / LAW/15/63, p. 205.

30. Testimony of Zeev Liron, Sept. 22, 1963, *Attorney General v. Barenblat*, ISA, RG / 32 / LAW/15/63, p. 288.

31. Testimony of Zeev Liron, Sept. 22, 1963, *Attorney General v. Barenblat*, ISA, RG / 32 / LAW/15/63, p. 292.

32. Testimony of Zeev Liron, Sept. 22, 1963, *Attorney General v. Barenblat*, July 4, 1963, ISA, RG / 32 / LAW/15/63, p. 289; *Maariv*, Sept. 23, 1963.

33. Testimony of Zeev Liron, Sept. 22, 1963, *Attorney General v. Barenblat*, July 4, 1963, ISA, RG / 32 / LAW/15/63, p. 299.

34. Testimony of Zeev Liron, Sept. 22, 1963, *Attorney General v. Barenblat*, July 4, 1963, ISA, RG / 32 / LAW/15/63, p. 289.

35. Testimony of Kalman Blachash, Aug. 30, 1963, *Attorney General v. Barenblat*, July 4, 1963, ISA, RG / 32 / LAW/15/63, p. 249.

36. Testimony of Kalman Blachash, Aug. 30, 1963, *Attorney General v. Barenblat*, July 4, 1963, ISA, RG / 32 / LAW/15/63, p. 250; *Davar*, Aug. 30, 1963; *Davar* and *Maariv*, Sept. 1, 1963.

37. See Chapter 1 for an account of Barenblat's first trial.

38. Testimony of Miriam Barenblat, Sept. 23, 1963, *Attorney General v. Barenblat*, July 4, 1963, ISA, RG / 32 / LAW/15/63, pp. 309–310.

39. Prosecutor's summation, Oct. 17, 1963, *Attorney General v. Hirsch Barenblat*, ISA, RG / 32 / LAW/15/63, p. 345.

40. Prosecutor's summation, Oct. 18, 1963, *Attorney General v. Hirsch Barenblat*, ISA, RG / 32 / LAW/15/63, p. 365.

41. Prosecutor's summation, Oct. 17, 1963, *Attorney General v. Hirsch Barenblat*, ISA, RG / 32 / LAW/15/63, p. 356.

42. Prosecutor's summation, Oct. 17, 1963, *Attorney General v. Hirsch Barenblat*, ISA, RG / 32 / LAW/15/63, p. 345; see similar statement in the prosecutor's sentencing argument, Feb. 5, 1964, *Attorney General v. Hirsch Barenblat*, ISA, RG / 32 / LAW/15/63, p. 395.

43. Prosecutor's summation, Oct. 17, 1963, *Attorney General v. Hirsch Barenblat*, ISA, RG / 32 / LAW/15/63, pp. 353–354.

44. Prosecutor's sentencing argument, Feb. 5, 1964, *Attorney General v. Hirsch Barenblat*, ISA, RG / 32 / LAW/15/63, p. 395.

45. Defense attorney's summation, Oct. 18, 1963, *Attorney General v. Hirsch Barenblat*, ISA, RG / 32 / LAW/15/63, p. 366.

46. Defense attorney's sentencing argument, Feb. 5, 1964, *Attorney General v. Hirsch Barenblat*, ISA, RG / 32 / LAW/15/63, pp. 396–399.

47. Defense attorney's summation, Oct. 18, 1963, *Attorney General v. Hirsch Barenblat*, ISA, RG / 32 / LAW/15/63, p. 367.

48. Verdict of Tel Aviv District Court, Feb. 5, 1964, *Attorney General v. Hirsch Barenblat*, ISA, RG / 32 / LAW/15/63, p. 3.

49. Verdict of Tel Aviv District Court, Feb. 5, 1964, *Attorney General v. Hirsch Barenblat*, ISA, RG / 32 / LAW/15/63, pp. 7–8.

50. Verdict of Tel Aviv District Court, Feb. 5, 1964, *Attorney General v. Hirsch Barenblat*, ISA, RG / 32 / LAW/15/63, pp. 10–11. For descriptions of felons as "sadistic" and "cruel," see, for example, verdict, Jerusalem District Court, Sept. 2, 1951, *Attorney General v. Joseph Paal*, ISA, RG / 31 / Law/48/51, pp. 147, 151; verdict, Tel Aviv District Court, Jan. 27, 1952, *Attorney General v. Jacob Honigman*, ISA, RG / 32 / Law/3/51, p. 31. See also verdict, *Jacob Honigman v. Attorney General*, *Piske Din*, vol. 7 (1953), criminal case 22 / 52, 296–305; and verdict, *Paal v. Attorney General*, *Piske Din*, vol. 6 (1952), criminal case 119 / 51, 498–510.

51. Verdict, Tel Aviv District Court, Feb. 5, 1964, *Attorney General v. Hirsch Barenblat*, ISA, RG / 32 / LAW/15/63, pp. 10–11.

52. Verdict, Tel Aviv District Court, Feb. 5, 1964, *Attorney General v. Hirsch Barenblat*, ISA, RG / 32 / LAW/15/63, p. 14. In a trial that took place ten years earlier, the court found Fischel an unreliable witness. See *Attorney General v. Siegel*, ISA, RG / 32 / LAW/475/52, p. 2.

53. Verdict of Tel Aviv District Court, Feb. 5, 1964, *Attorney General v. Hirsch Barenblat*, ISA, RG / 32 / LAW/15/63, p. 13.

54. Sentence, Tel Aviv District Court, Feb. 5, 1964, *Attorney General v. Hirsch Barenblat*, ISA, RG / 32 / LAW/15/63, pp. 1–2.

55. *Maariv*, Feb. 6, 1964.

56. *Davar*, Feb. 7, 1964; *Herut*, Feb. 4, 1964.

57. *Ha-Olam ha-Zeh*, Feb. 12, 1964.

58. In a postscript to her book *Eichmann in Jerusalem* (New York: The Viking Press, 1963 / 1973), Hannah Arendt makes a brief reference to Barenblat's trial (284).

59. *Ha-Olam ha-Zeh*, Feb. 12, 1964. In the second half of the article, Avnery tries to get at his political foes by arguing that the Jewish Agency heads, including Ben-Gurion, were culpable because they did not order Jews in Europe not to join the Jewish Councils and police. Also, the Kastner trial reverberated in newspaper opinion pieces published following the trial. *Herut*, which like *Ha-Olam ha-Zeh* was an opposition newspaper, pointed to the political implications of the trial and drew a parallel with the Kastner trial. See *Herut*, Feb. 7, 1964.

60. See, for example, verdict, *Jacob Honigman v. Attorney General, Piske Din*, vol. 7 (1953), criminal case 22 / 52, 296–305; and verdict, *Paal v. Attorney General, Piske Din*, vol. 6 (1952), criminal case 119 / 51, pp. 498–510.

61. *Maariv*, May 3, 1964.

62. Verdict, *Hirsch Barenblat v. Attorney General, Piske Din*, vol. 18 (2) (1964), criminal case 77 / 64, p. 75; see also Landau's opinion on 105–106. Ten years earlier, when Cohn stood before the judges in the Banik trial, he expressed the exact opposite opinion regarding the testimony of a twelve-year-old. A witness's memory of such traumatic events as those experienced by Holocaust survivors, he stated then, do not change easily, even if they occurred many years earlier. See Cohn, opening statement, May 14, 1951, *Attorney General v. Andrej Banik*, ISA, RG / 33 / LAW/121/51, p. 5.

63. Avihu Ronen, *Nidona le-hayim: yomana ve-hayeha shel Haikeh Klinger* (Tel Aviv: Yediot Aharonot, 2011), 162–163.

64. Verdict, *Hirsch Barenblat v. Attorney General, Piske Din*, vol. 18 (2) (1964), criminal case 77 / 64, 76.

65. Testimony of Reuven Wekselman, July 5, 1963, *Attorney General v. Hirsch Barenblat*, ISA, RG / 32 / LAW/15/63, p. 101.

66. Testimony of Hirsch Barenblat, Aug. 28, 1963, *Attorney General v. Hirsch Barenblat*, ISA, RG / 32 / LAW/15/63, pp. 213–214. Historian Avihu Ronen initially expressed the view that the case of the orphans did indeed occur, however, over time he had come to doubt it. See Avihu Ronen, "Yehudi Zaglembyeh be-tekufat ha-Shoah, 1939–1943," Ph.D. thesis, Tel Aviv University, 1989, 1:282–283; Ronen, *Nidona le-hayim*, 162–163; Avihu Ronen, email correspondence with author, June 23, 2017. As one historian pointed out in his book about the Judenräte, Cohn's views do not necessarily stand up to historical scrutiny: Isaiah Trunk, *Judenrat: The Jewish Councils in Eastern Europe under Nazi Occupation* (New York: Macmillan, 1972), 567–569.

67. Verdict, *Hirsch Barenblat v. Attorney General, Piske Din*, vol. 18 (2) (1964), criminal case 77 / 64, 81. Regarding other counts of assault, Cohn cast doubt on whether they fell within the requirement of the law that the assault take place in a "place of confinement." Regarding the sixth and seventh counts, see verdict, *Hirsch Barenblat v. Attorney General*, 77 / 64, *Piske Din*, vol. 18 (2) (1964), criminal case 86–88.

68. Verdict, *Hirsch Barenblat v. Attorney General, Piske Din*, vol. 18 (2) (1964), criminal case 77 / 64, 93 (emphasis in original).

69. Verdict, *Hirsch Barenblat v. Attorney General, Piske Din*, vol. 18 (2) (1964), criminal case 77 / 64, 96 (emphasis in original).

70. Verdict, *Hirsch Barenblat v. Attorney General, Piske Din*, vol. 18 (2) (1964), criminal case 77 / 64, 99.

71. Verdict, *Hirsch Barenblat v. Attorney General, Piske Din*, vol. 18 (2) (1964), criminal case 77 / 64, 101.

72. *Divrei ha-Knesset*, Mar. 27, 1950, 1148.

73. Prosecutor's summation, Dec. 7, 1951, *Attorney General v. Elsa Trenk*, ISA, RG / 32 / LAW/2/52, p. 138.

74. Verdict, *Hirsch Barenblat v. Attorney General, Piske Din*, vol. 18 (2) (1964), criminal case 77 / 64, 90–91. While in previous rulings judges did mention the

"sadistic" or "cruel" nature of the actions of those convicted for collaboration, it never served as a standard by which one determined whether to try someone or not.

75. "Collection of Evidence against the Nazis," letter to the attorney general, Apr. 10, 1964, ISA, RG/74/G/5274/11, note 27; Attorney General to District Attorneys, Jun. 15, 1964, ibid.

   In July 1966, a French new immigrant contacted a representative of Shin Bet with a sensational story. Her husband, a debilitated Holocaust survivor, had described to her how Pinchas Pashititzky, who was tried in the early 1950s (see Chapter 4), had ordered him to bury a woman alive. After consulting on the case, the investigators learned that Pashititzky had already stood trial and been acquitted, so the Shin Bet decided to drop the case. See Pashititzky police investigation, ISA, RG/79/L/2200. For additional police investigations that took place in 1967, see also Hanna Yablonka, "Ha-Hok le-asiyat din ba-Natsim u-be-ozrehim: hebet nosaf li-she'elat ha-Yisre'elim ha-nitsolim ve-ha-Shoah," *Cathedra* 82 (Dec. 1996): 151–152.

76. Police deposition of Sonia Punk, Aug. 12, 1971, in *Attorney General v. Lube Gritzmacher (Meskup)*, ISA, RG/32/LAW/116/71; testimony of Sonia Punk, Apr. 10, 1972, in *Attorney General v. Lube Gritzmacher (Meskup)*, ISA, RG/32/LAW/116/71, p. 62.

77. Police deposition of Sonia Punk, Aug. 15, 1971, in *Attorney General v. Lube Gritzmacher (Meskup)*, ISA, RG/32/LAW/116/71, p. 1.

78. Police deposition of Berta Schwartz, Aug. 28, 1971, in *Attorney General v. Lube Gritzmacher (Meskup)*, ISA, RG/32/LAW/116/71, p. 2. See also testimony of Dov Shilansky, Apr. 18, 1972, in *Attorney General v. Lube Gritzmacher (Meskup)*, ISA, RG/32/LAW/116/71, p. 86.

79. Testimony of Mary Daniels, Apr. 10, 1972, in *Attorney General v. Lube Gritzmacher (Meskup)*, ISA, RG/32/LAW/116/71, pp. 49–50; testimony of Sonia Punk, Apr. 10, 1972, in *Attorney General v. Lube Gritzmacher (Meskup)*, ISA, RG/32/LAW/116/71, pp. 62–63.

80. Testimony of Aryeh Segalson, Mar. 22, 1972, *Attorney General v. Lube Gritzmacher (Meskup)*, ISA, RG/32/LAW/116/71, p. 15. See also testimony of Shmuel Kelansky, Mar. 23, 1972, *Attorney General v. Lube Gritzmacher (Meskup)*, ISA, RG/32/LAW/116/71, pp. 37–38.

81. For more on the incident in which Itzik Gritzmacher escaped from the Bad Tölz movie theater, see Chapter 1.

82. Testimony of Lube Gritzmacher, June 6, 1972, *Attorney General v. Lube Gritzmacher (Meskup)*, ISA, RG/32/LAW/116/71, p. 145. See all defense attorney summations, Sept. 20, 1972, *Attorney General v. Lube Gritzmacher (Meskup)*, ISA, RG/32/LAW/116/71, p. 271. In correspondence, the German embassy in Tel Aviv mentions that Gritzmacher faced a French court. See Dietrich Granow to Dr. Adalbert Rückerl, Apr. 25, 1972, Bundesarchiv, Ludwigsburg, B162/30358, p. 2.

83. Testimony of Lube Gritzmacher, June 5, 1972, *Attorney General v. Lube Gritzmacher (Meskup)*, ISA, RG/32/LAW/116/71, 130–131; police deposition of Lube Gritzmacher, Aug. 19, 1971, in *Attorney General v. Lube Gritzmacher (Meskup)*, ISA, RG/32/LAW/116/71, p. 3. Some of these arguments are re-

peated in correspondence of German diplomats seeking to collect material. See Dietrich Granow to Dr. Adalbert Rückerl, Apr. 25, 1972, Bundesarchiv, Ludwigsburg, B162/30358, pp. 2–3, as well as other documents in that file.

84. Sentence, Sept. 20, 1972, *Attorney General v. Lube Gritzmacher (Meskup)*, ISA, RG/32/LAW/116/71, p. 2. While it is symbolic that the defendant in the last trial was a woman, that was clearly not an intentional choice by the prosecutors, who could not know that this would be the last such trial in Israel.

EPILOGUE

1. In addition to the case of *Attorney General v. Siegel* (ISA, RG/32/LAW/475/52), Valenstein had prosecuted the cases of *Attorney General v. Leon Hershkopf* (ISA, RG/32/LAW/672/52), *Attorney General v. Tsvi Shapshevsky* (ISA, RG/32/LAW/486/52), and *Attorney General v. Meir Shmuel Zoltan* (ISA, RG/32/LAW/398/53).

2. Yohanan Bader, *Ha-Keneset va-Ani* (Jerusalem: Idanim, 1979), 41.

3. Haim Cohn, *Mavo ishi: otobiyografiyah* (Or Yehudah: Devir, 2005), 332. Cohn makes only a brief and inaccurate reference to the Banik and Barenblat trials, focusing on their acquittals (336).

4. Two exceptions are Isaiah Trunk, *Judenrat: The Jewish Councils in Eastern Europe under Nazi Occupation* (New York: Macmillan, 1972), and a conference at Yad Vashem in 1977 that focused on the Judenräte; see Yisrael Gutman, ed., *Demut ha-hanhagah ha-Yehudit be-artsot ha-shelitah ha-Natsit, 1933–1945* (Jerusalem: Yad Vashem, 1977). These discussions, however, were limited to the Judenräte and did not consider other forms of collaboration.

5. Yitzhak Shamir, opening speech, Holocaust Remembrance Day, Apr. 28, 1984, YVA.

6. Yitzhak Shamir, opening speech, Holocaust Remembrance Day, May 1, 1989, YVA.

7. *Tokhnit ha-Limudim le-Beit ha-Sefer* (Jerusalem: Ministry of Education, 1970), 36; Elazar Stern, *Masa kumtah: nivutim be-govah ha-enayim* (Tel-Aviv: Yedi'ot aharonot, Sifre hemed, 2009), 105, 117; Dan Porat, "From the Holocaust to the Scandal in Israeli Education," *Journal of Contemporary History* 39, no. 4 (2004): 627. For a slightly different take on the reasons for the obliteration of the kapo trials from the memory of the Holocaust, see Idith Zertal, *Israel's Holocaust and Politics of Nationhood* (Cambridge: Cambridge University Press, 2005), 87–88.

8. Hayim Nahman Bialik, "City of the Killings," in *Songs from Bialik*, ed. and trans. Atar Hadari (Syracuse, NY: Syracuse University Press, 2000), 5.

9. Assaf Sagiv, "Bikoret ha-todaah ha-korbanit," in *ha-Sho'ah veha-nakbah: zikaron, zehut le'umit ve-shutafut Yehudit-Arvit*, ed. Bashir Bashir and Amost Goldberg (Tel Aviv: Van Leer Jerusalem Institute & Hakibbutz Hameuchad, 2013), 344.

10. For example, Benjamin Netanyahu, opening speech, Holocaust Remembrance Day, Apr. 7, 2013, http://www.pmo.gov.il/English/MediaCenter/Speeches/Pages /speechholocoast070413.aspx (last accessed July 7, 2017). For a similar use of

the expression of "in every generation, they rise up to destroy us," see also Ofer Shif, http://news.walla.co.il/item/2631174 (last accessed July 7, 2017); Stern, *Masa Kumtah*, 115.

11. Chaim Herzog, opening speech, Holocaust Remembrance Day, May 5, 1986, YVA.

12. Yehuda Elkana, *Haaretz*, Mar. 2, 1988; for a translation of the article, see "In Memoriam: 'The Need to Forget,'" *CEU Weekly*, Aug. 20, 2014, http://ceuweekly.blogspot.co.il/2014/08/in-memoriam-need-to-forget-by-yehuda.html (last accessed July 7, 2017). See also Avi Sagi, *ha-Masa ha-Yehudi-Yisreeli: sheelot shel zehut ve-shel tarbut* (Jerusalem: Shalom Hartman Institute, 2006), 123–129; Sagiv, "Bikoret ha-todaah ha-korbanit," 331–333, 348.

13. Adam Milstein, "Israel Air Force F-15 Eagles over Auschwitz," *Jerusalem Post*, July 6, 2016; *Haaretz*, Sept. 2, 2013, http://www.haaretz.co.il/magazine/.premium-1.2112587 (last accessed July 9, 2017); Stern, *Masa kumtah*, 123.

14. Victor Brombert, *In Praise of Antiheroes* (Chicago: University of Chicago Press, 1999), 8–9, 128.

15. Yisrael Gutman and Haim Shatsker, *ha-Shoah u-mashmautah* (Jerusalem: Merkaz Zalman Shazar, 1984), 127.

16. Giuseppe Grassano, "A Conversation with Primo Levi (1979)," in Primo Levi, *The Voice of Memory: Interviews, 1961–1987*, ed. Marco Belpoliti and Robert Gordon (New York: New Press, 2001), 132.

17. Primo Levi, "The Gray Zone," in *The Drowned and the Saved*, trans. Raymond Rosenthal (New York: Vintage, 1989), 37–40.

ACKNOWLEDGMENTS

Writing a book is a journey in which one encounters individuals who help make it even more fascinating and exciting. I was fortunate to meet many such people in the seven years of working on *Bitter Reckoning*, people who helped refine some of the bitterness inherent in the topic. They enlightened me with their knowledge and words. Most of all, I appreciate their genuine wish to help.

Morris Douglas, one of those outstanding people, demonstrated to me what it means to be truly committed to justice. I was blessed to get to know him at an academic conference, and from that point on he read and commented at length on anything I wrote. He very much enriched this book, and I thank him for both his friendship and his thoughts.

Another legal scholar who helped me tremendously was Joshua Schoffman, Israel's former deputy attorney general. Joshua—or as I know him, Yehoshua—was one of the first with whom I shared my interest in pursuing the kapo trials. All along the way, he advised me on how to obtain the files from the state archives, on the history of Israel's legal system, and on legal issues in general. He also read and commented on early drafts of the book.

The Israel Police History Unit was an important source of information, and I wish especially to thank Major Ori Kossovsky, who made many documents available and always shared with me information and thoughts. Although it was at times difficult to release some of the documents, Ori did his utmost to help speed up the process. At Magen David Adom, Susan Edel helped me locate relatives of survivors.

In long walks along the train-track promenade in Jerusalem, I consulted with my longtime friend Kimmy Caplan. His advice and connections always proved helpful. I cherish our friendship.

In research there are always some frustrating administrative and intellectual obstacles. Yael Shapira always heard me out and with her wisdom helped me put them in perspective.

Ilana Kurshan read and commented on early drafts of the book. Deborah Harris and George Altman encouraged me early on to pursue the topic. Avi Staiman and his professional team at Academic Language Experts helped bring my writing up to par. I would especially like to thank Rose Hadshar and Avi Kallenbach for going over the final draft and, in addition to editing my English, also asking important editorial questions. Esther Hecht, with whom I have been working on a regular basis, also did an excellent job in copy-editing earlier versions of the manuscript and the book proposal.

When I almost gave up on this project, my literary agent, Geri Thoma, believed in it and encouraged me to finish it. I wish to thank her for her advice and her continuous support. At Writer's House, Andrea Morrison responded promptly to all my queries and questions.

It's been an honor to work with my editor, Kathleen McDermott. A special thanks to Louise Robbins, who read the manuscript very carefully and made important suggestions. Years ago as a graduate student I used to look longingly at the website of Harvard University Press and wonder whether I would ever have the chance to work with one of those accomplished editors. Luckily, Kathleen showed interest in my project, and it was a pleasure to work with her and the entire team at Harvard University Press.

Several friends and colleagues have enriched me with advice or with comments on parts of the manuscript. I wish to thank them all: Avril Alba, Steven Ascheim, Yehudit Dori Deston, Tuvia Friling, Simon Perego, Avihu Ronen, Sharon Saban Ben-Safrai, Lachan Sarid, Igal Sarna, and David Silberklang.

Over the years I employed several research assistants on this project. They are all talented and promising young men and women and I wish to thank each of them for their efforts on my behalf: Raanan Forshner, Vered Hoshmand, Mor Sagi, Ayana Sassoon, Talia Shlomi, and Jonathan Winter.

I wish to thank the following institutions and their employees for allowing me to examine their collections and, in some instances, also for permission to use their photos: Israel State Archives; Central Zionist Archives (CZA); Israel Police History Unit; Knesset Archives; Ghetto Fighters' House Archives; Moreshest Archives; Yad Vashem Archives (YVA); Ben-Gurion Archives; Haganah Historical Archives; Yad Tabenkin Archive–Ramat Efal; Jewish Historical Institute (ZIH) in Warsaw; Bundesarchiv, Germany; Archiv Bezpečnostních Složek, Czech Republic; Ministry of Foreign Affairs Archive (MZV), Czech Republic; US Holocaust Memorial Museum; Jewish History Center in New York and its various archives, especially the YIVO archive; United Nations Archives and Records Management Section; National Archives (NARA), College Park; the Israel National Library; and Rare Books, Special Collections and Preservation, University of Rochester, New York.

I was fortunate that four foundations agreed to fund my research. I wish to thank the Aharon Barak Center for Interdisciplinary Legal Research at Hebrew University for providing seed money for this project. The Memorial Foundation for Jewish Culture provided funds for research and travel. The National Endowment for the Humanities provided a summer stipend, and the Gerda Henkel Stiftung a fellowship that allowed me to devote time to writing. Their assistance is acknowledged and appreciated. The arguments and words in this book are completely my own and do not represent their views. At the final stages of publication, the Lubin Prize provided funds for essential elements of the book, such as photo permissions and proofreading.

Finally, I wish to thank my family. My father, Shlomo Porat, followed my research and writing as it developed. Unfortunately, he passed away shortly before I completed this project. He is deeply missed. As always, my wife, Vered, and our children have tolerated my attraction to difficult topics. I thank them for that and for always being at my side.

ILLUSTRATION CREDITS

INDEX

Note: Italicized page numbers indicate illustrations.